Lights of Madness

Lights of Madness

In Search of Joan of Arc

Preston Russell, M.D.

Frederic C. Beil
Savannah

Published by
Frederic C. Beil
609 Whitaker Street
Savannah, Georgia 31401
http://www.beil.com

LIBRARY OF CONGRESS CATALOGING-IN-PUBLICATION DATA
Russell, Preston, 1941–
Lights of madness : in search of Joan of Arc / Preston Russell.
p. cm.
Includes bibliographical references and index.
ISBN 1-929490-24-0 (hardcover : alk. paper)
1. Joan, of Arc, Saint, 1412–1431.
2. Christian women saints—France—Biography.
3. France—History—Charles VII, 1422–1461.
I. Title.

DC103.R87 2005
944'.026'092—dc22

2005013841

First edition

Printed in the United States of America

To

my children

Lindsay and Alex

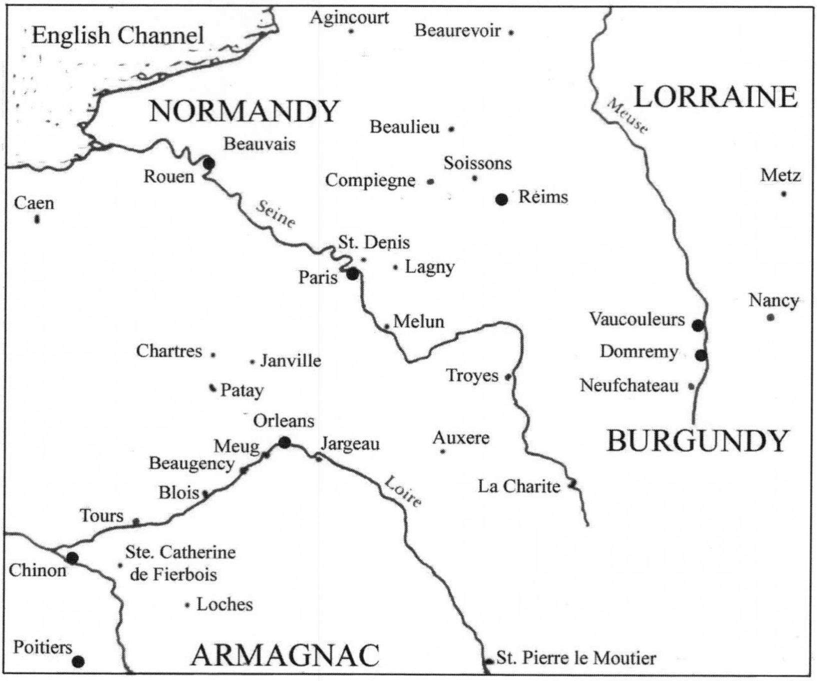

Jeanne d'Arc's France

Contents

Lights of Madness

Introduction

In the mid-1990s my wife, Barbara, and I were on vacation in the Lorraine area of eastern France. Not far south of the city of Nancy, my guidebook informed me, was the birthplace of Joan of Arc, Jeanne d'Arc in France, which after all was her own country—which it really wasn't at the time, I learned. Nor was she precisely clear about her last name, or even her age. My curiosity grew. We stopped at the little town of Vaucouleurs for lunch. The country *cuisses de grenouille* were plump and memorable, along with ample *vin de maison.* Finally pushing away from the table, we learned that the old town gate through which Jeanne d'Arc had passed into destiny to save France was just up the hill behind the rustic restaurant. Warding off somnolence, we strolled up the dirt road to a commanding view. Children wandered by with their dog after school. I tried to converse with them in my jarring French. They responded shyly with nervous laughter and moved on. Barbara and I walked further toward the arch, but the old fifteenth-century walls had long since disappeared. I then posed her standing beneath the old gate of Vaucouleurs, heroically pointing west, barely suppressing a smirk. It is an amusing little picture, which doubtless has been reproduced several thousand times by other tourists just like us. What a legendary little photo joke, some old stones still hanging around to feebly buttress what is largely legend too.

Then we drove a bit further south to tiny Domremy, Jeanne's birthplace. There stands the very house of her childhood, fantastically rediscovered in the early nineteenth century. Though it is now a tourist attraction, the most rabid pilgrim could not spend more than ten dollars in the homespun gift shop, which dispenses thin booklets, key chains, and other trinkets. Out back is the small garden where a remarkably serious girl, aged twelve or thirteen, first heard a frightening voice, to her right, toward the church—or so she claimed. She said she saw a light as well. There, to the right, stood the old church. Then and there I heard something like a voice myself. Was it true? Can it be?

From that instant I was hooked. I later learned that the records of her trials still exist, tomes of testimony, rediscovered in the nineteenth century and grist for countless books thereafter. Mark Twain had his go at them, in what he at least considered his finest work. George Bernard Shaw wrote his arresting *Saint Joan* over three hundred years after Shakespeare had coined his little pun about Jeanne the witch, the supposedly virginal La Pucelle:

> Pucelle or puzzle, dolphin or dogfish,
> Your hearts I'll stamp out with my horse's heels,
> And make a quagmire of your mingled brains.

Two hundred years after Shakespeare, Voltaire took another bawdy turn at sending up the Pucelle legend. What great company to argue with! Vita Sackville-West, a central biographer of the twentieth century, took on the evidence in the 1930s. What is fact and what is fiction? Let Sackville-West respond in her typically forthright way:

> I have observed a tendency to believe that very little is known of Jeanne beyond the cardinal facts of her inspiration, achievement, and death. Nothing could be less true. We know practically every detail of her passive existence as a child and, as to the few months of her active career, they are so thoroughly documented that we know

exactly where she spent each day, and in whose company; what she wore, what horse she rode, what arms she bore, what she ate and drank; and, more importantly still, what words she uttered. Scores of her friends, neighbours, followers, and companions-in-arms have left vivid testimony as to her appearance, manners, habits, character, and speech. The idea that there is any paucity of material for reconstructing her life and personality is fallacious in the last degree.

Now Jeanne d'Arc is officially a Catholic saint, made so 489 years after she was burned by the Church as a heretic. The little handwritten inscriptions by the ordinary I encountered on my visit, left in *Le Livre d'Or*, the visitor's book at Domremy, are more religious than secular. In their eloquent directness, they are the most moving testament to a phenomenon transcending mere history. Short and immediate, the sentiments express hope in the mystical, wishing Jeanne well, asking for her grace, sweetly caressing the face of modern cynicism. While something continued to stir in me, I added my own little prayer to the others.

As Jeanne was redefined by the nineteenth century, she has become literally—and confusingly—*une sainte pour tous*: spokesperson for both the French political left and right, Vichy puppet, first Protestant, first nationalist, proto-feminist. In the process Jeanne systematically has been shorn of any supernatural or spiritual implications, a guinea pig prodded through mazes of ideological and scientific dogma. Her own words have been ignored, or reshaped to fit specific secular needs. Was she anointed by God? Did she speak directly with angels and saints? Or was she mad, or a liar, or a witch, or a man, or even a lesbian haunted by penis envy, as she was ponderously diagnosed in 1933 in full Freudian drag.

Captivated, I set out on my own search for Jeanne d'Arc, driven by scientific curiosity, a thirst for sound history, and an open-mindedness to that divine mystery that has dumbfounded both her own contemporaries and her interpreters over the centuries—her *je ne sais quoi*. The following historical chronology is provided to facilitate the factual testimony covered in the first two chapters, before my personal quest for Jeanne's truth or madness begins. Perhaps the two will lead to the same place.

1337 Hundred Years War began between France and England.

1346 English defeated the French at critical battles of Crécy and Poitiers, and then began to conquer Normandy and northern France.

1412 Jeanne was born in Domremy in the Duchy of Lorraine, on the eastern border of France.

1415 Battle of Agincourt in France. The English under Henry V soundly defeated the French ruled by Charles VI, disputed father of the Dauphin Charles, born in 1403.

1416–19 The English formed an alliance with the French portion of Burgundy in middle France, which had been feuding with the Orléans faction under Charles VI. Prominent murders fueled both factions, including assassinations of both the Dukes of Burgundy and Orléans.

1420 Treaty of Troyes was signed among Henry V, Charles VI, and Philip the Good of Burgundy. The Dauphin Charles was disinherited, with France and England to be ruled by the son of Henry V, who was newly married to the daughter of Charles VI. Henry VI was born in 1421.

1422 Both Henry V and Charles VI died, leaving the English Duke of Bedford to act as regent for the infant Henry VI, until his maturity and dual reign of England and France.

1424 At age twelve or thirteen, Jeanne first heard a voice by her church in Domremy, Lorraine. She was progressively instructed to go save France from the English.

1429

January: Jeanne left Domremy to go to nearby Vaucouleurs to proclaim her mission to Robert de Baudricourt, to save France from the English and Burgundians, who were engaged in a lengthy siege of Orléans, last major stronghold of the Dauphin Charles and his faithful Armagnac party in the south.

February–March: Jeanne and a small party traveled nine hundred miles west across France to Chinon to meet Charles. He tentatively validated her after a trial conducted by his churchmen at Poitiers.

April–May: Jeanne marched to Orléans and relieved the English-Burgundian siege, fighting along with Dunois, the self-proclaimed Bastard of Orléans, and the Duke d'Alençon. She was first wounded. The attack on Orléans was lifted on May 8, to become the annual date remembering the feat of the Maid of Orléans through present times.

May–July: More French victories followed in the Loire Valley at Jargeau, Meung-sur-Loire, Beaugency, and Patay. The stronghold of Troyes reversed itself and recognized Charles as the legitimate dauphin.

July 17: Because of Jeanne's victories, the dauphin was crowned Charles VII at Reims.

August 29: Edict of Compiègne, declaring Franco-Burgundian truce until Christmas. Composed by advisers to Charles VII, this did not agree with Jeanne's messianic vision.

September: Against the wishes of Charles VII, Jeanne unsuccessfully tried to take Paris, and was wounded for the second time on September 8. On September 21, the king dissolved the main army.

October–December: Separating from Charles VII, Jeanne

began to experience other failures, along with occasional minor successes.

1430

May 23: Jeanne was captured by the Burgundians at Compiègne. No ransom was forthcoming from Charles VII. Imprisoned for months, she failed in several escape attempts and was finally sold to the English for clerical trial at Rouen, in Normandy.

1431

January 9: Trial of Jeanne at Rouen began, headed by Bishop Pierre Cauchon.

May 30: She was burned at the stake as a heretic.

1435 Treaty of Arras reconciled Charles VII and the Burgundians. Charles entered Paris in 1436. Gascony was conquered in 1442, Normandy by 1450.

1452–56 After the last battle of the Hundred Years War was fought at Castillion in 1453, virtually all of France was restored to Charles VII by subsequent uprisings. He initiated a trial of reclamation to clear Jeanne's name of heresy, thereby buttressing his own divine claim to the throne. In 1456 the original verdict of Jeanne's trial was annulled, claiming procedural flaws in the first trial at Rouen in 1431.

1591 William Shakespeare's play, *Henry VI, Part I,* politically derided Jeanne as a witch and loose woman.

1762 The French satirist Voltaire published *La Pucelle d' Orléans*, a bawdy farce deriding the Jeanne d'Arc legend. In the years after the French Revolution of 1789, Jeanne became more unpopular as a symbol of royalism. Eventually she became a footnote in history.

1804 Seeking resolution in a nation divided after the French Revolution, Napoleon Bonaparte encouraged a monument in Orléans to Jeanne.

1840s After several decades of research, Jeanne's original trial records were reconstructed by Jules Quicherat, renewing great public and literary interest. This inspired major revisionist works by Anatole France, Mark Twain, and George Bernard Shaw, among many others.

1869 Jeanne was first proposed for Catholic canonization by the Bishop of Orléans. The process officially began in Rome in 1894. By 1909 she had advanced to being beatified. France's humiliation in the Franco-Prussian War of 1870 added patriotic zeal to Jeanne's perpetuation, leading to political and religious reverberations into the twentieth century.

1920 Jeanne d'Arc was declared a saint at St. Peter's Basilica in Rome on May 16.

1

"Go! Go on! I Will Be Your Help—Go on!"

As the defendant began to respond, the scribe's quill moved across the parchment: "When asked about the place of her birth, she replied that she was born in a village called Domremy de Greux, and in Greux is the principal church."

She was basically from nowhere in a little duchy in the Lorraine, on the eastern border of France. Nothing good ever tended to come from that region. Her mother and father were Isabelle Romée and Jacques Darc, solid Catholic country *laboureurs*. "And it was from my mother," the girl continued, "that I learned the Pater Noster, Ave Maria, and the Credo. Nobody taught me my belief but my mother." She believed that she was around nineteen years old, "as far as I know," and could not recall her age when she had left home. Villagers called her Jeannette, "and since I came to France, Jeanne. As for my surname, I know of none." She was nothing much to look at, fettered in leg irons, short, with dark eyes beneath dark bangs, her hair cropped above the ears in a bowl-cut, *en ronde*. She was dressed in long hose and loose black tunic of a man, her breasts flattened beneath a snug quilted doublet. Except for her attractive feminine voice, this shabby adolescent offered little to arouse concupiscence.[1]

In English-occupied Normandy, Jeanne sat before her vast panel of judges in the Chapelle Royale in the castle of Rouen. Forty-three of them surrounded her, while scribes and other attendants receded into the shadows. Dour expressions covered a spectrum of dignity, concern, irritation, and occasional curiosity. The accused had been refused attendance at Mass because of her obstinacy toward proper authority, haughtily refusing to change from male attire. She complained of her chains, to no avail. Repeatedly, with mounting anger, she was commanded to answer all questions under sacred oath. Repeatedly the prisoner responded with caveats: "Perhaps you may ask of things that I will not answer. . . . As to some things I shall tell the truth, as to others, not. If you are well informed about me, you would wish that I were out of your hands. I have done nothing save by revelation."

But those revelations were not subject to a vow of total truth: "I shall willingly tell you what I know—but not all!" As far as Jeanne was concerned, her head could be cut off before she revealed all. At length she reached a compromise, by kneeling and placing both hands on the Scriptures in answers regarding her faith and deeds, "but I will not say all that I know." Her opening statements caused grumbles in the chapel. Master Jean Beaupère, a theologian from the University of Paris, was chosen to conduct the interrogation, his frustration mounting. He did not suffer fools gladly, believing that women were full of cunning and subtlety. This young woman in particular galled him. He sensed that her claims of some heavenly calling originated only from innate deviousness and pride. A man for all seasons, Beaupère received an annual honorarium from Jeanne's sworn enemy, the English. He was not alone in this among the judges, many of whom were in servile collaboration with their new masters.[2]

Enemy insults of *putain*—whore—to the contrary, Jeanne claimed to be a virgin. She said she confessed her sins annually. She took the Body of Our Lord every year at Easter. And at other times, Beaupère probed? *Passez outre,* "Go to the next question," she stiffened, knowing that she sought out the Sacraments at every opportunity, every day if it were possible. Priests were already concerned that ordinary folk were too commonly seeking the Holy Eucharist. Was Jeanne such a headstrong *faux dévoué?* Or was she one of those women whose fervor for frequent confession became a pretext for dalliances with priests? In the next breath she revealed—here the curious leaned forward—while the scribe bore down:

> From the age of thirteen, she received revelation from Our Lord by a voice which taught her how to behave. And the first time she was very afraid. And she said that the voice came that time at noon, on a summer's day, a fast day, when she was in her father's garden. She had not fasted the day before. "I heard this voice to my right, towards the church. Rarely do I hear it without it being accompanied by a light. This light comes from the same side as the voice." She said further that, after she had heard it three times, she knew that it was the voice of an angel. She said also that this voice had always taken good care of her. "Since I came into France, I have often heard this voice."

Beaupère asked, "But how can you see this light you describe, if it comes from your side?" The prisoner did not elaborate, deviating to claims she heard the voice more clearly in the woods. "It seemed to me to come from lips I should reverence," Jeanne concluded. "I believe it was sent by God."[3]

This maid named Jeanne, the virginal La Pucelle—Daughter of God, her voice proclaimed—must be deluded, a heretic, or a witch. She would hardly be the first, as women were coming forth periodically with mystical claims of visions, miraculous cures, levitations, and other heretical magic. There seemed to be a ground swell of *vieilles sorcières*, witches. All over Europe groups of them were proclaiming personal visions that exempted them from Church authority. Some even believed that they could indulge in carnal pleasures, free of sin. A leading Parisian theologian, Jean Gerson, expressed alarm that "false mysticism was ravaging the Church." Interpretation of mystical theology might become rampant among the *vox populi*, crudely discussed "in the vulgar language among servants, uneducated youths, slow-witted old people, the unlettered crowd, broken-down old women, at one time in the market place, at another in the back streets."

Only the year before, a woman from Britanny claimed she talked with God face-to-face, the Almighty dressed in a white robe with a red tunic beneath. She was burned at the stake. Seven years before, a woman was tried in Lyons for claiming God sent her to redeem souls from hell, and that she could read men's sins on their foreheads. Previously a woman diviner had confessed—under torture—to invoking a demon, one physical proof at the trial being a dead toad skewered with a spike. Yet another woman said that she frequently saw Christ flying through the air. "Unless I am mistaken," Gerson concluded, "she was out of her mind." In Paris, four witches had been burned after torture made them reveal bizarre relations with bodily demons. Witches could render men impotent, break their penises—*nouer l'aiguillette*—incite abortions, change the weather, induce grave illness. The times were indeed unsettling, full of magic and portent. An old visionary named Marie d'Avignon had even come forth to proclaim to the French court that a maiden in armor would come to save the country from its enemies.[4]

Jeanne was asked to explain stories about the mysterious Fairies' tree back in Domremy. The superstitious feared that witches might gather there in secret sabbats, meeting with the devil. The Lorraine frontier was said to overrun with such meeting sites. The notary continued to record her testimony:

> She answered that quite close to Domremy there was a tree which was called the Ladies' tree, others called it the Fairies' tree, and near it was a spring. And she had heard it said that persons suffering from fever drank of it, and she had seen them going to it to be cured. But she did not

> know whether they were cured or not. . . . She said that she sometimes went there with the other girls in summer time, and made wreaths for Notre Dame de Domremy. "I have seen the young girls putting garlands on the branches of this tree, and I myself have sometimes put them there with my companions. . . . Ever since I knew I should come into France, I have given myself up as little as possible to these games and distractions."[5]

Had Jeanne ever heard voices at the spring? Yes, she recalled, but their message in her childhood was unclear. Had she heard voices beneath the tree? She did not recall. Others had told her of seeing fairies or *faées* there—*maligni spiriti* to her judges—including one of her godmothers, Jeanne Aubry, wife of the Domremy mayor. "Whether this is true," Jeanne continued, "I do not know. I have never seen a *faée*, as far as I know, either at the tree or anywhere else." Asked if her godmother who saw the *faées* is considered a wise woman, Jeanne said that she is considered a sensible and upright woman, not a witch or a sorceress.

Jeanne said that she had to contradict her own brother that she had not received her revelations from any *faées* at the tree in the Bois Chenu, visible from the door of her house, only half a league away. It also was not true, she continued, that she believed the prophecy that some attributed to the folk figure Merlin, that a marvelous virgin would rise up from there to crush the English archers. Concerning such superstitions, "I hold all that to be sorcery." Despite outward appearances, the simple teen did not appear to be a folklore-riddled rustic. Jeanne recalled that she occasionally had danced in childhood around the great tree with other girls, but she quit such reveries after her revelations. After her voices came, Jeanne played very little, she emphasized, "the least that I could."[6]

Did Jeanne possess a mandrake, a mystical root tracing back to biblical times, used to cast spells, said to even shriek when ripped from the earth? Although she was told that one was buried near the old tree, she had never seen it, as the clerk recorded her bewilderment: "She had heard it said that it was a dangerous and evil thing to him who keeps it, but she does not know its purpose . . . she had heard it said that it attracts money, but she does not believe it." Despite having performed what others swore were miracles, she claimed no supernatural powers. No, she did not use a ring given to her by her family to hex her enemies. But the judges asked about an infant Jeanne supposedly resurrected from the dead in the cathedral at Lagny, full of villagers praying for it:

> The child was three days old. It was brought before the image of Our Lady. They told me that I might wish to go also and pray to God and Our Lady to give life to this infant. I went and prayed with them. At last, life returned to the child, who yawned three times, and was baptized. Soon after, it died, and was buried in consecrated ground. It was three days, they said, since life had departed from this child. It was black as my tunic when it yawned, and the color began to return to it. Asked if it was not said by the town that she had brought this about by her intercession, she replied, "I never inquired."[7]

Even the sword of this captured warrior-maid, discovered at her direction near a remote cathedral altar in the Loire, was surrounded by psychic aura. The tribunal had her repeat the tale of how she had known where to find it at Ste.-Catherine-de-Fierbois, where the French leader Charles Martel, according to legend, had left a sword in tribute to his victory over the Muslims seven centuries before:

> She said it was in the ground, all rusted, and upon it were five crosses. "I knew by my voice where it was. I had never seen the man who went to seek it." It was not deep in the ground behind the altar, so she thought, although

> in truth she was not certain whether it was in front of it or behind, but she believed that it was behind. . . . She added that as soon as the sword was found, the clergy of the place rubbed it and the rust fell off without any effort. . . . She said also that she greatly prized this sword, since it was found in the church of Saint Catherine, whom she much loved. Asked whether she had placed her sword upon any altar, she said no, nor would she have known how to do so. "I neither blessed it, nor had it blessed. I should not have known how to set about it." Asked if she sometimes prayed that the sword might be more fortunate, she answered, "It is good to know that I wished my armor might have good fortune!"

But Jeanne infinitely preferred her battle standard to actually using her sword. "Better, forty times better, my standard than my sword," she explained. "I bore my standard during an attack to avoid killing anyone. I have never killed anyone at all." Jeanne admitted that she had repeatedly told her troops to go boldly among the English, and that she had done so herself. *Hardiment*, boldly. It was a favorite word of hers, one that her voices, her *Conseil*, repeated to her over and over. Go *hardiment*, speak now *hardiment*. Toward the end Jeanne had adopted a less exalted captured sword, "useful for giving hard clouts, *bonnes buffes*," she offered mundanely—clouts that on occasion were applied to whores who followed her army. What became of the sword from Ste.-Catherine-de-Fierbois? she was pressed. Jeanne replied that there was no point in pursuing its disappearance. It was missing after she had left St.-Denis, where she had given an offering for recovering after her wound received at Paris.

The sword had nothing to do with her trial, she protested. Jeanne would dampen further inquiry on fantasies about her, explaining it was not true that butterflies magically clustered around her standard. Surely it were her enemies the Burgundians who had invented such a ridiculous tale, trying to label her a sorceress, who used insects as mediums. Did her voices tell her to hate Burgundians? Jeanne replied that she had only known one of them from her childhood. She would be happy to see his head cut off—"that is, if it pleased God."[8]

What had Jeanne's voice told her to do in the beginning? she was asked. Just be a good girl and go to church for the first several years, she answered. Then one day when she was tending cattle in a field, she learned she should go west and save France. Jeanne wept at the revelation, lamenting that she could neither ride a horse nor conduct war. Her mission was urgently repeated two and three times a week, she claimed, the voice convincing her of the misery of the French. Not honoring her father and mother, she had left home without their permission. Had she not committed a sin? she was asked. "Since God commanded it so, I had to obey." Jeanne stressed that if she had a hundred fathers and mothers—if she had been a king's daughter—she would still have left home on God's command. A command from God? Whom did this voice belong to?

> She said it was Saint Michel, whom she saw before her eyes. And he was not alone, but was accompanied by angels from heaven. She said also that she would not have come into France had it not been for God's command. Asked if she saw Saint Michel and the angels bodily and in reality, she answered, "I saw them with my bodily eyes, as well as I am seeing you."
>
> And when the host left, Jeanne wept and longed to go with them. Kissing the ground in reverence, then and there she vowed her virginity for as long as it pleased God.[9]

Saint Michel, whom Jeanne described as having wings, was the warrior angel who had driven Lucifer himself from heaven, the adopted symbol of French resistance against the English. Saint Michel's image was newly added to their banners, the sword-wielding archangel having aided the Franks under Clovis over a thousand years before. Emperor Charlemagne too had devoted himself to this defender against invaders. Saint Michel was the patron saint of Jeanne's region, with several churches dedicated to him. In her childhood fear Jeanne had first doubted that the voice really belonged to Saint Michel, but the voice relentlessly had returned to convince her, and then instruct her. What had Saint Michel instructed her over? "He told me to be a good child, and that God would help me. And among other matters, that I should go to help the King of France."

Were there other voices? After a while, she answered. Once Saint Michel had left her, Saint Catherine and Saint Margaret routinely appeared, wearing crowns. Over six long years they had greeted her warmly, even politely introducing themselves at first. Physical curiosity seized the clerics. Were Saints Catherine and Margaret dressed in the same clothes? Of the same age? Did they talk and appear at the same time? The judges tripped over one another, interrupting Jeanne's words in anticipation. "I have not leave to tell you that," she demurred. "I shall not now tell you anything else."[10]

Saints Margaret and Catherine had shared the same legendary fate in the fourth century A.D., both killed because they had refused marriage out of devotion to Christ. Margaret became the patron of childbirth, and Catherine, whom Jeanne loved more, the protector of virgins and philosophers. Catherine had once bested fifty pagan wise men from Egypt in debate, becoming the patron saint of the University of Paris for this forensic feat. Jeanne had grown up around their likenesses in churches around Domremy. The judges must know more. Jeanne reluctantly divulged teasing bits over the coming days:

> Asked what part of them she saw,
> She answered, the face.

Asked whether they had hair,
She replied: Assuredly—*Il est bon à savoir!*

Was the hair long? Did the saints have arms, legs, and other members? She could not answer them about such physical matters, but she described their voices as beautiful, sweet and low, speaking in French. But how could they speak if they had no other bodily members, came the next logical inquiry? "*Je m'en rapporte à Dieu*: I leave that to God," Jeanne answered, an unassailable refuge she would progressively cling to. Did the voices have eyes? Could they see? Jeanne would not reveal that yet, adding enigmatically, "there is a saying among little children that people are often hanged for telling the truth." Was Jeanne in truth hiding any crime herself to be hanged for? No, she answered.[11]

Did Saint Margaret speak English? "Why would she speak English?" Jeanne replied in surprise. "She is not on the side of the English." Do her saints hate the English? Her response was platitudinal. *"Elles aiment ce que notre Seigneur aime, et haient ce que Dieu hait*": "They love what God loves, and hate what God hates." Frustrated with such coyness, the judges persisted. Does God hate the English? "As to the love or hate that God has for the English, or what He would do for their souls, I know nothing. But I am well assured that they will be driven out of France—except those who die here—and that God will send the French victory over the English."

Jeanne was asked if she had ever been involved in defeating the English." *En nom Dieu*—surely," she proudly proclaimed. "How gently you put it! Have not many fled from France already?" And the rest of the English would all flee France within seven years, she had prophesied. This proud peasant girl sitting before her learned judges was clearly not awed by her opposition. Trying to drive the English out of France, who controlled nearly half the country? She had a messianic will that was dangerous and contagious. And successful. Jeanne had famously broken the siege around Orléans, and not even an arrow wound had slowed her down:

> Asked whether she knew beforehand that she would be wounded, she said that she well knew it, and had informed her king of it, but the wound notwithstanding, she would not give up her work. And this was revealed to her by the voices of Saint Catherine and Saint Margaret. She said also that she herself was the first to plant the ladder against the fort at the bridge, and it was while she was raising it that she was wounded in the neck by an arrow.[12]

After Orléans, Jeanne had inspired a thrashing of the English and their Burgundian allies at the battle of Patay a month later, driving them from the Loire Valley north to Paris. She had followed them and tried to liberate Paris, and despite receiving another wound, she did liberate much of the surrounding area. Far worse, she had escorted the discredited dauphin to Reims to be anointed with holy oil and crowned Charles VII, the legitimate king of France. Captured in battle, Jeanne was now before a panel of inquisitors in Rouen. It was February of 1431.

As a contemporary described the introspective Charles, he had three vices, "changeability, defiance, and above all, envy. He savored of the fruit all he could suck from it." Behind his vapid expression and calculating, narrow eyes lay a mind open to compromise. More devious were the key advisers to the dauphin, who, at twenty-eight years old, was wise to listen to experience. They stressed to him that diplomacy, not warfare, was the quickest way to bind Frenchmen together again. Jeanne had attacked Paris without his consent, being a single-minded liability who only listened to voices that no one else heard—ones who had told her not to take Paris, she confessed. As Charles's advisers argued, one must accommodate and negotiate the realities of conquest with the Burgundians in order to drive a diplomatic wedge between them and the English invaders. But not Jeanne. She seemed determined to win the Hundred Years War in six months. Jeanne's voices had told her that she had about a year to accomplish her mission. For her there was no time to waste in complying with temporal authority. Later her deadline was pinpointed to end before the Feast of Saint John. Though she admittedly would have avoided her fate if she could, the voices had assured her "that it had to be so, and I should not be cast down, but take it all in good part and God would help me."

A month before Saint John's Day, Jeanne d'Arc ingloriously was dragged off her charger into the mire by a Burgundian archer. She had trooped nearly three thousand miles around France, yet her path of glory had lasted but fifteen months. "Daughter of God, go on," Jeanne had recalled her message after Orléans. "Go! Go on! I will be your help—go on!" But weeks, months, half a year passed with no offer of ransom from Charles to free her. He had pleaded with the Burgundians for some tradeoff, then raged and threatened to extract retribution against the English. Both attempts proved futile. Finally the Duke of Burgundy sold Jeanne to the English for ten thousand livres in gold.[13]

It was a powerful but anxious coalition that gathered for judgment in Rouen, all wanting the elimination of this deluded and dangerous maid. Clearly the English wanted her militarily canceled out. So did their Burgundian colleagues. The Duke of Burgundy supported the English claim to the French throne by way of the child-king, Henry VI, who was eight years old at the time. Under his boyish signature a letter had been sent out denouncing Jeanne La Pucelle, "leaving off the dress and clothing of the feminine sex, a thing contrary to divine law and abominable before God, and forbidden by all laws, who wore clothing and armour such as is worn by men." But only the Church could denounce and disgrace this Daughter of God for heresy. Jeanne cited her authority as coming directly from heaven, from saints of the Church Triumphant.

With no shame and little fear, she presented a direct challenge to the medieval authority on earth, the Holy Church Militant, with its batteries of bishops and clerics to enforce orthodoxy, over a people only a few steps removed from Gallic paganism. If the Pan of nature was supposedly dead, occult folk ceremonies to crops and wine still lived. Special trees and rocks were sacred, cats were burned as evil on Saint John's Day, and many a goodwife left a drink of milk outside for *faées* before retiring to pray to the Virgin. Village wise women practiced magic like shamans. From the beginning of time, it seemed, the Church had tried to cloak ancient pagan symbols, planting fig leaves over fertility rites, developing a ceaseless religious calendar. But there was no end, like energy transformed but never destroyed. Anticlerical revolts always threatened. Several bishops had been killed in Paris in 1418. Perhaps the learned churchmen could expose Jeanne as satanic, thus halting any martyrdom before it spread among the gullible. An English trial could kill her body, but not her soul. Nor could it stamp out her dangerous claims from God Himself.

What if Jeanne's rebellious example spread further? "Many people were glad to see me," she admitted in sweeping understatement. As La Pucelle had passed by in new hope, the oppressed reached out to kiss her hands, her feet, her garments, hugging even the muddy legs of her horse. At the holy site of St.-Denis she was said to have allowed children to offer candles to her on bended knee, then engaged in sorcery by dripping candle wax on their heads in occult benediction. She denied that she had affixed a round device above her helmet, resembling a halo. Although she claimed she tried to prevent such manifest adulation, women still clamored to touch their rings with Jeanne's for good fortune—the blessed ring that had touched Saint Catherine. Such idolatry was an affront to the Church. "Did the French people firmly believe you were sent by God?" Jeanne was challenged. "I do not know whether they believe it," the fettered youth responded. That was not an answer. Beaupère persisted. "If they *thought* you were sent from God, do you think it was well thought?" Jeanne's response was defiant. "If they believe that I am sent from God, they are not deceived. But even if they do *not* believe it—still I am sent from God!"[14]

There you have it—heresy. As she stood on trial for her life, Jeanne continually requested *le Conseil* from her voices. She averred that she could summon them with a plea to Christ and the Virgin Mary, requesting answers to give to her accusers. Often the voices came without being called. Did Jeanne always make the sign of the cross when the saints appeared? Sometimes yes, sometimes no. She had no doubt that the voices came directly from God. She consulted them daily, as she divulged early on: "Questioned since when had she heard her voice, she answered she had heard it both yesterday and today. . . . Questioned as to what she was doing yesterday morning when she heard the voice, she answered she was asleep, and that the voice awoke her. Asked whether the voice awoke her by its sound, or by touching her on the arms or elsewhere, she answered that she was awakened by the voice without being touched. Questioned as to whether the voice was still in her room, she replied that she thought not, but that it was in the castle. Asked if she did not thank the voice, and kneel down, she answered that she thanked it, being seated on her bed. And she said that she joined her hands together, and begged and prayed that it might help and advise her in what she had to do. To which the voice told her to answer *hardiment*."[15]

After eight months of weary imprisonment, alone Jeanne faced her voluminous prosecution, a rotating battery of six bishops, fifty-five theologians and doctors, plus their extended retinue. Some came and went, but daily they sat, by the dozens. The theological and legal nucleus was sent to Rouen from "our Mother, the University of Paris," as they referred to that institution of learning, which had been founded in the twelfth century. Clustered around the rue de Sorbonne on

Mount Ste. Geneviève, rising from the left bank of the Seine River, it was the towering intellectual center of Christendom. The university had the finest libraries in the world, "abundant orchards of all manner of books," one visitor typically enthused. "What a mighty stream of pleasure made our hearts glad when we visited Paris, the paradise of the world!" Students flocked from across Europe to sit at the feet of masters in theology and law, studying the sacred Scriptures to become proud wrestlers in words. The pope in Rome might enforce dogma, but the theological scaffolds of dogma were erected in Paris.

And what of once-mighty Rome? There was no university there. That decayed eternal city was on the verge of collapse, wild animals dwelling among the deserted ruins of antiquity, which were covered in weeds. Livestock were stabled in abandoned churches. The Black Plague from the previous century had devastated Rome's population to twenty thousand—scarcely a third of what it had been. Pope Martin V was under siege, huddled defensively in St. Peter's Basilica, cut off from those who wanted to depose him by the Fortress of St. Angelo. Other popes challenged the authority of the Holy See, one of whom had resided in southern France for decades at Avignon, with a different set of cardinals and bishops. Pope Martin had just died on the eve of Jeanne's trial, to be replaced by a sickly Eugene IV, who remained equally isolated and desperate. Papal power was eroding in the face of a rebellious Europe, which included competing Italian duchies, some of which were conspiring to unite with France. In Britain a popular taunt went, "the pope has become French, and Jesus has become English."[16]

The University of Paris, too, was fractured by war and politics, losing prestige as many students left to study in Oxford, England. Those doctors from Paris who went to Rouen were loyal to the Burgundian party and in league with the English. A letter from the university had been sent to the Burgundian

John of Luxembourg, who held Jeanne after her capture. It was Luxembourg's holy obligation—"under penalties of law, which are grave"—to turn over for trial "a certain woman called La Pucelle, by whom God's honor has been immeasurably offended, the Faith greatly wounded, and the Church much dishonored."

The authors of this letter were the *litterati*, in their Latin self-description, pitted against Jeanne, an unlettered *illitterata,* a blasphemous pretender, *ignorans Scripturas*. Pierre Cauchon, Bishop of Beauvais, presided, claiming the right because Jeanne had been captured near his diocese. The prestigious Archbishopric of Rouen was dangling before the impatient Cauchon if he succeeded in satisfying English desires. He already received a thousand pounds a year as a member of the Council of Henry VI, the English king. Cauchon had been the chief negotiator with the Burgundians in selling Jeanne to the English. Indeed England was financing the cost of many of the principals for their presence at the trial. Cauchon, however, also wanted to fulfill his religious office. He seemed genuinely committed in his task of thwarting this new threat to Christianity. In a letter to Luxembourg and the Duke of Burgundy, he described Jeanne as one "suspected and defamed of having committed several crimes, such as spells, idolatries, invocations of demons, and several other acts concerning our faith and opposed to it." Conflict of task and conscience was no dilemma for the Bishop of Beauvais. Regardless of secular motivation, ridding heretics and trying to save their souls was the proper task of the court. The finest minds in France were gathered to accomplish this, all before a watching Europe.[17]

Some clergymen had balked over such a mongrel procedure against this threat to orthodoxy, which they alone, by office, should help stamp out. The Bishop of Avranches challenged Cauchon's competence to preside, believing that such profound articles of faith were a matter for the pope in Rome. Cauchon struck his name from the list of assessors. A Norman priest claimed that the trial was invalid. He was sped out of town. A theologian from the University of Paris pointed out that Cauchon was the sworn enemy of Jeanne. The Bishop of Beauvais dismissed him. Jean Massieu, the priest in daily charge of escorting Jeanne from her prison cell to the trial chamber, was threatened with prison because he—once—had allowed her to stop on the way for prayer. Others who tried to interrupt the testimony were told loudly by Cauchon to hold their tongues—*de par le diable!* One judge soon complained that evidence favorable to Jeanne was being suppressed. He left Rouen under threat. Jeanne herself finally confronted Cauchon over the mounting farce: "Oh, you write the things which are against me all right, but not the things which are in my favor!"[18]

Often Jeanne's answers were sublime beyond guile or forensics, dumbfounding the learned *litterati*. In the process of denying any psychic powers, she inadvertently volunteered that without the grace of God, she could do nothing. So might any other Christian believer pray. But in that statement waited a steel-jawed trap, the pious conceit that she was in a state of holy grace. If one claimed to be in it, blasphemy beckoned. If not in a state of grace, mortal sin. Letting her innocent slip of the tongue lay dormant through several unrelated tangents, the unanswerable question was then sprung. State of grace—tell us about your state of grace—how do you *know* if you are in a state of grace? "It is not a proper question to put to such a woman," one judge protested. Another rose to agree. Cauchon commanded silence, while the court strained for her response: "If I am not, may God put me there. If I am—*que Dieu m'y tienne*—may God keep me there."

Some crossed themselves, amid murmurs that Jeanne might be truly inspired. "You have answered well, Jeanne," one exclaimed. She despaired that if she knew she were not in the grace of God, she would be the most miserable person in the world. And if she were in mortal sin, she believed, surely her voices would desert her, lamenting, "I would that everybody might hear my voices as well as I do." One of the scribes noted that her interrogators were stupefied by this response. They ceased their traps for that session.[19]

Jeanne continued to answer her interrogators boldly—too boldly—as her trial wore on, but at other times she refused to answer. Or she did not know. Or she had forgotten, delaying to seek *le Conseil* of her voices. "She could speak well on occasion," one priest recalled, "but sometimes varied her answers, and sometimes did not reply to the questions." Progressively Jeanne seemed tugged and confused, as direct testimony suggested during her fourth tedious interrogation:

> Asked whether she had heard her voice since Saturday, she answered, "Yes, indeed, many times." Questioned as to whether she heard it in this hall on Saturday, she answered, "That has nothing to do with your trial," and afterwards said yes. Asked what it said to her on Saturday, she answered, "I did not well understand it. I understood nothing that I could tell you until my return to my room." Asked what it said to her when she was back in her room, she replied, "I should answer you *hardiment*."[20]

Jeanne admitted that in captivity she had to listen closely to overcome the noise made by her harassing guards, and did not always recognize her voices at once. Other times she could not understand the voices until she was fully awake. Even the most sympathetic judge might have wondered whether this disturbed teen was only dreaming and talking in her sleep.[21]

Jean Le Maitre, Vice-Inquisitor of the Heretical Evil for the Realm of France, reluctantly participated as cochairman of the trial. He insisted that he be ordered to participate by higher authority, to legalistically salve "the serenity of his conscience." This morally reticent official addition took a tepid part in the proceedings, knowing Jeanne had already been tried two years before by Church authority at Poitiers, before she had taken

Orléans. The dauphin himself, who was residing at Chinon when Jeanne first met him, had had his doubts about this obscure maid, starting with her alleged virginity. She was examined and found to be virginal—a first crude indicator that she might not be a witch—before she was sent to Poitiers for her theological examination. At Poitiers in 1356 superior French forces had suffered yet another ghastly defeat at the hands of the English. Thousands of soldiers had been killed or captured before the city walls as they attempted to flee.

Charles, forewarned of Jeanne's coming by a letter she had sent ahead, was already wary when she arrived at Chinon. He was counseled against receiving a young female peasant prone to flighty fantasies, and urged "not to make himself ridiculous in the eyes of foreign nations, the French having quite a reputation for the ease with which their nature leads them to be duped." Jean Gerson also wrote Charles that he should rely less on court astrologers, to avoid a flighty reputation. It was even suggested that Jeanne might be an assassin, and therefore it would be safer that the dauphin not be alone with her. Coming from the Lorraine, she could even be demonic, as that region was particularly notorious for witchcraft. Women were said to be transformed into wolves there, and to devour hapless travelers. Better to keep her languishing for a spell, since outwitting the devil by outwaiting him was considered wise policy. "Dissimulated evil must make some visible eruption," one archbishop advised. Charles called a council to decide about receiving Jeanne. Some advised that he at least grant her an audience, since she claimed to be sent by God. From afar Jean Gerson noted that "If we deny, ridicule or reject everything immediately, we shall appear to weaken the authority of divine revelation, which is as authoritative now as it was then, for God does not lack the power to make a revelation." The ecclesiastics now had to walk a thin line: be taken in by a false prophet, or reject God's prophet to save France. All of them believed that divine Providence lay behind human events, although all human effort must be expended before beseeching God for solutions. In the fifth century Saint Jerome had declared Gaul the freest from heresy. Since that time its monarch had carried the mantle of the most Christian of rulers. Under the current downtrodden condition, therefore, the times must be a sign that the kingdom clearly had lapsed morally. But then so often had the children of Israel strayed, yet God had not abandoned them. A verse from 1 Corinthians was repeated as most prescient: "God chose what is weak in the world to shame the strong."

At her full examination in Poitiers, Jeanne had faced a group that Jean Gerson had called "spiritual money changers," wise in the coin of divine revelation. They were largely refugees from the University of Paris loyal to the crown, who had left when the Burgundians took over the city in 1418. Their assigned task was that of *discretio spirituum*, the discernment of spirits. Time-honored rules of this exercise dictated that they should research the subject for an exceptional truth, *manifestando occulta,* divining demonic falsehood for some heavenly *signum*—a sign—or something *monstrum, prodigium, portentum—miraculum.* It might be a physical *signum.* Moses had turned a rod into a serpent, for example. That objective *signum* lacking, a compelling biblical prediction might suffice. Jeanne had been full of predictions favorable to the kingdom, and was found at Chinon to be "devout, sober, temperate, chaste, who customarily confessed and took communion once a week."

Still, there was no *signum.* Weeks of ecclesiastical examination followed at Poitiers, guided by the admonition from the Bible, "test the spirits to see whether they are of God, for many false prophets have gone out into the world." Their investigation focused on one who had admitted that "I do not know A from B." Jeanne was illiterate, *idiotae sine litteris*. Beyond the Lord's Prayer, Ave Maria, and Catholic Credo taught to her by her mother, she was otherwise ignorant of religious matters, claiming her counsel came from childhood voices. What tongue did her voices speak in? one examiner had asked. "Better than yours," Jeanne impishly responded, inducing a ripple of laughter over the theologian's own thick regional *patois*. Did she believe in God? "Yes—and better than you," came her impudent reply, the answer reflecting her rude impatience to get on with her mission. Relentlessly the examiners probed for a divine *signum* to legitimize her mission. *"En nom Dieu,"* Jeanne finally protested, "I have not come to Poitiers to perform signs. Lead me to Orléans and I will *show* you the signs I was sent to make." Why the need for soldiers, Jeanne was asked, if it was already God's will that Orléans be liberated? *"En nom Dieu,* the soldiers will fight and God will give them victory!"

Commanding that a letter be fired off telling the English to leave France, Jeanne had promised that Orléans would be freed, and the dauphin anointed at Reims. Paris would also return to the rule of Charles one day. The doctors appeared satisfied. If they could find nothing overtly *miraculum* about her, they had discerned no *maligni spiriti*. They made a decision of blind faith, tempered by desperation. As stated in the conclusion at Poitiers, rejecting Jeanne with no evidence of evil was to repel the Holy Spirit, rendering France unworthy of God's aid. Additionally there was no worldly alternative to salvation from the English. "I believe that Jeanne was sent by God," one recalled, "because the dauphin and the people under his rule had lost all hope and everybody else thought only of retreat." One contemporary described her as like a second Saint Catherine, having momentarily overcome such a large number of learned skeptics.[22]

Politically the present demolition of this sorceress at Rouen was also a demolition of the king she had legitimized by having Charles anointed, one whose legitimacy to the throne was even thrown into question by his own mother. According to the unfortunate Treaty of Troyes (a result in 1420 of the startling English victory over French knighthood at Agincourt in 1415), the son of the victorious Henry V would succeed the vanquished Charles VI of France, that son to come from the loins of Charles's own daughter, Catherine. This royal union was consummated in 1422 by an infant Henry VI, heir-apparent to England and France. But conflict began when both kings died in that same year. Charles VI had already sired a son—though some whispered that the king's brother, the Duc d'Orléans, was the real father. This teen Charles—the so-called pretender, or *soi-disant Dauphin*, as he was branded by the Treaty of Troyes—was whisked from Paris in his bedclothes when the Burgundian party had taken over the city in 1418. Charles then wandered about his own divided kingdom with his paternity officially a *blague, canard*—a joke abetted by his icy mother, Isabeau de Bavière. She further helped to split the kingdom by maintaining her own little court at Troyes, aligned against her *soi-disant* son.[23]

Although the English were standing behind the trial, it nevertheless was a thorough ecclesiastical interrogation of one accused of heresy, blasphemy, idolatry, and sorcery. If rife with political motives to condemn Jeanne, many of the judges seemed both fascinated and horrified by her celestial claims. *A priori*, the young woman must be either a holy mystic or a demon, with no middle ground for one who claimed regular physical contact with God's angels. In titillating facets of inquiry, Jeanne was interrogated about kissing or embracing Saint Catherine or Saint Margaret. The scribes took down her words: "She said she had embraced them both. Asked whether they smelled pleasant, she replied: *'C'est bon à savoir;* assuredly.' Asked whether in embracing them she felt warmth or anything else, she said she could not embrace them without feeling or touching them. Asked what part she embraced, whether upper or lower, she answered: 'It is more fitting to embrace them below rather than above.'"[24]

Was Saint Michel naked? Jeanne was asked. Her answer was

rhetorical. "Do you not think that Our Lord has the means to clothe him?" If she were to lose her virginity, would her voices and good fortune disappear? "That has not been revealed to me," she responded.

The voyeuristic line of inquiry was quite real in the minds of some judges. At sabbats, witches worshiped the devil by first praying for his presence, then kissing his left foot or genitals, before he might become fully incarnate to make love to them as an incubus, often in the form of a smelly goat, or large black beast with glowing eyes. Unlike angels, demons could assume flesh—could stink, retch, break wind. They also felt icy cold to the touch, and to embrace them caused ecstatic pain. Erotic dancing, spitting on and trampling crucifixes, cursing Christ, flying about, devouring bats or infants, all were manifestations of a sabbat. No one claimed to have ever witnessed such demonic orgies, or knew of anyone who had—except witches.

Nevertheless the physical reality of demons was paradoxically a theological proof of God's existence. Inverse logic was used, with Satan on one pole of the *just milieu,* the golden mean that spanned God's creations. God was on the invisible opposite pole. No theologian could prove that God materially existed, including the greatest of the age, Saint Thomas Aquinas, who had trained and taught at the University of Paris. Instead the dilemma of proof was approached by endless scholastic argument, *disputatio*, proving that God does not *not* exist, by logical deductions of what God is *not,* like evil. Whatever those double-negative proofs of what God was not, Satan and his minions *were*. Mankind's condition was tossed about in that arc of the *just milieu* between ultimate good and evil. Man was trapped in the Doctrine of Original Sin, and it was unassailable which pole of the arc he was born into: eternal damnation—except through salvation. Only the Church could provide this watershed against Satan, dismissing the ancient fable that Adam had mourned a hundred years, and thus had expunged original sin by this atonement. Demons served as physical manifestations of God's enemies, the cause of evil in this world, which otherwise could only be assigned to God. This was unthinkable, leading to that paradox of opposites, the necessity of darkness to define the presence of light, *nullus Deus sine diabolo*: no God without the devil.

In this world one could actually get one's hands on human witches, the brides of Satan, seduced in the very physical acts of incubus and succubus. Their own words, whether forced by torture or not, affirmed the physical reality of evil. Therefore the opposite pole of the *just milieu* must exist as the source of goodness, which was an incorporeal God and his airy minions, angels and saints. Only decades before, the University of Paris had issued a twenty-eight-point article buttressing the existence of demons. In diverse old ways they were attempting to recapture heaven, and force Saint Michel and the angels to replace them in hell. Building for several centuries theologically, God's creatures presently were at war to the death. A popular evangelist who had been run out of Paris was still enthralling thousands of people who packed into French fields, preaching for days on end that the world would end in 1430.[25]

In contrast to demons, angels were not physical but ethereal, sent from God's nonphysical world. According to Aquinas' refinements of Church thought in the thirteenth century, angels might appear to have variable bodies when appearing to humans for divine purposes, but they were incapable of being touched or scented. "Angels do not need bodies for their own sake, but for ours," he stated in his exhaustive *Summa theologica.* Like Jeanne, the adolescent Aquinas had had a visitation of angels while he slept, who told him that they would clothe him with a white girdle of virginity. Jean Gerson reaffirmed the function of angels, who could be useful to humans under proper conditions and pure motives. But a devout non-heretic who claimed a holy vision should speak only of such spiritual encounters in obscure, non-corporeal terms. It was shocking that this country teen claimed she could actually see, touch, and even *smell* Almighty God's totally spiritual beings, who were above such physical degradation.

The theologians continued to probe to no avail, to help reverse Jeanne's mounting corporeal heresies: "Asked if Saint Michel and Saint Gabriel had natural heads, she said, 'Yes, I so saw them. And I believe it was they, as certainly as I believe that God exists.' Asked whether she believes that God made them with heads as she saw them, she answered, 'I saw them with my own eyes. I will not say anything more.' Asked again whether she believes that God made them with heads as she saw them, she answered yes. . . . Questioned whether she ever had received letters from Saint Michel or her voices, she said, 'I have not leave to tell you this.'"[26]

The Inquisition format had evolved over centuries, predominantly in Spain. Now, however, magic and sorcery were on the rise all over Europe, increasingly among women, the fresh face of heresy. The black arts must be stamped out. The accused were not presumed innocent of specific charges until proven guilty: Quite the opposite. Questions were layered remorselessly until the heretic stumbled into error or contradiction. Those were then used to formulate charges after the fact. "I remember," said one priest, "that incomplete questions were often put to Jeanne, and many difficult ones at the same time. Before she could answer one, another would come." Bluff was part of the proceedings, too, with the inquisitor theatrically implying a mountain of evidence already gathered for damnation. Enormous portfolios of papers would be shown to the accused, or ominously fingered in search of some fake evidence at the worst moment, to unnerve the heretic into confession. It was best to first extract confession in small errors of doctrine, which were easier for the accused to admit, and then build toward damnation. Rapid-fire questions by multiple questioners were meant to break down defenses, with fatigue on the side of the prosecution. A lie was harder to maintain than the truth: it was only a matter of time. By design, questions were not asked in logical sequence. Another participant stated that the seemingly disorderly, hodgepodge assault on Jeanne was calculated indeed.

When trying heinous witchcraft, a judge might even promise escape from death upon confession, only to retract it, or maintain the letter of the law by having another pronounce the final sentence. Guile was necessary to unmask Satan's guileful, who might try to save themselves by involving others—often friends and family—all of them consigned to the flames. Proof was a closed circle that proved itself. Confession was *ipso facto*, no matter how obtained, no matter how incredulous. Even suicide was self-evident proof, compounded by mortal sin. Pangs over false judgment were minimal: if an innocent person happened to be burned by mistake, it was believed that his soul went directly to heaven. God's direct guidance was considered present with such a body of deliberation. In a pure council of clerics and *litterati*, as some judges believed at Rouen, such a mystical body was incapable of erring by divine grace of the Holy Spirit. Their authority even exceeded that of the pope in Rome. This guidance was infallible, known as *Unam Sanctam*. By the time of Jeanne's trial, however, procedural precedents had appeared that began to uphold the right to remain silent on personal matters, the right to answer only to specific charges, and to counter against blatant self-incrimination. *"Ce n'est pas de votre procès,"* Jeanne instinctively and repeatedly protested—"That has nothing to do with your trial. Must I tell you this? Is *that* in your case?" Pierre Cauchon, having trained in canon law at the University of Paris two decades before Jeanne's trial, had personally been part of "causes by faith" inquisitions. He fully knew that the accused could not be subjected to blanket oaths and random interrogations without a statement of prior charges.[27]

Jeanne's imperious posture toward the Church Militant did little to help her case. *"Passez outre, continuez*—go on to the next question," became a litany as she switched to unrelated matters, dissembled, delayed, did not understand, or referred the question to her prior answers: "It is written down at Poitiers." Her obstinacy also contained threats in the beginning, starting with Cauchon, who badgered her to reveal all. She refused:

> Beware of saying that you are my judge. For you take upon yourself great responsibility, and you overburden me . . . consider well what you do, for in truth I am sent from God, and you are putting yourself in *en grand danger*.

As questioners began to ensnare her, Jeanne redoubled her messianic warning:

> You say that you are my judge. I do not know whether you are. But I warn you not to judge me wrongfully, for you would put yourself in great peril. But I warn you, so that if Our Lord punish you for it, I shall have done my duty in warning you.[28]

From the first day of the trial, Jeanne refused even to recite the Pater Noster. Some believed that one in league with the devil could not get through it without stumbling. "Hear my confession," Jeanne countered to Cauchon, "and I will say it willingly." But to hear her confession would mean granting solace to a heretic, possibly trapping the bishop into confidentiality about whatever she revealed. Cauchon offered two other priests to hear her recite the Pater Noster, but Jeanne's *quid pro quo* remained: no Pater Noster without confession. She also refused to vow that she would not escape. "It is the right of every prisoner," Jeanne maintained. She had twice tried to do so, jumping from the tower of her prison to what should have been certain death. Had her saints promised her freedom within three months? "Ask me in three months and *then* I will give you my reply," she answered. Was this a joke or a threat? Jeanne added that those who wished to remove her from this world might well leave it before her. Pressed further on a miraculous escape, she admitted, "By my faith, I know neither the hour nor the day. God's will be done." In vain, she prayed often for escape. Her Lord would send deliverance, but if not she recited the French proverb, *Aide toi, Dieu te aidera*—"help yourself and God will help you."[29]

From the beginning Jeanne's adoption of male dress was an affront to man and God, as her judges would remind her from Old Testament scriptural law: "A woman shall not wear anything that pertains to a man, nor shall a man put on a woman's garment; for whoever does these things is an abomination to the Lord your God." Her short hair also ran afoul of Saint Paul's admonition in the New Testament: "It is disgraceful for a woman to be shorn or shaven." As Pierre Cauchon wrote before the trial, "This woman, completely forgetting the honesty that is proper to the female sex, breaking all the restraints of shame, oblivious of all female decency, by an astonishing and monstrous deformation, wore unusual garments proper to the male sex."

Thomas Aquinas had taught that transvestism without purpose was not allowed, although permissible in case of necessity, "for instance to hide from enemies, or because there are no other clothes, or for some other good reason." Religious tradition had accepted prior examples of women who adopted male dress to escape seductions or forced marriages, or to enter monasteries disguised as a man, for a purely spiritual end. But Jeanne, as the clerics at Rouen charged, dressed "in the manner of fops," with a stylish male haircut, fine raiment, "sumptuous and magnificent clothes of precious cloth of gold and also furs." It was true that she had been dragged from her horse at Compiègne by her elegant long gold surcoat. Perhaps this little touch of prideful foppishness had contributed to her downfall. Described as full of hubris, she was "suspect of idolatry and the consecration of your person and your clothes to the devil in imitation of the rites of pagans." And the rites of men as well, by wearing their *habitus,* a bifid word meaning both clothing and deportment. Indeed she had forsaken normal female pursuits, "comporting herself in all things like a man rather than a woman." This had led her to corrupt social hierarchy, riding before an army of thousands of men, "in which there were princes, barons, and many other noblemen whom she made serve under her as under a principal captain."

Who had advised Jeanne to take on blasphemous male appearance? she was asked. She implied that it was God's will, like all of her acts—then she clouded this by asserting the idea was her own choice. Jeanne stressed that it was absolutely essential to adopt male attire when beginning her campaign in the exclusive company of men, sleeping beside them in the field. Did her voice specifically order her to wear men's dress? Jeanne dismissively replied that the subject was a very small matter to God—"nay, the least thing. I did not take it by the advice of any man. I did not take this male dress nor do anything at all, save by the command of Our Lord and the angels." When pressed further whether her voices told her to wear male attire, Jeanne repeated warily, "Everything good that I have done, I did by the command of the voices."[30]

On Tuesday, March 13, a more startling topic recurred, which was God's physical sign of revelation to the dauphin, provided through Jeanne. The bizarre subject was first brought up by the judges themselves weeks before. Was there an angel above the king's head the first time Jeanne saw him? they inquired. "Forgive me. *Passez outre,*" she declined. During the first of her trial Jeanne had been adamant about not discussing her revelations, explaining that her voices forbad it. "If the voice forbade me, what would you say?" When asked later about an angel above the king's head, Jeanne seemed flabbergasted at the very idea, responding, "By Saint Mary, if there were any, I did not know, nor did I see one." By March 1, Jeanne was asked if she had seen a crown on the king's head when she showed him his sign from God. "I cannot tell you without perjuring myself, and you would not want that," she maintained."Spare me that. Continue." She had heard of a heavenly crown, but had not yet seen one. The physical sign remained elusive for weeks.

But the crown as sign began a metamorphosis, becoming in Jeanne's words beyond price and description, to reign more than a thousand years. It was now physically in the king's treasury, she testified on March 10. "Go *hardiment*," her voices had instructed," for when you stand before the king, he will have a sign which will make him receive you and believe in you." She claimed that none other than an angel of God had given the sign to the king. Then Jeanne had asked Charles if he was content: "And he answered yes. And then she left him and went into a little chapel near at hand. She heard it said that after her departure more than three hundred people saw the sign. She said also that for love of her, and that they might cease questioning her, God was willing to allow those of her party to see the sign."[31]

Thus ended Jeanne's fantastic testimony for that day. The next day being Sunday, there was no session. Curiously the judges did not directly follow up on Monday. That session was occupied with pursuing more mundane subjects, like her leaving her mother and father, her father's dreams about her leaving, his threat to drown her if she did, her pledge of virginity, her heaven-sent title of La Pucelle, daughter of God—and, yet again, her reasons for wearing male clothes. On one minor sally into the subject of angels, Jeanne volunteered that she also had seen them mingling among other people: "Asked if the angels stayed long with her, she answered, 'They often come to Christians who do not see them.' She added that she had often seen them among Christian folk."[32]

On March 13, the subject of the sign dominated the day. Indeed it formed the opening question of the morning. Jeanne would not answer. Had she promised Saint Catherine not to reveal the sign? No, she responded, contradicting her prior claim. "Of my *own* accord I have sworn and promised not to reveal this sign. Too often I have been urged to do so." She muttered to herself that she would never speak of the episode again. But in the next breath she did so, in the windiest of detail. If the churchmen sought a tall tale, they should have it. Jeanne explained that the sign the angel gave Charles when he brought the crown was this: the promise that all of France would be his through God's help and Jeanne's efforts. The king should support her with troops to fulfill his anointing, and the sooner the better.

Had the angel put the crown directly on the king's head? No: First it was given to an archbishop, the Archbishop of Reims, if she was not mistaken. And the archbishop presented the crown to Charles in his castle at Chinon. It was late in the day, some time after Easter two years ago, she recalled. Did the angel come along the ground or descend from on high?

> He came from on high . . . and he entered the room by the door. . . . When he came to the king, he did him reverence, bowing before him, and saying the words that Jeanne had already mentioned concerning the sign, and together with this, the angel recalled the great patience the king had shown in the great tribulations that had come upon him, and from the door he walked across the floor to the king. Asked how far it was from the door to the king, she said she thought about a lance's length, and he went out by the way he came in. Jeanne said also that when the angel came she accompanied him, and went with him up the stairs to the king's chamber, and the angel entered first. Then she herself said to the king, "Sire, here is your sign. Take it."

Saint Catherine had instructed Jeanne several times to speak boldly that day. She did so, continuing in mounting allegory, blurring angel and La Pucelle, Daughter of God and messenger of God. The angel, she elaborated, first had come to her at her lodging in Chinon:

> And then they went together to the king, and the angel was accompanied by a number of other angels whom no one could see . . . as for the crown, several churchmen and others saw it, who did not see the angel. Asked what appearance the angel had, and how tall he was, Jeanne said she had not leave to answer this, but will do so tomorrow. Asked whether those who accompanied the angel all had the same appearance, she said that some of them were like each other, and others not, as far as she could see, and that some of them had wings, and some had crowns, and others not, and there were amongst them Saint Catherine and Saint Margaret, who went with the angel and the others right into the king's chamber. Asked how the angel left her, Jeanne replied that he departed from her in a little chapel and she was much disturbed by his leaving, and wept, and would have gladly have gone with him, that is, her soul would have gone.

Surely everyone present had lost faith in Jeanne's faculties by now. Why was she chosen over others to deliver this sign? "It pleased God to do so," she replied, "by means of a simple maid to drive back the king's enemies."[33]

It was quite a story, and Jeanne exceeded herself on each revelation. Probably more than one observer concluded that this not-so-simple maid had enraptured her fantasy with archangels and archbishops bearing golden crowns, when in reality it was merely Jeanne alone who had been the sign to her king. Did she herself actually believe such gilded fabrications, or was she trying to end her questioning with a ludicrous fantasy? The scent of mendacity stayed in the nostrils of the churchmen, conjuring up a long memory of similar types, those who still claimed to practice the *Ars Notoria*. Challenged centuries before by Aquinas, this manifestation of the divine arts persisted among charlatans, who claimed mystical visions with angels induced by prolonged fasts, which granted them special powers of insight and wisdom. Could Jeanne hail from this mystical school of angel-guided aestheticism? Tellingly she had been asked on several occasions how long she had fasted, or last eaten, in relationship to her own angels. [34]

Jeanne was also digging her grave with a spade of endless finalities. One notary recalled a tactically shrewd insight regarding the nature of the proceedings that was dragging her into the abyss. "You see the manner of their proceedings. They will catch her with her own words if they can, that is in the assertions where she says 'I know for a *certainty*' touching on her apparitions. If she said 'it *seems* to me' instead, no man living could condemn her." For Jeanne's judges the implications of "it seems that it is so," *Videtur quod,* was the language of the scholastics in their lengthy dialectics on God, semantically implying "it is," but leaving a theological loophole. At the start of the trial two sympathetic priests sat near Jeanne, trying to guide her away from her headlong plunge of certitudes with gestures and grimaces, and even an occasional touch. They were soon threatened away. Others who yearned to counsel her were equally scared off, or so they claimed after it was too late. [35]

Wednesday, March 14, was dominated by interrogations over Jeanne's death-inviting leap from her prison tower at Beaurevoir, after four months of imprisonment. In terms of physical miracles, she had survived without major injury. Why had she leapt? Jeanne said she had feared that all the people of Compiègne, down to the age of seven years, would be killed by the English. Asked whether she had said to Saint Catherine and Saint Margaret, "Will God allow these good people of Compiègne to die so wretchedly?" she replied, "How can God let the good people of Compiègne die, who have been so faithful to their Lord?"

She would rather have died herself than live after such a slaughter. "That was one of the reasons," the scribe recorded. "The other was that she knew she had been sold to the English, and she would much rather have died than be in the hands of her enemies." Saint Catherine had told Jeanne that God would spare the people of Compiègne, but Jeanne admitted to being angry. She repeatedly ignored the admonition of her voices not to jump, because she wanted to be at Compiègne to see for herself: *Aide toi, Dieu te aidera,* she had maintained. And worse—as she had berated her voices—she would soon be in the hands of her enemies if she did not escape. She pleaded to her Burgundian captors that she would rather surrender her soul to God than become an English prisoner. There was only one solution. Jeanne put herself physically into the hands of God and jumped, plunging a full sixty feet to solid earth.

She was unconscious for a period, but Jeanne, as she described it, recovered after three days of fasting, "comforted by Saint Catherine, who told me to confess and beg mercy from God for having leaped, and that certainly the people of Compiègne would receive help before Saint Martin's Day in winter. Then I began to get well and eat, and was soon cured." Had she not expected to kill herself? "No," she denied. "In leaping, I recommended myself to God, and believed that by means of this leap I could escape and avoid being handed over to the English." Had she denied and cursed God after her recovery? "I do not remember," she hesitated. "I do not admit to this. I cannot remember exactly what I said or did." Jeanne asserted that, by religious habit, she never abused God's name. *Bon gré Dieu*—"God be willing"—was the extent of her oaths. This was nothing compared to the *goddon* English—so called because of their blasphemous string of "God damns."

Did Jeanne confess to mortal sin after her suicide attempt? "I did not do it out of despair," she pleaded, "but in the hope of saving my life and going to the help of a number of good people who were in need." Save her life by a fatal jump? Jeanne admitted that she was wrong to have leaped, and on Saint Catherine's advice she made her confession. After that her saint told her she was forgiven. Would Saints Catherine and Margaret take bodily vengeance for Jeanne's offense? She did not know, not having asked them. As for lingering mortal sin, she did not know of that either: "*Je m'en rapporte à Dieu*: I refer myself to God."[36]

After this round of interrogation, it might have become clear to the most cynical judge that the torn youth's voices were not merely invented justifications of her own desires, telling her only what she wished to hear. She had questioned her voices, argued with them, ignored, and finally defied them. She herself seemed of two minds; she was willing to admit error, but her voices—never. When accused that she had followed her voices in everything, Jeanne corrected, "Everything *good* that I did." To credulous churchmen she had no doubt blasphemed her voices. She had hurled herself defiantly into the Godhead and survived, claiming she was forgiven. It was a miracle that baffled the judges, especially since Saint Catherine's prophesy had come true. Compiègne was relieved before November 11, Saint Martin's Day.

Jeanne, however, was still firmly in the hands of the *goddon* English. Surely her voices had deserted her there. She faithfully maintained that if she was a prisoner, it must be pleasing to Christ. Only days before, she had been defiant in speaking of deliverance to her tribunal, stating, "The sign that you need is that God should deliver me out of your hands. And it is the most *certain* one that He could send you." Since being told of her capture over a year before, Saints Catherine and Margaret had assured Jeanne that she would not be cast down, and urged her to accept her destiny in good faith. God would help her. She had begged them to let her die swiftly instead of suffering a lengthy imprisonment. Jeanne still believed that deliverance was at hand, by a great victory in fact. Saint Catherine had told her so, and much more: "Later my voices said to me, 'Take it all cheerfully. Do not despair on account of your martyrdom, for in the end you will come to the Kingdom of Heaven.' Her voices had told her this message of eternal salvation simply and clearly. She interpreted her martyrdom as her suffering in prison. 'Now I do not know, God willing, how much longer I must suffer.'"[37]

A promise to enter the Kingdom of Heaven? If any judges crossed themselves on that declaration, it was from trepidation, slack-jawed in their reaction to such martyred presumption. Did Jeanne really believe herself saved from purgatory or hell already? Clearly she did. "I firmly believe what my voices have told me, that I will be saved. I believe it as firmly as if I were already there." The judges tried to counsel her that this assertion carried great weight. Jeanne remained dogmatic in her response: "I *too* count it as a great treasure."

Great weight? There clearly was no great weight hanging over Jeanne in this crystalline moment of her belief. Instead of searching for the most politic response to this weightiest of questions concerning her immortal soul, she did not understand the threat—the question itself—did not understand theological rules of salvation. How could she? Jeanne did not, could not, answer but with her own direct understanding, the understanding of an unlettered child who had been promised salvation simply and directly: "I too count it as a great treasure." From God, His messengers had spoken to her from a shining light, and it was a great treasure, beyond earthbound theological machinations. Given her promise of eternal salvation, did she really believe it was still necessary to make religious confession? "One cannot cleanse one's conscience too much," she admonished, seeking confession of her sins repeatedly. This chained youth did not yet appear to believe herself beyond heaven's judgment. But what of the terrible judgment of the earthly Church Militant? It was not only La Pucelle's tendency to respond *hardiment* that began to unhinge her mortal judges. It was the sublime confidence about her calling, her mission, her fate—the uncluttered simplicity with which she *knew* them—that gripped, pricked, and ultimately angered the churchmen. Such certitude must be corrected, humbled, or destroyed.[38]

The distinctions between the Church Militant and Church Triumphant were explained to Jeanne. "I do not understand these terms," she admitted, "but I am willing to submit to the Church, as a good Christian should." If only it could be so simple. By stages she was informed of the Church Triumphant above, where God, the saints, and all saved souls dwelled. The head of the Church Militant below was the pope, "God's Vicar on earth," it was stressed, with his "cardinals, the prelates of the Church, and the clergy, and all good Catholic Christians, and this Church when assembled cannot err, and is governed by the Holy Spirit," *Unam Sanctam.*

Did this distinction sink in? Jeanne began the session on March 1 with a promising assertion to her judges. "I will tell you as much as I would to the pope in Rome, if I were before him." That, too, was not so simple. Which did she believe to be the true pope, the one in Rome or France? "Are there *two* of them?" she responded. Which of the popes had her voices told Jeanne to obey? It might not have been merely a trick; perhaps the churchmen at Rouen welcomed a celestial suggestion from her *Conseil*, since the rival popes were diluting Church authority for all claimants, while the University of Paris had become splintered in attempting reconciliation. Jeanne could not help the doctors of theology and law. Her voices had not specified. As for herself, she believed in the pope in Rome. Indeed, the tribunal at Rouen could take her there if her answers were not sufficient for them. "I demand to be brought to him," Jeanne challenged. "Then I will answer everything I ought to answer."

But Rome was far away. Was Jeanne willing to submit her actions to the present judgment of the Church Militant? "All my deeds are in God's hands," she maintained, "and I commit myself to Him. I assure you that I would neither do nor say anything contrary to the Christian faith." If the churchmen could show her where she transgressed the faith established by Christ, "I should not wish to uphold it, but would cast it from me." Was Jeanne willing to submit absolutely to the will of the Mother Holy Church—at least the splinter faction before her at Rouen? She repeated her hierarchy of love and support for the church—but when it came to her own works and calling, she first obeyed the King of Heaven.[39]

Beginning on March 10, the trial sessions were moved from the palace chamber to Jeanne's prison. After a meeting at Bishop Cauchon's residence, it was decided that many of the judges were becoming fatigued. Master Beaupère was one of them, being replaced as principal interrogator by Jean Delafontaine, another member from the University of Paris, one a little more sympathetic to Jeanne. It was Delafontaine who had to thread through Jeanne's byzantine rendition of the sign and crown given to Charles. But a full week later he made no headway in inducing her to yield to the Church Militant. Jeanne would yield only to God and the Church Triumphant. "In my opinion," she repeated wearily, "it is all one, God and the Church, and one should make no difficulty over it. *Why* do you make such a difficulty?"[40]

Starting in mid-March, Cauchon and his assessors began to prepare the Articles of Indictment to be pressed on Jeanne. The five-day effort produced seventy, declaring in stultifying length that Jeanne:

> shall be denounced and declared as a sorceress, diviner, pseudo-prophetess, invoker of evil spirits, conspiratrix, implicated in and given to the practice of magic, wrongheaded as to our Catholic faith . . . superstitious, schismatic, sacrilegious, idolatrous, apostate, accursed and mischievous, blasphemous toward God and His saints, scandalous, seditious, disturber of peace, inciter of war,

> cruelly avid of human blood, inciting to bloodshed, having completely and shamelessly abandoned the decencies proper to her sex, and having immodestly adopted the dress and status of a man-at-arms . . . having in contempt and disdain of God permitted herself to be venerated and adored, by giving her hands and garments to be kissed, heretical, or at any rate vehemently suspected of heresy, for that she shall be punished and corrected according to divine and canonical laws.[41]

If convicted of being a heretic, death by fire was in the balance. But this was only the introduction to the seventy charges. According to Article two, Jeanne had been captured while in the midst of her sorcery and invoking of demons, *in flagrante delicto*. Article four alleged that she had not been properly instructed in the faith by her mother, but rather by old women sorcerers and evil *faées*. Articles five and six perverted her girlish reverie about the old Fairies' tree, "accompanying her dances with songs mingled with invocations, sorceries, and witchcraft." Jeanne protested that she did not understand what the nonsense about *faées* was about. "As for my instruction," she added in distress, "I learned to believe, and was duly taught how to behave, as a *good* child should."

Jeanne was implicated in Article eight of being an adolescent whore, sleeping with other whores at an inn frequented by lusty soldiers. She had even boasted that she would sire three sons, all by the Holy Spirit, after having "entered into intimate relationships" with a man who volunteered to be one of the fathers. The vile mandrake accusation was again dredged up, by then worn in Jeanne's bosom for good fortune. "I deny it completely," she answered for the second time. Contrary to ordinary procedure, no witnesses to Jeanne's alleged infamy were considered necessary. Her own perverted words were damning enough. On Wednesday, March 28, 1431, fully three dozen mature reverends, bishops, doctors of law and theology, all surrounded a nineteen-year-old illiterate like demons. They spat out charges serious enough to burn her ten times over. But even this did not appear sufficient demolition, for the *litterati* knowingly poured personal filth on childhood, truth be damned. In an orgy of *nostalgie pour la boue,* they willfully smeared unneeded mud on innocence in a black farce of righteous panic, for reasons only accountable to collective poverty of simple decency. There could be no other earthly explanation for their stooping so low. Yet with unctuous platitudes, they had assured Jeanne that very morning that they would treat her with "all piety and meekness, as we have always been disposed." For unmasked prurience, this was the nadir of the trial.[42]

From among the tribunal that had just crafted this scathing indictment laced with cruel lies, Jeanne was "allowed" to choose counsel to assist her in answering the remaining seventy charges—something at least one judge, Jean Lohier, had previously suggested, concerning such a simple girl legally in need of an advocate. "As to the counsel you offer I am grateful," she replied, "but I have no intention of departing from the advice of God." Jeanne's prior responses were read to her, so that she could not deny anything later. She was adjured to swear that she would add nothing untrue. To save time, she asked that the charges be read without interruption, unless she herself interrupted in disagreement, which she repeatedly did. Jeanne took her usual limited oath on the Scriptures to respond to matters of fact and faith. She replied in detail to the first article, regarding the court's authority to punish heresy. She conceded that the pope and his clergy existed to protect the Christian faith and to punish those who transgressed it, "but for myself and my deeds, I will submit myself only to the church in Heaven, that is to say, to God, the Virgin Mary, and the saints in Heaven. And I believe firmly I have not failed in the Christian faith."[43]

It required two days to cover the seventy articles. Jeanne

had repeatedly answered most of the inquiries before: "I refer to my previous answers. . . . I refer to what I said elsewhere. I deny the rest. . . . I refer to what I have already said." Articles twelve through sixteen again brought up her male dress. Whose command had she followed? Was it not blasphemous, an abomination to God? Jeanne referred to her seven prior statements on the subject. If the panel wished more, she requested a delay. She testified that she had often been admonished to wear a woman's dress, but had refused, on one occasion with a touch of disdain: "As for womanly duties, she said there were enough other women to do them." She was asked if she would assume women's dress to receive Easter Communion. Jeanne replied that mode of dress should make no difference to Christ. The Body of Our Lord should not be refused her for this reason. Jeanne was charged with being a false prophet, indicted by words from the book of Matthew: "By their fruits ye shall know them." The passage ends ominously: "Every tree that does not bear good fruit is cut down and thrown into the fire."[44]

The first two weeks of April were involved with condensing the articles to twelve. Diced up at the University of Paris, the truncated version returned with devious convolutions, perversions of testimony that had preceded, missing testimony, and phrases altered to imply the opposite of Jeanne's words. This mattered little to the obedient judges at Rouen. As one cowed notary later observed, "It pleased them to have it like that." Armed with this new bludgeon, on April 18 Cauchon returned to Jeanne's cell with half-a-dozen colleagues. Again he offered her benefit of counsel. She refused, believing that she was to die soon from apparent food poisoning. Jeanne suspected Cauchon of having sent her contaminated fish to eat. One priest shouted, "*Paillarde,* lewd slut, you have eaten other things to make you sick!" Jeanne denied it, while more heated insults flew. As they drove her further into a fever, she begged to have her confession taken and to be buried in consecrated ground. She was instructed that her fear of death was an even more compelling reason to mend her ways and submit to the Church. "If my body dies in prison," she beseeched, "I trust you will bury it in consecrated ground. But if you do not, then I put my trust in Our Lord." Asked whether she believed the Holy Scripture was revealed by God, Jeanne answered, "You know this! It is certain that it was." As she refused steadfastly to submit to the Holy Church, one judge tried to convince her to do so with examples of biblical authority, returning to the Gospel of Matthew for the fate of those who neglect to listen to the Church: "Let him be unto thee as a heathen and a publican." Thus Jeanne too would be abandoned as an infidel. "I am a good Christian," she protested, "and was baptized so. I will die a good Christian."[45]

By May 2, Jeanne had recovered enough to be brought back to Rouen Castle. Before over sixty assessors, she was given an admonition by Jean de Chatillon, another theologian from the University of Paris. With thirty years of experience behind him, Chatillon commenced his attempt to remove "the cunning of the devil" and save her soul. Jeanne was instructed about the perils of excessive *curiositas*, persuaded how dangerous it was to examine things beyond one's own understanding. Nonclerics all over Europe were increasingly demanding to examine the Holy Scriptures for themselves, in their own vulgar tongues, and coming to conclusions heretical to the Latin-fortified Church Militant; they even questioned the *Unam Sanctam*.

For the learned, *curiositas* could lead to vanity; for the ignorant, to folly and perdition. Women in particular tended to become confused by such fervor, "which leads them to gazing about and talking," as Jean Gerson had described. Chatillon cautioned Jeanne that in believing or inventing new things, "demons have a way of introducing themselves into such curiosities," perhaps even appearing as saints. A verse from 2 Corinthians was cited: "For even Satan disguises himself as an angel of light. So it is not strange if his servants also disguise themselves as servants of righteousness." Aquinas had affirmed this: "All changes capable of occurring naturally and by way of genus, these the devil can imitate." Deception was the only real power that demons abundantly possessed, who otherwise were bound by the same natural laws as man. It was said that Satan had even appeared once as a righteous abbot at the Cluny monasteryin Paris. A more recent dabbler in magic, Jehan de Bar, had gone too far in occult *curiositas* by conjuring up a host of demons, who had first tricked him by appearing as "good angels." Before his execution de Bar had admitted his error of deception. Biblically and theologically no human being could tell the difference without further proofs or signs—which Jeanne clearly lacked. She already had displayed her ignorance, even arrogance, when asked if she could discern if the evil one were to appear as Saint Michel. "She said she could easily tell whether it was indeed Saint Michel, or a counterfeit in his likeness."

The noose tightened, but Jeanne remained unfazed. If she would not submit, she was threatened with the fate of a heretic, death by fire. "I will tell you nothing else," she reiterated. "And even if I saw the fire, I should tell you what I have told you—and nothing else." In the margin of the transcript the scribe added, *superba responsio*. Would Jeanne submit to the authority of the pope? "Take me to him," she again requested, "and I shall answer him!" Otherwise she refused to submit further to the present trial. Reminded finally of the flames on earth and in hell, she flared with a warning herself. "You cannot do as you say against me without suffering evil, both of body and soul."[46]

Jeanne's line was drawn indelibly between obedience to God over the Church. A week later, on May 9, she was taken not to the usual hall of judgment, but to the great tower of the castle. Inside the thick stone walls, light filtered through arched windows onto instruments of torture, which unsettled her. By laws of the Inquisition, torture could be applied if discrepancies existed, "to restore her to the way and knowledge of truth, to procure the salvation of her body and soul." After confession had been extracted in excruciating screams, the torture would cease, so that the accused might confess a second time, as if voluntarily—or face more torture. While the executioner prepared the instruments before her, Jeanne was warned a final time to recant, or torture would begin immediately. Composing herself, she recoiled. "Truly, if you were to tear me limb from limb and make my soul leave my body, I would not say to you anything more. And if you do so, then afterwards I shall say that you made me say so by force."

The judges removed the physical threat as they went away to deliberate. Two decided that torture was expedient, while ten others argued that it was not required—yet. One warned that torture could only cast a shadow over such an orderly trial. In what was intended as holy benevolence, another priest, Nicolas Loiseleur, suggested that a little torture might be healthy for Jeanne's soul, to save her from eternal damnation. The vice-inquisitor, Jean Le Maitre, ended discussion by suggesting that she be given one more chance to submit to the Church Militant. She told her tribunal that she had asked her voices if she would be burned, "and that the voices had told her that she must wait on Our Lord and He would help her."[47]

The reduced Articles of Accusation were taken back to the University of Paris for final formulation. On May 23, Jeanne was formally censured by having the finalized articles against her publicly read. The remonstrance was delivered by young Pierre Maurice, yet another from the University of Paris, who was described to Jeanne as "the light of all knowledge and expunger of errors." Addressing her at first as "dearest friend," Maurice soon began to unnerve Jeanne with the final charges—which were withering against "the woman commonly called La Pucelle," whose poison threatened to infect all of Christendom. Her claims to have heard voices since age thirteen "are lies, untrue, pernicious, and evil, and all such revelations are superstitious, and proceed from evil and diabolical spirits." As to believing that Saint Michel had come to her, it was not so: "You believed too lightly and affirmed your belief too rashly." Her pledge of virginity was "presumptuous." She had not honored her father and mother. In adopting men's clothes, "you blaspheme God and despise Him in His sacraments," defying sacred Scripture. Her sign to her king was a lie, her promise to him both rash and sanctimonious, also blaspheming God. Likewise the claim that God had forgiven her for attempted escape from the tower at Beaurevoir, showing "that you wrongly understand the doctrine of Free Will and man's right to choose." Her leap was an act of "cowardice, tending to despair and suicide." As for implying that God favored the French over the English, Jeanne had transgressed Christ's commandment to love thy neighbor. In sum, "you are an idolater, an invoker of demons, a wanderer from the Faith, having rashly taken an unlawful oath."[48]

After being charitably admonished at length to repent or die, Jeanne repeated her stance. "If I saw the fire lit and the executioner who was to burn me ready to cast me into the fire, still in the fire would I not say anything other than I have said. And I will maintain what I have said until death." Again the scribe wrote in the margin of the transcript, *Responsio Johanne superba.* Jeanne was asked if she had anything final to say before the trial ended. She said no.

The next day, Thursday, May 24, Jeanne was taken by cart to the cemetery of St. Ouen. There two platforms had been erected,one for her and the other for her judges. With Father Jean Massieu standing beside her for comfort, she heard herself threatened with excommunication, cast out of the Church by words from the Gospel of St. John:

> As the branch cannot bear fruit of itself
> except it abides in the vine,

neither can you, unless you abide in me.
I am the vine, you are the branches.
He who abides in me, and I in him
he it is that bears much fruit
for apart from me you can do nothing.
If a man does not abide in me
he is cast forth as a branch and withers
and the branches are gathered,
thrown into the fire and burned.

The crowd was immense and turbulent. Among the many prelates present was the cardinal of Winchester, England, along with the Bishop of Norwich, private secretary to Henry VI. The Earl of Warwick stood behind the Bishop of Beauvais, as other Englishmen in the throng impatiently waited for Jeanne to be condemned. In a sermon Guillaume Érard, the canon of Rouen, started by calling Jeanne a monstrous heretic. "Oh, royal house of France, you have never known monsters till now. But you are dishonored for giving your faith to this woman, this sorceress, heretic, and child of superstition." Jeanne's simpleminded patriotism caused her to protest. "Speak of *me*, not the king!" Raising his finger, Érard glared at her. "I *am* speaking of you, Jeanne, and I tell you that your king is a heretic and a schismatic." She retorted that Charles was the noblest of all Christians—"He is not what you say!" Érard ordered Massieu to shut her up, then pointed from Jeanne to the platform of prelates. "Look at my lords the judges, who have time and again summoned and required you to submit all of your words and deeds to our Holy Mother Church." Jeanne cried out, "I will answer you! I have already told you that concerning all that I have done I appeal—after God—to our Holy Father the pope in Rome. Let a report be sent to him. As to my own words and deeds, I have done everything at God's command. I charge no one, neither the king nor any other. If there is any fault, it is mine alone!" Érard repeated his exhortation for Jeanne to submit to authority. "I appeal to God," she persisted, "and to our Holy Father the pope!"[49]

Yet again the prospect of appealing to distant Rome was dismissed. The judges believed they possessed sufficient godly authority. Cauchon began reading the sentence of excommunication, "as a limb of Satan severed from the Church." Massieu begged Jeanne to recant. To be placed in English secular hands meant certain, horrible death. "Oh—you take great pains to lead me astray," she accused the conflicted body. "I saw well that Jeanne neither understood the situation nor the danger which threatened her," Massieu described. She was pressed to sign a prepared article of recantation, the Latin *Cedula*. She answered, "Let this paper be seen by the clerks and the Church, into whose hands I must be put. If they advise me to sign it, and to do as I am told, I will do it willingly." Érard commanded her to sign: "Do it *now*—if not this day you shall end your days by fire!"

For whatever reason—the final reality of burning, the crushing words—Jeanne's nerve and pride dissolved. She relented. The crowd erupted. A few stones arched in the direction of the judges. A short document of confession suddenly appeared, read to her by Massieu. Jeanne seemed to be mouthing its words to understand, at one point laughing at what she heard. An Englishman scolded Cauchon that Jeanne was making a mockery of the affair. Cauchon angrily responded that it was his duty to save her, not burn her. Jeanne asked Massieu to read the abjuration again. Amid confusion, she made her mark at the bottom of the page, a Burgundian testifying that her hand traced a round O. Then he saw her hand redirected by an English official, Laurent Calot, who "made Jeanne make a mark which I no longer remember." Others believed the sign of a cross was forced. Nothing was clear. Threats and murmurs festered in the mob. Had she truly signed the confession or not?[50]

Whatever the truth amid the confusing drama, a disputed

document of confession entered the records of the trial, from "a miserable sinner," concluding that "I do confess that I have grievously sinned, in falsely pretending that I had revelations from God and angels, Saint Catherine and Saint Margaret." It is signed JEHANNE †. This confession is forty-seven lines long. The official trial transcript, so heavy-handed in unconvincing elaboration, recorded that she then recited the whole thing on her scaffold, which would take several minutes at the least, and longer still for an illiterate. Three witnesses, including Jean Massieu, recalled that the original recantation he read to Jeanne was not nearly as long—about the length of a Pater Noster—and also differed in content and calligraphy. "It was given to me to read to Jeanne," Massieu said, "and I remember well that in that letter it was noted that in the future she would neither carry arms, nor wear men's clothes, nor would she cut her hair short, and other things I do not remember anymore. And I know well that it contained eight lines and no more, and I know absolutely that it was not registered in the transcript of the trial, because what I read her was different from that which was inserted in the record."[51]

Nevertheless her torment seemed over at last. After Jeanne's recantation, her new sentence was read to her. *Carcer perpetuas*—life imprisonment—morbidly sustained "with the bread of sorrow and the water of affliction, that you may weep for your sins, and nevermore commit them." Crushed, Jeanne was led down from her platform and out of the cemetery. One priest, Nicholas Loiseleur, urged her to accept their kind sentence. "You have spent a good day, Jeanne," he assured her with Christian piety. "Please God, you have saved your soul." Jeanne responded, "Well—as to that—then some of you churchmen take me into your prison, so that I am no longer in the hands of these Englishmen." Cauchon curtly refused: "Take her where you brought her from." The bishop and his minions left amid threats from the English, who felt cheated out of death. "The King has spent his money very badly on you," one of them grumbled to Cauchon. Jeanne was instructed to forsake her revelations and men's dress. She agreed to put on a woman's dress, which was provided to her. The Earl of Warwick complained to the judges that Jeanne was slipping out of their jurisdiction. "Do not worry," one answered, "we shall catch her, all right."[52]

When Cauchon and a small party returned on May 28, Jeanne was again in men's clothes, wearing a tunic, short robe, and leggings. When asked why, she said she had done it of her own will. She preferred them because male habit was safer among male guards. Jeanne claimed that she had never intended to take such an oath. "I did not understand the abjuration," she pleaded. "If you wish, I will resume a woman's dress. As for the rest, I can do no more." She charged that the court had not kept its promise to allow her to receive Mass and Holy Communion, and she was still in chains. Her face streaked with tears, she stated she would rather die than be kept in irons. Had Saints Catherine and Margaret talked to her recently? she was asked. Yes, Jeanne responded, they had admonished her for the last four days over her recantation:

> They told her that God had sent her word by them that she had put herself in great danger of perdition in that she had consented to make the renunciation in order to save her life, and that she was damned for doing so. . . . She said further that in saying that God had not sent her she had damned herself, for truly God had sent her. And since Thursday her voices had told her that she had done great wrong to God in confessing that what she had done was not well done. She said also that everything she had said and revoked, she had done only through fear of the fire. Asked if she believes that the voices are those of Saint Catherine and Saint Margaret, she answered yes, and that they come from God. . . . She also said that she

would rather do penance by dying than bear any longer the agony of imprisonment.

In the margin of the trial transcript the scribe recorded his final reaction, *responsio mortifera*: deadly response. As he left the prison, several recalled that Cauchon assured the English, "Farewell, make good cheer. It is done." Behind the scene, other judges joined in a joyful sigh of relief.[53]

Although Jeanne agreed to assume a woman's dress again, Cauchon decided after proper counsel that since she had relapsed, being persuaded by the devil through her voices, she should be considered a heretic and left to secular justice. At seven in the morning of May 30, two priests, Martin Ladvenu and young Jean Toutmouillé, visited Jeanne to prepare her for death. Jean Massieu was present. Ladvenu asked him to go seek permission for Jeanne to receive Holy Communion. Cauchon granted this, a remarkable act of charity for one not in absolution but pronounced a heretic; but it was now time to consider the soul in eternity. "Give her the Sacraments and all that she asked for," Cauchon instructed. Ladvenu heard Jeanne's last confession. He became disturbed by the lack of complete reverence with which a clerk had brought the Sacraments, and commanded that the stole and lights be brought as well. Candles lit, the transubstantiation ceremony became proper for the spiritual transformation of bread into flesh, with Latin liturgy. Massieu watched while Jeanne prepared to receive Communion "with great devotion and many tears."

In nomine Patris et Filii et Spiritis Sancti Misereatur vestri omnipotens Deus et dimissis peccatis vestris perducat vos ad vitam aeternam Christe eleison Gloria in excelsis Deo Et in terra pax hominibus bonae voluntatis Dominus vobiscum Sanctus Sanctus Sanctus Dominus Deus Sabaoth Qui pridie quam pateretur accepit panem in sanctas ac venerabiles manus saus et elevatis oculis in caelum ad te Deum Patrem suum omnipotentem tibi gratias agens bene dixit fregit deditque suis dicens Accipite et manducate ex hoc omnes

HOC EST ENIM CORPUS MEUM

Haec quotiescumque feceritis in Mei memoriam facietis Haec commixtio et consecratio Corporus Domini nostri Jesu Christi fiat accipientibus nobis in vitam aeternam

The Consecrated Host held above her head, Jeanne was asked:

"Do you believe that this is the Body of Christ?"

"Yes, and I believe that He alone can deliver me. I ask that it may be administered to me."

Putting the bread on her lips for consumption into one flesh, Ladvenu delivered the final benediction:

Ecce Agnus Dei ecce qui tollit peccata mundi Corpus Domini nostri Jesu Christi custo'diat a'nimam tuam in vitam aeternam
Amen

Mingled with her tears, Jeanne received the Body of Christ. Ladvenu then confirmed that she would die by burning. She broke down in horror, *doloreusement et piteusement,* lamenting that her pure body was to be burned to ashes. "Oh, I protest before God, the great judge, the great wrongs and griefs they have done to me."

Cauchon entered. "Bishop—I die because of you!"

Cauchon replied, "Jeanne, take it patiently, you will die because you have not held to what you promised us, and because you return to your first witchcraft."

"If you had put me in the prison of a church court," she protested for the last time, "this would not have happened to me. That is why I complain to you before God!"

Jeanne turned to Pierre Maurice. "Where shall I be tonight?"

"Have you no faith in Our Lord?" he asked.

"Yes," she recovered. "God helping me, today I shall be with Him in Paradise." [54]

After eight o'clock Jeanne was taken to the crowded marketplace to face her judges and the stake, which was in the square across from the Holy Savior Cathedral. Massieu and Ladvenu were at her side. Fish stalls lined the square, opaque eyes and lifeless fins mute witness. The judges began trudging toward their places around nine o'clock, gathering in a stand facing the scaffold. Several chose to stay away. On hearing that the Church would no longer protect her, Jeanne fell to her knees and prayed aloud in sobs for mercy, begging that all pray for her soul, as she forgave her enemies. "Oh Rouen," she cried, "must I die here?" She continued in frenzied lamentation, until many joined her weeping. This stricken scene lasted for half an hour. Some clergy were led away in tears. "I never wept as much for anything," one recounted, "and could finally not stop weeping for a whole month." An Englishman protested—"Priest, are you going to let us get done in time for dinner?" Amid the horror Massieu described an English soldier, who handed Jeanne a crude little cross, fashioned from two sticks. She pressed it to her breast while Nicolas Midi gave the last sermon, based on a verse from Corinthians. "Whether one member suffers, all the members suffer with it . . . In the name of the Lord. Amen." Dropping his script, Midy looked toward Jeanne with a human face. "Go in peace," he said at the end. "The church can no longer defend you." Cauchon formally declared her excommunicated as a rotten member, pernicious viper, infected with the leprosy of heresy. "Time and again you have relapsed, as a dog returns to its vomit. We do cast you forth and reject you from the communion of the Church as an infected limb, and hand you over to secular justice."[55]

Finally, impatient English hands thrust Jeanne toward the stake, on a high stone scaffold surrounded with wood. They attached her. A tall paper cap was placed on her shaved head, denoting a heretic. The executioner was told to do his duty. He lit the fire. Jeanne told Ladvenu to back away. A crucifix was held before her bulging eyes. As the flames leapt, she cried out for her voices. Saint Michel—Saint Catherine—Saint Margaret. Pain seared higher, her feet, her legs, her loins. Merciful flames began to devour her breath. In terminal agony she shrieked over and over to her Christ:

Jhesus! Jhesus! Jhesus! Jhesus Jhesus *Jhesus* *JHESUS*

Jeanne's hideous face sank forward in release. Her final howl to Jesus hung in the air, haunting many for the rest of their lives. After a stench-filled interval of burning flesh, the executioner was ordered to part the flames to display Jeanne's nude, charred body to the superstitious. Those in charge were still afraid of her powers. The fire was restarted. What refused to perish after a second burning—her heart and entrails according to legend—were thrown into the Seine. Many said they saw the name of Jesus written in flames that consumed her. Among other miracles reported that day was the shaken testimony of an English soldier, who swore he saw a white dove arise from the flames and fly away from France. An excess of drink failed to console him, or to assuage the executioner, who believed he was damned because he had killed a saint. "We are all lost. We have burned a Saint," a secretary to the king of England blurted out. This was only hours after the victory that had taken so many hard months for everyone to achieve, all in the name of God.[56]

A week after Jeanne's immolation, the disputed document of Rouen appeared, revealingly named the *Acta Posterius*. It purported that she had confessed on the morning of her death to having been deceived by her voices. In terms of human understanding, there appears holy truth in that: My God, my God, why have you forsaken me?

But Martin Ladvenu believed that Jeanne had died a good Christian. She had vowed to him unto the last day that her voices were from God. Tearfully led away from the flames across the marketplace, the canon of Rouen expressed a prayer for himself: "I wish that my soul were where I believe this woman's soul to be."[57]

CORPUS DOMINI NOSTRI JESU CHRISTI CUSTODIAT ANIMAM TUAM IN VITAM AETERNAM

2
Rehabilitation

Nineteen years later, on February 15, 1450, Charles VII wrote to Guillaume Bouillé, canon of the Noyon Cathedral in Rouen: "Whereas formerly Jeanne the Maid was taken and apprehended by our ancient enemies and adversaries the English, and brought to this town Rouen, against whom they caused to be brought proceedings by certain persons . . . and committed many faults and abuses . . . they brought about her death iniquitously and against right reason, very cruelly. Therefore we would know the truth of the said trial proceedings."[1]

Charles was in control at last, having entered Paris in triumph in 1437. The English had been driven out the year before—within the span of Jeanne's seven-year prophesy—but Normandy was not free of English influence until Rouen was repossessed in 1449. Over the channel in England, Henry VI, now twenty-eight years old, was offering up the crown jewels as collateral for another try in France. The last English bastion in Guyenne fell to the newly united French in 1451.

But Charles's claim of legitimacy still rested partially on the resurrection of Jeanne d'Arc's reputation, her charred heretical remains notwithstanding. Another political trial offered, with reverse motivation to un-damn the ghost of La Pucelle. Pleading on her knees in Notre Dame Cathedral in Paris, Jeanne's decrepit mother made a moving petition to agents of Pope Calixtus III in Rome for her daughter's rehabilitation. Previously the pope had tried to maintain a studied neutrality because he hoped to enlist English aid against a threat from the rising Muslim empire. "I demand that my daughter's name be *restored,*" Isabelle Romée ended. Her plea was successful. The Holy Father could more gracefully grant this request from an aggrieved family. The first witnesses were called in 1452, to answer a prepared questionnaire. After the process moved around France for four more years, 115 witnesses were interrogated, some of them multiple times.

Childhood Recollections of Jeannette

In retrospect young Jeannette grew more saintly with each recollection from those who had known her childhood in Domremy, as attested to by her godfather among many others. "Jeanne was as well-behaved a girl as any one of her kind can be, for her parents were not very rich . . . she was such a good girl that almost everyone in Domremy loved her. And Jeannette knew her creed, her Pater Noster and the Ave Maria the way little girls of her age do . . . she used to go out ploughing and sometimes she looked after the cattle in the fields, and she did woman's work, spinning and all that." One of her godmothers recalled that Jeannette "applied herself to all the different jobs in her father's house, and sometimes she spun flax or wool, or went to the plough, or to the harvest fields when it was time, and sometimes when it was her father's turn, she watched the village beasts or herds." For whatever reason, when Jeanne had been asked at her condemnation trial whether she had ever tended herds in childhood, she was vague, claiming loss of memory.[2]

"Jeannette often went of her own will to church and sacred places, caring for the sick and giving alms to the poor," a forty-four-year-old farm worker recalled. "This I saw myself, for when I was a child I too was sick and Jeanne came to comfort me." "Willingly did she give alms," another described, "and gathered in the poor, and she would sleep beneath the hood of the hearth, that the poor might sleep in her bed." A girlfriend in her mid-forties, who grew up next door to Jeannette, recalled that "she was bought up in the Christian religion and was *remplie de bonnes moeurs*, full of good ways. She went of her own will and often to church to give alms out of her father's property and was so good, simple, and pious that I and the other young girls would tell her that she was *too* pious."[3]

Adolescent Jeannette clearly stuck out in stern piety. "I myself," recalled a male comrade, "and other young men used to tease her." A woman related that "often she was ashamed because of people remarking how she went so devoutly to church." Her priest delighted over what an exemplary Catholic Jeannette was, "that he had never met a better, and had none better in his parish." She was continually either at daily Mass or working. "She did not dance," a fifty-year-old woman testified, "so that we, the other girls and young men, even talked about it." On many Saturdays Jeannette would walk to the hermitage of Notre Dame de Bermont with her older sister, Catherine, bearing candles. "For the love of God she gave away willingly all that she could get gladly," one companion testified. The word "gladly" littered descriptions of one who radiated benevolence. Gladly Jeannette worked, gladly she gave, gladly she worshiped. When she heard the church bells in Domremy ring for Mass and the evening Compline, she gladly fell on her knees in prayer wherever she might be. "I was, in those days, church warden at the church of Domremy," Perrin Drappier recalled, "and often I saw Jeannette come to church, to Mass, and to Compline. And when I did not ring the bells for Compline, she would catch me and scold me, saying I had not done well. She even promised to give me some wool if I would be punctual in ringing the bells."[4]

Any superstitious powers in relation to the Fairies' tree were played down by Jeannette's godparents and friends, who claimed that romantic fairies no longer visited now that the locale was routinely cleansed by Christian ceremonies and biblical readings from the gospel of Saint John, which was considered efficacious in purifying pagan superstitions. On a particular Sunday each year, the young people of Domremy went to sing, dance, and feast beneath the great tree beside the road to Neufchâteau, sometimes in spring and summer too, gathering flowers. Young lovers were attracted to the site as well. Her godfather among others testified that Jeannette had gone along with her companions, "and did all that the others did. I have never heard that she went there alone, or for any other reason, except for a walk and to play with the other girls." "I never heard that she had a bad reputation because of that tree," another godmother added. Jeannette had six godparents, a common practice until the Protestant Reformation began to reduce such numbers in the next century.[5]

Jeanne Sets Out for France

Jeanne then was called to leave Domremy in her red working surcoat. "I did not know when she went away," a close friend named Hauviette recalled, "but I cried very bitterly about her going. I loved her very dearly because she was so kind, and I was her friend." Jeanne traveled the few miles up to Vaucouleurs to convince the head of the town, Robert de Baudricourt, of her divine mission. Although Jeanne had pleaded ignorance of fulfilling folk prophecy at her condemnation trial, others remembered her as both messianic and a child of prophecy. According to one Michel Lebuin, Jeanne herself told him "that there lived a maid between Coussey and Vaucouleurs who, before the year was out, would have the king of France crowned. And in truth, the following year the king was crowned at Reims." "Has it not been said that France will be lost by a woman," Jeanne assured her uncle, "and shall thereafter be restored by a virgin?" In this she referred to the quasi-mother of Charles VII—and to herself. She explained that she was being sent by her Lord to tell the dauphin that help was coming, and that Charles should place his kingdom at her command. [6]

Who was her Lord? Robert de Baudricourt first inquired at

Vaucouleurs. "The King of Heaven," Jeanne replied. Baudricourt did the prudent thing, having her exorcized. He called in a priest named Jean Fournier, who was protected in his righteous stole, according to a villager named Catherine Le Royer. Fournier insisted, "If there was any bad thing in her that she go hence from them, and that if there was a good thing, then let her approach them. And Jeanne approached this priest and went down on her knees, and said that this priest had not done well, since he had heard her confession. And when Jeanne saw that Robert would not escort her, she said—I heard her say it—that she must go to where the dauphin was." Jeanne repeated to Catherine Le Royer the legend that France would be saved by a maid. "I remember having heard this, and I was flabbergasted." Jeanne told Catherine's husband that if she was obliged to go on her knees—her legs worn to stumps—go she would to Chinon and the dauphin. In Vaucouleurs a future priest named Jean le Fumeux marveled at Jeanne's religious devotion. "She used to hear the morning Mass and stay behind a long time praying. I saw her kneeling before the Holy Virgin under the vault of that church, sometimes with her face bowed, and sometimes looking straight above her."[7]

"This Maid spoke very well," others recalled. "Certain inhabitants of the town caused a tunic to be made for her, hose, leggings, spurs, a sword, and other things, and bought her a horse. Jean de Metz, Bertrand de Poulengy, Colet de Vienne, with three attendants, took her to the place where the dauphin was. I saw them mount their horses to set off." Colet de Vienne was a messenger provided by Baudricourt, who knew the roads and perils to reach Chinon, where the dauphin resided. Thirty-one-year-old Jean de Metz had become fully convinced of Jeanne's mission from God, pledging himself to her by taking her hand as a sign of personal commitment. "I asked her when she wanted to leave. She answered, 'Rather today than tomorrow, and rather tomorrow than later.'" The remains of the arched gate that Jeanne and her few followers passed through still stand on a commanding hill above Vaucouleurs in front of the ruined cathedral. "Go," Baudricourt told her, "go and let what is to be come to pass." [8]

As Jeanne's party made the dangerous eleven-day passage westward across France toward Chinon, she recalled her prophecy about France being saved by a Pucelle. Jeanne also insisted "that she feared no men-at-arms, for her way was open, and if there were men-at-arms on her road, she had her Lord who would clear the way for her to go to the lord dauphin, and that she had been born to do this." The group usually traveled by night to avoid English and Burgundian patrols, and experienced several close calls. Rivers were forded in midwinter. Jeanne was dissuaded from attending Mass along the way because it was too dangerous. She did stop to receive Mass at Auxerre and Ste. Catherine de Fierbois, below Tours. She repeatedly assured Jean de Metz not to be afraid, as he recalled: "for her brothers in Paradise told her what she had to do. . . . I had great trust in what the Maid said, and I was on fire with what she said, and with a love for her which was, as I believe, a divine love. I believe that she was sent by God. She never swore, she loved to hear the Mass, and crossed herself with the sign of the cross. And thus we took her to the king at Chinon, as secretly as we could."[9]

Some who had escorted Jeanne to the dauphin thought her a bit presumptuous, "and their intention was to put her to the proof," one testified. "They said in the beginning they wanted to require her to lay with them carnally. But when the moment came to speak to her of this, they were so much ashamed that they dared not say a word of it to her." "Every night she lay down with Jean de Metz and me," Bertrand de Poulengy recalled, "keeping on her surcoat and hose, tied and tight. I was seventeen years old then, yet I had neither desire nor carnal movement to touch woman, and I should not have dared to ask such a thing of Jeanne, because of the abundance of goodness which I saw in her. . . . She never swore, and I myself was much stimulated by her voices, for it seemed to me that she was sent by God." Jean de Metz echoed the teen's overpowering awe. "I myself would never have made advances to her, and I say upon oath that neither did I have desire for her nor carnal motion. . . . I had great confidence in the Maid's sayings, and I was fired by her sayings and with love for her."[10]

Another witness recalled this pervasive stunting of carnality, *coitus reservatus*, in Jeanne's presence, marveling that "when helping to arm her or at other times, I have often looked at her breasts, which were beautiful—and I was strong, young and vigorous in those days—yet I never had *volonté charnel* for her." Her squire later had the impression that Jeanne did not menstruate, indicating that when women watched her undressing, there was never any index of blood on her undergarments. Jeanne usually slept with one or more female attendants when they were available, and preferred those closer to her own age. "She did not like to sleep with old women," one noted. If women were not present, she slept in her clothes on the straw, unmolested by men. If these recollections had been available to the judges at Rouen, they might have been used to demonstrate witchcraft, twisted into the ability to render men impotent.[11]

JEANNE'S RECEPTION BY THE DAUPHIN AT CHINON

Laughter and mockery greeted Jeanne's arrival at Chinon. The grandmaster of the king's household, by then in his eighties, dismissively recalled that on her first audience this "poor little shepherdess" boldly announced, "Very noble lord Dauphin, I am come—sent by God—to bring succor to you and your kingdom." The legendary moment, when Charles hid himself among his courtiers to test if this psychic youth could recognize him, gains support from the story told to Simon Charles. "When the king knew that she was coming, he withdrew apart from the others. Jeanne however knew him at once and made him a reverence and spoke to him for sometime. After hearing her, the king appeared radiant." Jean Chartier, historian of the court at Chinon, also recorded that Jeanne had recognized the dauphin at once and made the proper curtsies. Charles replied, "What if I am not the king?" and pointed to a more impressive-appearing courtier. *"En nom Dieu,"* Jeanne replied, "it is you and none other."

Jeanne said that her voices had revealed Charles to her, assuring her that she would be received by him. She later told her confessor and companion, Jean Pasquerel, that she had assured Charles that he was the true heir to France and that she would escort him to Reims for his coronation. "That heard, the King told those who were present that Jeanne had told him certain secrets that none knew or could know, excepting only God. That is why he had great confidence in her. All this I heard from Jeanne's mouth, for I was not present." One contemporary recorded how Jeanne moved from a subject of suspicion and ridicule after convincing Charles. "She, seeing that no one put any faith in her words, told him things it is said were known only to God and the dauphin. This caused the dauphin to gather many wise men, and they began to dispute with her, to test her in all kinds of matters."

Decades later a former gentleman of the bedchamber named Guillaume Gouffier said Charles afterward had described Jeanne's sign to him. In his anguish before her appearance, the dauphin had prayed that, if he were truly the heir to France, God might keep and defend him. If not, God should allow him to escape to Scotland or Spain. Jeanne repeated Charles's prayer to him, which convinced him that she was a sign from God. There were no alternatives. Before Jeanne's miraculous arrival, one of Charles's desperate courtiers recalled, "there was no hope but in God . . . so the king might as well take her in aid."[12]

At Chinon, as Jeanne told her confessor Pasquerel, a man approached her, inquiring if she was indeed the so-called

Pucelle. Being told yes he swore to God that she would not remain a maid after one night with him. *"En nom Dieu,"* Jeanne recoiled, "do you take His name in vain when you are so near death?" Shortly afterward the man drowned in the Loire River. Her fifteen-year-old page, Louis de Coutes, described her otherwise sublime periods in a castle tower. "I often saw Jeanne on her knees and engaged in prayer, as it seemed to me. However I was never able to hear what she said, although sometimes she wept."[13]

The Duke of Alençon, returned by ransom after five years in English captivity, was greeted by Jeanne on their first meeting. "You, be very welcome," she told the twenty-five-year-old regal. "The more royal blood of France that shall be together, the better." Alençon's great-grandfather had died against the English at the battle of Crécy in 1346, and he himself had lost his father at the battle of Agincourt in 1415. Alençon saw Jeanne implore the king to offer his kingdom in order to be restored by the King of Heaven. After a meal together Alençon was amazed as he watched while Jeanne "galloped atilt with a lance, and seeing her behave in this manner, bearing a lance and tilting, I gave her a horse." A woman also noted, "I saw her riding on horseback and bearing a lance as the best soldier would have done it, and at that the men-at-arms marveled." Remarkably, at the beginning of her Rouen trial, Jeanne had given no indication of prior experience in military arts, saying that when her voice had told her she must go into France, "she answered that she was only a poor woman, who knew nothing of riding or making war." To this day historians still cannot explain Jeanne's mysterious acquisition of equestrian and military skills.[14]

Irritated at her continued interrogations by churchmen over her mission from God, Jeanne afterward confided to Alençon that "she had been very closely examined, but that she knew more and could do more than she had told her questioners." Jeanne also carped to Pasquerel. "She was not pleased with all these interrogations, . . . they were preventing her from accomplishing the work for which she was sent." Taken to Poitiers for further investigation, Jeanne was both mentally and physically tested, "to know how it was with her, whether she was a man or a woman and whether she was corrupt or virgin," one witness testified. Jeanne's attendant, Jean d'Aulon, related how women of the court "visited and secretly regarded and examined in the secret parts of her body. But after they had seen and looked at all there was to look at in this case, the lady said and related to the king that she and her ladies found with certainty that she was a true and entire maid in whom appeared no corruption or evil. I was present when the lady made her report." After three weeks of interrogation, theologians also judged her spotless, *virgo intacta,* and "publicly said that they saw, knew, nor were aware of anything in this Maid whatsoever but only can be in a good Christian and true Catholic. It was their opinion that she was a very good person." Nevertheless the head of the investigation, the Archbishop of Reims, would continue to have doubts about the Maid, and actively counsel Charles to distance himself from her. He finally succeeded with the help of equally wary advisers in the court.[15]

Jeanne as Transformed Warrior

Jeanne received her first suit of costly armor from Charles, fashioned at Tours to her diminuitive specifications. She sent for her famous rusted sword, to be found at the Church of Ste.-Catherine-de-Fierbois. Jeanne also had her standards made, a small one for herself with a painted image of Christ sitting in the clouds, flanked by an angel holding the fleurs-de-lis. Charles assigned Jeanne another attendant and two heralds, their duty being to convey diplomatic messages without fear of reprisal. She now had an assembly of a dozen horses, including five stout warhorses. On March 22, 1429, Jeanne dictated a bold letter, summoning the English to abandon France:

> Surrender to La Pucelle who is sent here by God. She is come here by God's will to reclaim the blood royal . . . go back to your own country, *de par Dieu*. And if you do not do so, expect tidings from La Pucelle who will come to see you shortly, to your very great injury. . . . I am sent from God, the King of Heaven, to chase you out of all of France, body for body. . . . If you do not wish to believe this message from God and La Pucelle, then wherever we find you we shall strike you there, and make a great uproar *(hahay)* greater than any made in France for a thousand years, if you do not yield to right. Know well that the King of Heaven will send greater strength to La Pucelle and her good men-at-arms than you in all your assaults can overwhelm, and by blows it will be seen who has greater favor *(meilleur droit)* with the God of Heaven. . . . Answer if you wish to make peace in the town of Orléans, and if you do not, you will be reminded shortly to your very great harm. Written this Tuesday of Holy Week.[16]

Gathering her troops at Blois in the eastern Loire valley, Jeanne set out with her army for besieged Orléans, which had suffered under withering English pressure for seven months. If Orléans fell, the remainder of southern France would be open to conquest. The French had experienced a crushing defeat several months before at the Battle of the Herrings, so-called because it had involved an attempt to stop an English convoy from delivering a large supply of fish to their troops at Orléans. On February 12, 1429, a large body of French cavalry attacked the English, who maintained their traditional defensive tactic of placing archers behind a row of sharpened stakes. As at Crécy and Agincourt, a smaller group of Englishmen had slaughtered a larger force of French knights with the terrible effect of their longbows, disrupting an impetuous French charge at a distance, before finishing off by hand the remnants that made it through the arrows. News of the setback further disheartened the French, causing more soldiers to desert the defense of Orléans and go home.[17]

But new hope was marching toward Orléans in the name of Jeanne. Priests marched before the army, ten thousand strong, under a large banner of the crucified Christ that Jeanne also had painted. On the three-day march the faithful sang a hymn, *Veni Creator Spiritus*. Livestock and other victuals dragged behind in wagons, to sustain the troops and help relieve famine in Orléans. Exuberant followers increased along the way, including Jeanne's two brothers, Jean and Pierre. She insisted that her troops either take confession or she would depart from them. Jeanne took daily confession herself. "She waxed very wrathful when she heard the name of God blasphemed, or if she heard anyone swear," Louis de Coutes attested: "Nobody in the army dared, before her, swear or blaspheme for fear of being reprimanded by her. She would allow no gambling or have any women following the army. Jeanne declared that such women would bring the army low, causing God to allow the war to be lost."

The Duke of Alençon was a target of her puritanical rage as well: "Jeanne was chaste, detesting the women who follow soldiers. I saw her once . . . pursue with drawn sword a girl who was with the soldiers, and in such a manner that in chasing her she broke her sword. She became very incensed when she heard the soldiers swear, and scolded them much, and especially me, who swore from time to time."[18]

Jeanne also despised looting, once trying to slap a soldier who had stolen a calf. Though he never met her, theologian Jean Gerson wrote of Jeanne's aura, as towns began joining the Armagnac side even before her great victory at Orléans. Gerson's description is most remarkable, verifying contemporary essentials that were building around Jeanne's legend:

> A certain young girl, the daughter of a certain shepherd, who herself is said to have tended the common

flock, asserts that she has been sent by God, so that through her the kingdom might be restored to his obedience. That however this claim of hers might not be considered rash, she also employs supernatural signs, such as revealing the secrets of hearts and foreseeing future events. It is further reported that she has her hair cropped in the manner of a man and, eager to sally forth to military actions, she mounts her horse clad in male attire and armor.

While she is on horseback carrying her banner, she is immediately infused with a miraculous activity, as if she were a general experienced in the strategic employment of the army. At that time her men too become highly spirited, but her enemies on the other hand are as fearful as if devoid of strength. As soon as she dismounts from her horse, however, and reassumes ordinary female attire, she becomes very artless, as ignorant of worldly events as an innocent lamb. It is said furthermore that she lives in chastity, sobriety and moderation, devoted to God.[19]

First Victory at Orléans

Thus Jeanne's popular effect, which was attested from afar and by personal witnesses. On approaching Orléans from the west, it became necessary to make a detour over the Loire River to reach the eastern gate, the only one not occupied by the English. Jeanne became furious at the delay and took it out on Count Dunois, the self-proclaimed Bastard of Orléans. Though only in his late twenties, he was an experienced commander, having barely escaped with his life at the Battle of the Herrings. According to Dunois, she inquired on their first meeting:

"Are you the Bastard of Orléans?"

I answered her, "Yes, I am so and I rejoice at your coming."

> She said to me, "Did you give the counsel that I should come here, to this side of the river, and that I not go straight there where Talbot and the English are?"
>
> I answered that myself and others wiser had given this counsel, thinking to do what was best and safest.
>
> Then Jeanne said to me, "In God's name, the counsel of the Lord your God is wiser and safer than yours. You thought to deceive me and it is yourself above all whom you deceive, for I bring you better succor than has reached you from any soldier and any city. It is succor from the King of Heaven. It comes not from love of me but from God Himself who, at the request of Saint Louis and Saint Charlemagne, has taken pity on the town of Orléans."
>
> Forthwith and at the same moment, the wind which was contrary and absolutely prevented the boats from moving upstream, in which were laden the victuals for Orléans, changed and became favorable. . . . From that moment I had good hope in her, more than before. I then implored her to consent to cross the Loire and to enter into the town of Orléans where she was greatly wished for.[20]

The magical shifting of the wind was enough to convince the Bastard of Orléans: "It seems to me that Jeanne and also what she did in warfare and in battle was rather of God than of men." Dunois described Jeanne and the army entering Orléans on the evening of April 29, 1429:

> At eight o'clock, despite all the English soldiers, who never attempted to prevent it, Jeanne entered. She was armed at all points, riding upon a white horse. She had her standard borne before her, which likewise was white. . . . And there was a marvelous crowd and press to touch her or her horse. So much so that one of those bearing a torch drew so near to her standard that the pinion took

> fire. Wherefore she struck spurs to her horse and turned him right gently toward the pinion and put out the fire.[21]

By the next day Jeanne was stewing for action, as witnessed by Louis de Coutes. "Jeanne went to see the Bastard of Orléans and spoke to him, and on her return she was in great anger, for she said he had decided on that day they would not go out against the enemy." Jeanne went to the battlements and yelled across to the English to withdraw in God's name—or be driven away:

> One called the Bastard of Granville spoke many insults to Jeanne, asking her if she expected them to surrender to a woman, calling the French who were with her miserable pimps. . . . Glasdale and those of his company answered basely, insulting her and calling her *cow girl!*, shouting very loudly that they would have her burned if they could lay hands on her. At which she was much enraged and answered them that they lied.[22]

After four more days of inactivity, La Pucelle was beside herself in frustration. She heard that English reinforcements were approaching under John Fastolf. Jean d' Aulon recalled that she rushed on Dunois:

> "Bastard, Bastard, in God's name I command you that as soon as you know that Fastolf is come, you will let me know, for if not, I promise you I will have your head taken off!" To which the lord Dunois answered that she should doubt not, for he would indeed make it known to her. After these exchanges, I was weary and fatigued, and cast myself down on a mattress in the Maid's chamber, to rest a little. And likewise did she, with her hostess, on another bed, to sleep and rest. But while I was beginning to take my rest, suddenly the Maid rose from the bed, and making a great noise, roused me. At that I asked her what she wanted.

> She answered me, "In God's name, my *Conseil* has told me to go out against the English and I know not whether against their fortification or against Fastolf, who is to relieve them."
>
> Upon which I arose at once and as swiftly as I could put the Maid into her armor.[23]

Jeanne's other attendant, Louis de Coutes, continued the story after she woke up and aroused him with a start:

> "Ah, wicked boy, you did not tell me the blood of France was spilling!"
>
> She urged me to fetch her horse. In the interval she had her armor put on by the lady of the house and her daughter, and when I came back from saddling and bridling her horse, I found her ready and armed. She told me to go and fetch her standard which was upstairs and I handed it to her through the window.
>
> After taking her standard, Jeanne hastened, racing toward the Burgundy gate. Then the hostess told me to go after her, which I did. There was at that time an attack or skirmish over toward St.-Loup. It was in this attack that the boulevard was taken, and on her way Jeanne encountered many French wounded, which angered her. The English were preparing their defense when Jeanne came in haste at them, and as soon as the French saw Jeanne, they began to cheer and the fortress of St.-Loop was taken.[24]

Though combatively messianic, Jeanne did not believe herself immortal. When told that it must be reassuring to enter battle because she could not be killed, she answered that she was no safer than any other soldier. Nor was she stupid, denying that she boasted that no one need worry, because she would personally absorb all the arrows and stones shot from the enemy. When asked to bless pious objects by touching them, she laughed at the idea. "Touch them yourself," she told some women, "they will be as good from your touch as from mine." As she did for her own comrades, Jeanne lamented those English first killed on entering Orléans, because they had died without the benefit of confession. "She wept much upon them and at once confessed herself to me," Jean Pasquerel recalled.[25]

The day after capturing the important defense at St.-Loup gate, Pasquerel described how Jeanne had a letter tied to an arrow and shot to the English to inform them that "the King of Heaven orders and commands you through me, Jeanne La Pucelle, that you quit your fortresses and return to your own country, or if not I shall make you such *hahay* that the memory of it will be perpetual." The English were enraged. "Having read it, they began to utter great shouts, saying 'News from the Armagnac's whore!' At these words, Jeanne began to sigh and to weep copious tears, calling the King of Heaven to her aid. And thereafter she was consoled, as she said, for she had had news from her Lord."

Another important English bastion was taken by a spirited assault led by Jeanne, not with her standard in hand, but a lance: "When they perceived that the enemies were coming out of the bastion to charge their men, La Pucelle and La Hire, who were always before them to guard them, couched their lances and were the first to strike among the enemies. Then everybody followed them and began to strike out at the enemy so effectively that they drove them back."[26]

On Friday, May 6, Jeanne instructed Pasquerel, "Rise tomorrow early in the morning, earlier than you did today, and do your best. Be always at my side, for tomorrow I shall have much to do, more than I ever did. Tomorrow the blood will flow out of my body above my breast." Pasquerel rose early on Saturday, celebrated Mass, and was part of a day-long assault:

> Jeanne, as she had predicted, was struck by an arrow above the breast, and when she felt herself wounded she

> was afraid and wept, and was consoled as she said. And some soldiers, seeing her wounded, wanted to apply a charm to her wound, but she would not have it, saying "I would rather die than do a thing which I know to be a sin or against the will of God."
>
> And that she knew well that she must die one day, but knew not when or how or at what time of the day. But if a remedy could be applied to her wound without sin, she was very willing to be cured. And they put onto her wound olive oil and lard. And after that had been applied, Jeanne made her confession to me, weeping and lamenting.

The Bastard of Orléans told a more marvelous version of the famous wound:

> Jeanne was wounded by an arrow, which penetrated her flesh between her neck and her shoulder for a depth of six inches. Despite this, she did not retire from the battle and took no remedy against the wound. . . . I was going to break off, and intended the army to retire into the city. Then the Maid came up to me and requested me to wait a little longer. Thereupon she mounted her horse and herself retired into a vineyard at some distance from the crowd of men. She remained in that vineyard at prayer for the space of eight minutes.
>
> When she came back, she immediately picked up her standard and took up her position on the edge of the ditch. The moment she was there the English trembled with terror. And the king's soldiers regained courage and began to go up, charging against the boulevard without meeting the least resistance.[27]

Jean d'Aulon described the final assault, in which he covered himself with his shield for fear of hurled stones. Jeanne's precious standard was being momentarily carried off, until she grabbed it in a fury:

> She waved the standard in such a manner that I imagined that in doing so the others would think that she was making them a sign. . . . This occasioned all who were of the Maid's army to come together and rally again. . . . No sooner had the attack recommenced than the English lost all power to resist longer, and thought to make their way from the boulevard into the Tourelles, but few among them could escape, for the four or five hundred soldiers they numbered were killed or drowned, except some few who were taken prisoners, and these not great lords. And thinking to save themselves, the bridge broke under them.

One of the many drowned was Sir William Glasdale, who had called Jeanne a cow girl and whore. Jeanne was moved by pity for those who had drowned. Glasdale's armor-weighted body was pulled out of the river, to lie in state before being transferred to England for burial. As the next day was Sunday, Jeanne ordered that the enemy be allowed to retire unmolested. "Let them go," she instructed. "It is not the Lord's pleasure that we should fight them today. You will get them another time." After both armies stood facing each other, the English retreated westward to Meung-sur-Loire. The Duke of Bedford wrote of the defeat, ascribing it to "a disciple and follower of the Fiend, called the Pucelle, who used false enchantments and sorcery." As this legend built, soldiers back in England even became afraid to cross the English Channel, lest they confront a witch.[28]

One account described Jeanne's triumphal return into Orléans: "She was received with as much joy and enthusiasm by all, men and women small and great, as if she had been an angel of God. For they hoped that with her help they would be delivered from their enemies." She went to the cathedral to give glory to God, continually spurning personal glory: "she liked to be alone and solitary." When men declared to Jeanne that never had such feats been recorded in books, she replied, "My Lord has a book which no clerk has ever read, being perfect in its instruction."

Jeanne remained exasperated at the adulation showered on her by men and women alike. But one month after the stunning victory at Orléans, she began to enter legend, propelled there at least in the letter of Perceval de Boulainvilliers, the king's councillor. He wrote the Duke of Milan, describing Jeanne as if he might well have seen her:

> This Pucelle has a certain elegance. She has a virile bearing, speaks little, shows an admirable prudence in all her words. She has a pretty woman's voice, eats little, drinks very little wine. She enjoys riding a horse and takes pleasure in fine arms, greatly likes the company of noble fighting men, detests numerous assemblies and meetings, readily sheds copious tears, has a cheerful face. She bears the weight and burden of armor incredibly well, to such a point that she has remained fully armed during six days and nights.

The letter continued with invented descriptions of magical attributes Jeanne had supposedly possessed in childhood, but this portion is mundane enough to be credible. It also conforms to the evaluation of Marguerite de Touroulde: "Jeanne was very simple and ignorant and knew absolutely nothing, it seems to me, excepting in the matter of war." And to that of the knight Thibaut d'Armagnac: "Apart from the matter of war, she was simple and ignorant."[29]

Unbroken Victory After Orléans

After taking Orléans, Jeanne went to Charles's headquarters at the castle in Loches. She fell at his feet and begged him to proceed immediately to his coronation, as her voices had urgently instructed her to do. She was asked by the dauphin and others to reveal the message from her *conseil*, according the Bastard of Orléans. She gladly answered that when people did not really believe that she was sent by God, she prayed: "complaining to Him that those to whom she spoke did not really believe her and, her prayer to God made, she heard a voice which said to her, *'Fille Dieu*, Daughter of God, go, go, go, I shall be your aid—go.' And when she heard this voice, she felt a great joy and desired to always be in that state. And what is more impressive, in thus repeating those words of her voices, she herself exulted in a marvelous fashion, raising her eyes to Heaven.[30]

Each day in Loches Jeanne went to chapel, where she had the bells rung for half an hour while priests sang hymns to the Virgin Mary. Her voices clearly animated her with boldness, according to young Guy de Laval, who was welcomed into her growing army. "I went to her lodging to see her," Laval wrote to his grandmother:

> She sent for wine and told me that she would soon have me drinking wine in Paris. This seems a thing divine by her deeds, and also from seeing and hearing her. . . . I saw her mount her horse, armed all in white armor (plain and unadorned) excepting her head, a little ax in her hand, riding a big, black charger which, at the door of her lodgings, cavorted very wildly and would not let her mount. Then she said, "Take him to the cross," which was before the church beside the road, and there she mounted without the horse moving, as if it were tied.
>
> The Pucelle told me at her lodgings, when I went there to see her, that she had sent to you, grandmother, a very small golden ring, that it was a very small thing and that she would rather have sent you better, considering your renown.[31]

A Burgundian, Jean de Wavrin, described the despair that began creeping into the bones of La Pucelle's enemies: "The courage of the English was much impaired and fallen off. They saw, it seemed to them, their fortune turn its wheel sharply against them, for they had already lost several towns and fortresses. . . . Thus they were all very desirous of withdrawing to the Normandy marches, abandoning what they held in the country of France."

The English gathered their forces east of Orléans at the town of Jargeau, on the southern bank of the Loire River, with a fortified bridge as the main entrance. Their commander was the Earl of Suffolk. It was well defended, with a wall and a ditch surrounding most of the town, except for a small suburb outside. The French, under Alençon, were reluctant to attack such an obstacle. Jeanne entered the war council with her usual impetuosity, haranguing that God was on the side of the French. "Jeanne said that unless she was sure that God was leading this work, she would have chosen to herd her sheep rather than expose herself to such dangers." In an earlier meeting with Alençon's family, Jeanne had promised his wife that she would return her handsome young husband intact. "Lady, fear not," Alençon recalled her saying, "I will bring him back to you safe and sound, in such state or better than he now is."[32]

Jeanne sent an offer to the Earl of Suffolk and citizens of Jargeau to either leave without harm, or face the consequences of a direct assault. It was refused. As the bombardment of Jargeau commenced from across the river, Jeanne warned Alençon to move from a certain spot, where she predicted that a return English artillery shot was going to land. "I withdrew and shortly after, at that very spot where I had withdrawn, someone was killed, who was called my Lord de Lude. That put me into great fear and I marveled at the sayings of Jeanne after all these events." In a surprise move the English came out from behind their defenses and attacked the French in the suburb, who began to fall back. But Jeanne rallied them with her standard, forcing the English back into the town. French cannon began reducing the walls, toppling one of the defensive towers. Alençon was content to continue the bombardment, but La Pucelle as usual was impatient for offense. "Jeanne herself said to me, 'Forward, gentle Duke, to the attack!' and as it seemed to me premature to begin the assault so swiftly, Jeanne said to me, 'Doubt not, the time is come when it pleases God,' and that one must act when God wills—'Act and God will act.' Oh, gentle Duke, are you afraid? Do you not remember that I promised your wife to bring you back safe and sound?"

Along with Jeanne, French soldiers entered the ditch with scaling ladders to mount the walls. The English maintained a stout resistance, pushing back the ladders and hurling objects down on those below. One large English soldier in particular fought like a demon, until a French artillery piece was specifically aimed to kill him. The contest raged for hours. Jeanne was constantly in the middle as the French finally began to breech the walls. As Alençon described it:

> Jeanne was on a ladder, holding her standard in her hand, when the standard was struck, and Jeanne was also struck on the top of her head with a stone, which broke on her helmet. She was stricken to the ground, and when she rose up, she said to the soldiers, "Friends, friends—up—our Lord has condemned the English, in this hour they are ours, be of good heart!" And at once the town of Jargeau was taken and the English withdrew toward the bridges and the French pursued them and in the pursuit were killed of them more than 1,100.[33]

Among the heavy English losses was the Earl of Suffolk, who was captured. He knighted his captor on the spot, because it would be ignominious to surrender to one of a lesser station, a mere squire. Jeanne and the army returned to Orléans before marching further west toward the English-occupied towns on the Loire River, Meung-sur-Loire and Beaugency. Like Jargeau, both had a fortified bridge across the river, further buttressed by stout, walled castles in town. At Meung the

French were content to capture the bridge fortifications, blocking off easy movement from the town. The Armagnacs accomplished the same feat at Beaugency, having been reinforced by a large force under Arthur de Richemont. Although he was lord constable of the dauphin, Richemont had been banned from Charles's court because of conflicts over the conduct of the war. Richemont wished to fight with abandon, while a favored adviser to Charles, Georges de la Trémoille, continued his council of diplomacy and delay. Trémoille had continually advised against the wild adventures of Jeanne, in which caution he agreed with the Archbishop of Reims, Regnault de Chartres. Jeanne overcame her own reservations and accepted Richemont. As Alençon recalled her saying, "Ah, good Constable, you have not come on my behalf, but because you have come, you are welcome." According to Richemont's scribe, the constable had a saltier reply for Jeanne: "I do not know if you come from God or not. If you are from God, I do not fear you, because God knows my good will. If you are from the devil, I fear you even less."[34]

There was new reason for the French to band together, for on the horizon had finally arrived thousands of troops from Paris, under the command of Sir John Fastolf. They began joining the fragmentary remnants of the English setbacks from Jargeau, Meung-sur-Loire, and Beaugency, heading north ostensibly back to Paris. Among these was the Earl of Talbot. Talbot wanted to turn and attack the French, but Fastolf feared that defeat could undo all the conquests of Henry V in one day. Talbot overruled his subordinate, and the English and Burgundians returned south. They encountered the French above Beaugency, arrayed for battle on a rise of ground described as *une petite montagnette*. Both armies observed each other at length as English archers assembled behind their sharpened stakes to repel a cavalry charge. The English sent heralds across the field to goad the French into descending from their hill to do battle. According to the Burgundian chronicler, Jean de Wavrin, Jeanne responded, "Go and camp for today, because it is quite late. But tomorrow, at the pleasure of God and our Lady, we will look more closely at you. "[35]

Seeing the bellicose Richemont in the equally aggressive company of Jeanne, the English moved off north of Orléans toward the fortified town of Janville. By the next morning the French had lost contact with the enemy. Scouts rode out on their best horses to locate the English, but there were ample forests for them to disperse in. By midday, the Armagnacs had become stricken with caution. As the Bastard of Orléans recalled:

> The Duke of Alençon, in the presence of the lord constable, myself and several others, asked Jeanne what he ought to do. She answered him in a loud voice, saying "Have all good spurs," which on hearing, those present asked Jeanne, "What say you? Are we going to turn our backs on them?" Then Jeanne answered, *"No!* It will be the English who will not defend themselves and will be vanquished—and you will need good spurs to run after them."

Jeanne promised that very few Frenchmen would fall on this glorious day. *"En nom Dieu*—we must fight them," she exhorted. "Even if they were hanging in the clouds, we should get them. For God has sent them to us to punish. The dauphin shall have the greatest victory today that he has had for a long time. My *Conseil* tells me they are ours!" Her confident exhortation electrified the troops, who set off.[36]

English pickets fell back toward their main body with word that an advance force of French cavalry was bearing down upon them. Lord Talbot turned south again down an old Roman road, to deploy five hundred archers in woods and hedges by a narrow passage where Jeanne's advance force should pass. They waited to ambush them in a hail of arrows, which could pierce armor at three hundred yards. Horses would be caught in this rain of death, which was even better: knights would tumble to the ground, and others charging behind them would topple into the maelstrom. Unhorsed knights flailing on the ground were as helpless as turtles in their heavy armor, to be finished off with a dagger to the throat or an axe blow to the head. It was said that a battle's outcome could be told by the time the sixth arrow was loosed.

While the archers set up, a stag was startled from the woods. It plunged into the hidden English, causing an outcry that gave their position away. Confusion set in as John Fastolf arrived with the English vanguard. Talbot's men began to fall back, which Fastolf took to be a retreat. In such disarray, mounted French knights hit the archers on their flank. Having avoided their deadly longbows, they overwhelmed them in minutes. Mounted soldiers in armor trampled and slashed the helpless footmen. The bulk of the French army followed immediately behind the cavalry and caught the English in total panic, crushing their ranks. Jean de Wavrin recounted that Fastolf,

> knowing that all was going very badly, had the notion of saving himself and it was said to him in my presence that he should take care of his person, for the battle was lost for them. And before he had gone, the French had thrown to the ground the Lord de Talbot, had made him prisoner and all his men were dead. The French were already so far advanced in the battle that they could take or kill at will whomever they wanted to. And finally the English were there undone at small loss to the French.[37]

The slaughter was over in less than an hour. "And so it was," the Bastard of Orléans recalled, "for they took to flight and there were killed or captured 4,000." The English estimated their loss at half that number, but the Battle of Patay was Jeanne's most sweeping victory, avenging the English one at Agincourt fourteen years before. She was deeply distressed, however, by the carnage she saw, and, according to her page, dismounted to receive the confession of a wounded English soldier, "raising his head and comforting him as much as she could,"[38]

Orléans reclaimed in the month of May, Jargeau taken on June 12, Meung abandoned on the fifteenth, Beaugency on the seventeenth, capped the next day by Patay—all of them in lightning sequence, with Jeanne as both symbol and substance. The entire Loire valley was clear. The dauphin rejoiced while Paris fortified its walls for the coming storm. Jeanne reminded her monarch that her time of glory would last little more than a year. A week after the victory at Patay, Jeanne dictated a letter to various towns, proclaiming:

> She has chased the English out of every place they held on the River Loire. Many of them are dead or taken prisoners and they are discomforted in battle. . . . Hold yourself fast, loyal Frenchmen, I pray you. And I pray and demand that you be ready to come to the anointing of the gracious King Charles at Reims, where we shall soon be. Come before us when you hear that we are approaching. I commend you to God.

The French humiliation at Agincourt had been avenged. Bedford, Exeter, and Warwick were momentarily foiled; Salisbury was dead, Talbot and Suffolk were captured, and John Fastolf was in disgrace. Indeed he would wind up a drunken buffoon as Falstaff in the hands of William Shakespeare, who with poetic license would look past Jeanne the witch and Patay to buttress the English sweetness of Agincourt, with the immortal words he put in the mouth of Falstaff's student Prince Hal, Harry the King:

> He that shall see this day and live old age,
> Will yearly on the vigil feast his neighbors
> And say "Tomorrow is Saint Crispian."
> Then will he strip his sleeve and show his scars,

And say "These wounds I had on Crispin's day."
Old men forget; yet all shall be forgot,
But he'll remember with advantages
What feats he did that day. Then shall our names,
Familiar in their mouths as household words—
Harry the King, Bedford and Exeter,
Warwick and Talbot, Salisbury and Gloucester—
Be in their flowing cups freshly rememb'red.
This story shall the good man teach his son.
And Crispin Crispian shall ne'er go by
From this day to the ending of the world
But we in it shall be remembered
We few, we happy few, we band of brothers.[39]

Road to Coronation at Reims

At Orléans the Armagnac army had further increased because of Jeanne's inspired successes. As she said to Alençon, "Sound the trumpets and mount your horse. It is time to go to the gentle King Charles to put him on the path of his consecration at Reims." But still the advisers of Charles demurred, particularly his chief councilor, Georges de la Trémoille, who continued to preach diplomacy with the Burgundians. He himself had been part of the Burgundian court before joining the Armagnacs. Others argued that Charles should instead head toward Normandy, not Reims, to induce more victories there. But there were still English-occupied towns threatening the way to Reims. Jeanne argued, as the Bastard of Orléans recalled, that coronation at Reims was primal, "that when the king had been crowned and consecrated, the power of his adversaries would continue to diminish, and that they finally would not be able to hurt him or his kingdom." Becoming frustrated at the stalemate, Jeanne stormed out of town to spend two days camping with the army in the field.[40]

Jeanne's position held sway. In late June of 1429 the dauphin set out toward Reims. The first significant town under Burgundian rule he encountered was Auxerre. It surrendered to Charles after three days of contemplating his large army, also supplying him with troops. Other villages along the way paid their homage until the Armagnacs reached the fortified city of Troyes. The question arose whether to besiege Troyes or bypass it. According to the Bastard of Orléans, Jeanne burst into Charles's council of officers to demand an attack in God's name, "because within three days I will take you into the city of Troyes by love, or by force, or by courage—and false Burgundy will stand *toute stupéfaite.*" On July 4, 1429, Jeanne sent a letter to Troyes offering mercy if the city opened its arms to Charles. If not, *Responce bref*—reply soon.[41]

While the French army surrounded Troyes for four days, a fiery eccentric named Brother Richard was finally sent out to consort with the fearsome La Pucelle. Among other things he had preached that she had direct access to God and the saints, and could penetrate any city's defense. Brother Richard had also predicted that the biblical millennium was at hand. Indeed the world would end next year, in 1430. These and other proclamations had caused him to be driven out of Paris. At Troyes, however, he approached Jeanne with trepidation, sprinkling holy water in his wake and making the sign of the cross—appropriate actions against a witch. With a sense of cosmic comedy in the face of another exorcism, Jeanne coaxed him closer. "Approach *hardiment,*" she beckoned, "I shall not fly away." Jeanne proved to be no witch capable of flight, and Brother Richard was no fool. He promptly took up with the Armagnacs.[42]

Jeanne arrayed the army so expertly for a pending attack that by the next day the unnerved defenders of Troyes made obedience to Charles. The Bastard of Orléans and Alençon both marveled at Jeanne's uncanny military tactics, which rivaled those of an officer with decades of experience, "and especially in placing the artillery, in which she acquitted herself magnificently . . . the positions that she took up were so admirable that even two or three of the most famous and experienced captains would not have made as good a plan of battle." Charles's party entered Troyes in triumph, while Jeanne carried her standard beside him.[43]

Two days later the army resumed the march to Reims with fresh provisions, encountering Châlons-sur-Marne along the way. As at Auxerre and Troyes the keys to the city were presented to Charles without resistance. There the dauphin confidently informed his subjects that his coronation was imminent, inviting all to attend by sending out criers. Jeanne's parents were among the subjects who responded, traveling west from Domremy. While emissaries from Reims were sent forth to welcome Charles, those in the city loyal to his enemies fled—including Pierre Cauchon. On July 16, the dauphin triumphantly entered the traditional site of French coronations in current Burgundian territory.

The next day Charles VII was crowned in the cathedral, a swift preparation impeded because most of the trappings of high service had been transferred to the Cathedral of Notre Dame in Paris. Not the most precious *saint ampoule,* however: the holy oil, the Holy Vial to anoint the new king, which four mounted knights ceremoniously made their way to the abbey of St.-Rémi to retrieve. This oil had been used to baptize all monarchs since Clovis, who was declared first king of the Franks in A.D. 496. Entering the wide-open doors of the cathedral, the knights, still mounted, clattered down the granite aisle to present the ointment. Prostrated on the steps of the altar and dressed only in shoes and a loose shirt, Charles was anointed, marked on the head, chest, shoulders, elbows, wrists, and hands. Afterward, publicly dressed in more regal trappings of office, Charles, amid chants to the saints, was given the ivory scepter representing the hand of justice. The gold crown was taken from the altar seat and held above the monarch's head, transforming him into royal majesty. When the crown was settled on his head,

> Every man cried out *Noël!* And the trumpets sounded so that it seemed as though the walls of the church should have crumbled. During this mystery, La Pucelle was always at the king's side, holding his standard in her hand. It was fine to see the elegant manners not only of the king but also of the Maid. God knows we wished them well.

Another observer revealed that Jeanne added most to the moment by tearfully embracing the legs of Charles, praising God that His true will had been fulfilled through her. But not all were transfixed by her display, even among the friendly court of the Armagnacs, who believed her too conspicuous. The Archbishop of Reims, Regnault de Chartres, was antagonistic toward Jeanne. Having presided over her theological trial at Poitiers, he maintained that her impulsiveness was disruptive to future accommodation with the Burgundians. Such prominence at the coronation was later challenged at Jeanne's trial of Condemnation, asked why she egotistically thought that her little pinion should stand out at the king's side before all others. Jeanne resolutely replied, "It has borne *la peine,* the toil. It was quite right that it receive *l'honneur.*"[44]

DISOBEDIENCE AND DOWNFALL AT PARIS

After Charles's coronation Jeanne was ecstatic. She was moved by the people's new allegiance everywhere she went. Without being confronted, the Burgundian towns of Soissons, Château-Thierry, Compiègne, Provins, Senlis, Laon, Crècy-en-Brie, Coulommiers, and Lagny—just east of Paris—switched over to the Armagnacs. Passing through the hilly Soissons region, Jeanne enthused, "These are good folk. I have never seen other people so greatly rejoice at the coming of so noble a king. May I be so fortunate, when my days shall be done, as to be buried in this ground." The Archbishop of Reims inquired where Jeanne wished to die? "Where it shall please God," she answered, "for I am not sure of the time or the place, anymore than you are."

King Charles offered a truce to the Burgundians for two weeks. The Duke of Bedford used the time to better fortify Paris—countering the new politics by naming the Duke of Burgundy the city governor. On August 7, Bedford wrote a scolding rebuke to Charles, "who now without reason, call yourself king." Bedford charged him with taking advantage of ignorance and superstition, relying on "that deranged and infamous woman who goes about in men's clothes and is of dissolute conduct . . . according to Holy Scriptures, abominable to God." Meanwhile an inventory including one thousand cannon balls was brought to Paris, while Bedford had its moats cleaned of debris.[45]

Without the advice of her voices, Jeanne moved toward Paris, her followers convinced that she would put the king there. She urged Alençon to gather the troops, for "I would go to see Paris, closer than I have seen it before." Charles achieved a new aura of command, while Jeanne, on the morning of his coronation, naively sent a letter to the Duke of Burgundy. Why was he making war on his own country? she asked. Why instead was he not at Reims paying homage to Charles? "As for the gentle King of France," Jeanne coaxed:

> he is ready to make peace with you, saving his honor, if it has to do with you alone. And I must make known to you from the King of Heaven, my rightful and sovereign Lord, for your good and for your honor and upon your life, that you will win no more battles against loyal Frenchmen, and those who wage war against the holy kingdom of France are warring against King Jesus, King of Heaven and all the earth, my rightful and sovereign Lord.

There was no reply. Meantime the king's council advised him to cease putting up with Jeanne's saber-rattling and further negotiate with the Duke of Burgundy. Without her knowledge emissaries speaking for Charles met with the Duke's representatives at Compiègne. The delegation was led by the Archbishop of Reims. A longer four-month truce was in the offering, along with the return of Compiègne and three other towns that recently had surrendered to Charles. The Duke of Burgundy proffered a neutral position in coming conflicts between the French and the English for this period, while also diddling with the English for tradeoffs after the truce ended.[46]

None of this was shared with Jeanne, who rode ahead of the king and set up cannon to bombard Paris. In preparation for assault she sent skirmishers out to probe around the strong Parisian defenses, with walls over twenty-five feet high all around, and massive towers guarding all six gates to the city, with a recently cleared moat ten feet deep and over one hundred feet wide in certain places. Meanwhile Charles was taking his time inching toward Paris, filled "with great regret" according to a number of sources. Alençon was sent several times to induce him to come to St.-Denis, within view of Paris, so that the attack might commence. By September 7, Charles finally arrived.

In an assault on the city the next day, the Armagnacs tried to cross the moats and storm the St.-Honoré and St.-Denis gates. Jeanne was in the moat at St.-Honoré with her standard, constantly dodging arrows and cannon missiles, as the noisy explosions became too numerous to count from inside the walls. Toward sunset she was wounded. According to a defender's account, the city was demonically attacked by an army of twelve thousand:

> on the word of a creature in the form of a woman . . . . Their Pucelle was there on the edge of the moat and said, "Yield to us quickly for Jesus' sake, for if you do not yield before night, we shall enter by force whether you will or not, and you will all be put to death without mercy." "Here's for you!" cried one—"Cackling bawd!" He shot straight at her with his cross bow, piercing her leg, and

> she fled. Another transfixed her standard bearer's foot who, feeling himself wounded, raised his visor to try to withdraw the bolt from his foot, but another shot and wounded him mortally between the eyes.[47]

For the first time the Armagnacs were repulsed. A page of Jeanne's named Raymond was killed on the spot by a crossbow bolt through his skull. Despite her own wound Jeanne urged her troops to press on—to no avail. By nightfall she was carried away from the moat against her will. Still she wanted to attack the next day, vowing she would never leave until she had taken Paris. But Charles sent word for the army to withdraw north to St.-Denis.

It took five days for Jeanne's leg wound to heal at this hallowed burial site of French kings, repository of such legendary relics as a piece of the true cross and the infant clothes of Jesus. Jeanne offered a suit of captured armor and a sword at the cathedral in homage to Saint Denis, according to the custom of wounded soldiers. She was made a godmother of several children while there, naming the boys Charles and the girls Jeanne, anointing children with candle wax in the cathedral. When asked several times at her Rouen trial whether she had attacked Paris on a holy feast day, Jeanne finally admitted she believed that she had. Was this a righteous thing to do? *Passez outre,* she evaded. Despite her letter she denied that she had commanded Paris to blasphemously surrender in Jesus' name.[48]

Jeanne's power was waning, and the numerous casualties suffered in the attempt on Paris were put on her head. Yet she and Alençon hoped to attack the city again from another direction, by way of a bridge across the Seine that Alençon had constructed. To prevent them King Charles had the bridge destroyed. Acting on the council of the Archbishop of Reims and Georges de la Trémoille, Charles soon separated Alençon from Jeanne, sending the duke reluctantly home, never to see the Maid again. When she finally realized that the king would not pursue the war with vigor, Jeanne separated from him to go her own way and fight the English. She said bitterly that she feared nothing but treason.[49]

Away from the battlefront, Jeanne had a bizarre encounter with an *illuminata* named Catherine de la Rochelle, who claimed to see visions and wished for Jeanne to share them with her, particularly a white lady dressed in gold who appeared at night with directions on how to find boundless hidden treasure to pay the army. Jeanne balked at first. "To this I answered this Catherine that she return to her husband and do her housework and feed her children. And to have certainty in the matter of this Catherine, I spoke with Saint Catherine and Saint Margaret and they told me that Catherine de la Rochelle was mad and a liar." Nevertheless Jeanne was clearly curious:

> I asked Catherine whether this white lady appeared to her every night, telling her that I should like to sleep with her in her bed, to see her. And in fact I lay down and watched until about midnight and I saw nothing, and then I fell asleep. And when morning came I asked this Catherine whether the white lady had come to her. She answered me yes, while I slept, and that she had been unable to awaken me. And I asked her if this lady would come the following night, and this Catherine answered me, yes. Therefore that day I slept in the daytime to be able to watch all the following night, and I lay down that night with Catherine and I watched all night long, but I saw nothing, although often I questioned Catherine to know if the lady was going to come or not. And Catherine answered me, "Yes, presently."[50]

No apparition appeared. Jeanne continued to falter, her army becoming smaller and more threadbare. In fact she was not even after the English anymore. Instead she was diverted far to the south to try to track down a renegade mercenary named Perrinet Gressart. This self-proclaimed nobleman held sway over several little towns, one of which was St.-Pierre-le-Moutier in the Loire Valley. Jeanne set out to take it by siege, which bogged down until she decided to attack the walls directly. Jean d'Aulon described her in a fleeting moment of delusion. Her attendant was wounded in the heel by an arrow, and Aulon saw her nearly alone while her men withdrew:

> I mounted a horse and immediately made my way to Jeanne and asked her what she was doing thus alone, and why she did not retreat like the others. After she had removed her light helmet, she answered me that she was not alone, and that she still had in her company fifty thousand of her men, and she would not leave there until she had taken the town. At that time, whatever she might say, she had not with her more than four or five men, and this I know certainly, along with many others who likewise saw her.
>
> I told her once more that she must come away and retreat as the others did. Then she told me to have them bring faggots and hurdles to make a bridge over the town moats so that we could better get at it. And as she spoke thus to me, she cried in a loud voice, "Faggots and hurdles—everyone—to build a bridge!" This immediately was done. At this thing I marveled greatly, for immediately the town was taken by storm without encountering too much resistance.[51]

This was Jeanne d'Arc's last significant conquest. The following siege at La Charité-sur-Loire was a failure that lasted a month. Catherine de la Rochelle had warned her not to go there, because the season was too cold in November. Instead she counseled an approach to the Duke of Burgundy to make peace. Jeanne replied that peace could only come at the tip of a lance. Before her attempt to take La Charité, she had written surrounding towns for new supplies. At her Rouen trial, Jeanne had been evasive about what her voices told her, denying that she had had holy water sprinkled before the abortive attempt:

> question: Why did you not enter the town of La Charité, since you had God's commandment to do so?
>
> answer: Who told you I had God's command to enter?
>
> question: Did you have *Conseil* from your voices or not?
>
> answer: Me, I wanted to go into France, but the men of war said that it was better to go first before the town of La Charité.[52]

Jeanne returned northwest to Jargeau on Christmas Day, 1429. She received word that she and her family had been ennobled, and given a coat of arms consisting of a sword mounted by a crown, flanked by fleurs-de-lis. Nevertheless she was desultory and inactive over the winter. On March 16 of 1430 she wrote a letter to the people of Reims with her old bravura, addressing their fears about being besieged by the Burgundians: "I will be very direct with you. If they come there, I will make them fasten their spurs so fast that they will not know how to put them on and get out of there, and very quickly at that." A second letter implied forlornly that Charles would be fully behind her in her rescue, should "many wicked people" in Reims try to turn the city back over to the Burgundians. "He will deliver you, *au plesir Dieu,* very soon."

News reached Jeanne from the north that Compiègne was about to be besieged by the Duke of Burgundy. That town had had a whirlwind allegiance of late, having voluntarily switched back to the Armagnacs that summer—after Charles had returned it to the Duke of Burgundy in furtive negotiations the preceding fall. Without court permission Jeanne, described as "very irritated," left the Loire and returned north to Lagny, on the road to Compiègne. It was late March, and at this time the miracle of having momentarily revived a dead infant was ascribed to her—the infant that she described as having been "black as my tunic" at her Rouen trial. By Easter, as she described at her Rouen trial, Jeanne's voices told her that she would soon be captured. "She said that after she heard by revelation at Melun that she was going to be taken prisoner, she handed over most of the conduct of war to the captains. She did not however inform them that she had had a revelation that she would be captured."[53]

Jeanne participated in one last small military success against a group of several hundred soldiers from Paris, who were surprised and nearly wiped out near Lagny. She captured their commander, Franquet d'Arras, adopting his surrender sword, the one that she preferred to give "hard clouts" with. When she learned that one of her men, for whom she had hoped to exchange Arras, had been executed in captivity, Jeanne turned the Burgundian over to local townspeople for execution. As she testified later at the Rouen trial, "she had agreed to his being put to death since he deserved it, because he had confessed that he was a murderer, a thief, and a traitor. . . . 'Since my man is dead, the one I wanted to have, then deal with this man as justice requires.'"[54]

Capture and Imprisonment

Finally Jeanne was captured at Compiègne. She had sneaked into the town at night; the next morning she took communion at the church of St. James. According to tradition, Jeanne told a group in the sanctuary that she was to be captured and put to death. She asked for their prayers. At midday she prepared to attack her enemies outside the town walls. "She put on her armor and ordered her men to arms and horse, and went out to join in the *mêlée,*" Alençon's chronicler related. "As soon as she came, the enemy fell back and were put to flight. La Pucelle charged hard against the Burgundian side." But the Burgundians rallied and got between Jeanne and the bridge to the town. Jeanne was warned of impending danger, but angrily screamed for silence. "Think only of striking hard at them," she shouted. "Whatever she might say, her men would not believe her and by force made her return directly to the bridge. And when the Burgundians and the English saw that she was coming back to get into the town, with a great effort they gained the edge of the bridge." In panic the drawbridge was pulled up, leaving Jeanne's outnumbered group stranded and overrun. According to one Burgundian, a rough-hewn archer, "angry that a woman should have surpassed so many valiant men, dragged her to one side by her cloth-of-gold and pulled her from her horse, throwing her flat on the ground." Her brother Pierre and Jean d'Aulon were among those captured with Jeanne. The day after her capture the Duke of Burgundy wrote, "By the blessed Creator, the woman called La Pucelle has been taken, and from her capture will be recognized the error and mad belief of all those who became sympathetic and favorable to the deeds of this woman."

At her Rouen trial, Jeanne was asked if she would have gone to Compiègne if her voices had warned her that she would be captured:

> If I had known the hour, and that I must be taken, I should not have gone willingly. Nevertheless, I should have done their commandment in the end, whatever was to happen to me . . . that day I did not know that I should be taken . . . still it had been told me that I must be made prisoner . . . I crossed by the bridge and the boulevard and went with a company of my men against the men of the lord John of Luxembourg and twice drove them back to the Burgundians' camp, and the third time as far as half way there. And then the English who were there cut the road behind me and my men. And me, in retreating, I was captured between the river and Compiègne.[55]

A Burgundian witness described the elation after the downfall of Jeanne. "The Burgundians and English were very joyous at it, more than if they had taken five hundred men, for they feared no other chief in war as much as they always had done, until that day, this Pucelle." After her capture Jeanne was taken to a castle in Beaulieu, where she attempted her first escape, as she described later in the Rouen trial. "Being in that castle, I had shut up my keepers in the tower, except the porter who saw me and encountered me. It seems to me that it did not please God that I should escape that time, and that I must see the king of the English, as my voices told me." Jeanne was then moved further north to a castle at Beaurevoir, being under the guard of John of Luxembourg. She was offered women's clothes by Luxembourg's wife, but refused them, stating that God had not yet given her permission. Jeanne stated at her trial, "Had it been that I was to wear women's clothes, I should have so more willingly at the request of those women than any other woman in all France, excepting my queen."

During Jeanne's imprisonment at Beaurevoir, a Burgundian knight talked with her periodically. "I tried several times," Haimond de Macy admitted, "playfully to touch her breasts, trying to put my hand on her chest, which Jeanne would not permit, but repulsed me with all her strength. Jeanne was indeed of decent conduct both in speech and act." Witnesses recalled how afraid the English were of the supernatural La Pucelle. "They were more afraid of her than of a large army," one testified. "I heard an English knight say that the English feared her more than a hundred men-at-arms. They reckoned that while she was alive they would have no glory or success on the field of war." Luxembourg's wife asked her husband not to turn Jeanne over to the English, but after four months she was ransomed to them for ten thousand livres. Pierre Cauchon was the intermediary.[56]

Trial and Execution

Jeanne was transferred to Rouen to begin her trial. After she was again physically examined to certify her virginity, the three-month rain of questions began. "Before she had given her answer to one," Jean Massieu recalled:

> another of the assistants interjected a different question, whereby she was often precipitate and confused in her answers . . . sometimes at the moment when one was questioning her and she was answering his question, another interrupted her answer so much that she several times said to those who were interrogating her, "Fine lords—ask one at a time" . . . And I was astonished to see how she could answer the subtle and capricious questions which were put to her, which a lettered man would have had difficulty in answering.[57]

Tiny Jeanne perched alone in a large chair surrounded by judges, which notary Guillaume Manchon described:

> Nearly every day there were interrogations in the morning which lasted three or four hours. Sometimes they extracted difficult and subtle questions from what Jeanne had said, and faced her with them after lunch in a second interrogation which lasted two or three hours. And sometimes they switched from one translation to another, while changing the manner of questioning as well. And despite this change, she answered prudently and with a very good memory, for often she said, "I have already answered on that point," or again, "I refer to the clerk," pointing at me.[58]

Witnessing such a confusing maze of procedure, a few assessors had the temerity to agree out loud that Jeanne was correct to protest, exclaiming, "You are quite right, Jeanne." Manchon himself became confused by all the hidden clerks taking down bogus testimony, and he complained to Bishop Cauchon. "On this subject, my lord Beauvais was greatly enraged at me. . . . Myself, I sat at the judge's feet with Guillaume Colles and the clerk of master Jean Beaupère, who wrote. But there were great differences between our writings, so much so that lively disagreements arose between us." Manchon testified that Master Nicolas Loiseleur went to Jeanne's cell, pretending to be from her country and offered to be her confessor. What Loiseleur learned in this underhanded manner was buttressed by Manchon and others, who were listening through a hole in the wall.[59]

The old interrogator Jean Beaupère was still alive by the time of the Reclamation trial. He recalled with a touch of misogyny that Jeanne "was right subtle, with a subtlety pertaining to woman." He was not alone in his day in believing that females were more wily and devious than males; Eve in the Garden of Eden provided the first great example. Beaupère doubted Jeanne's heavenly apparitions, believing instead that "they rose from natural causes and human intent, more than from anything supernatural." During the first phase of the trial, Jeanne's faculties were so sharp that she correctly recalled her answers from the week before. One notary named Guillaume Boisguillaume challenged her memory. Pierre Daron testified that "The answer for that day was read and it was found that Jeanne was right. She rejoiced greatly at it, saying to this Boisguillaume that if he made a mistake again she would pull his ears." No laughter was recorded at this simple rustic humor.[60]

As for the procedure of the trial, it became clear from the testimony of the surviving notaries that reducing the seventy charges down to twelve articles had been a Procrustean farce. Jeanne's answers had been altered to fit the mold. Guillaume Manchon was shown a trial folio in his own hand, noting many discrepancies. He was asked for an explanation at the trial of Reclamation:

> Question: "Do you believe that these articles were composed in a spirit of truth, for there is a great difference between these articles and Jeanne's answers."

> Manchon: "What is in the text of my proceedings is true. As for the articles, I refer them to those who did them, for it was not I who did them."

Two other notaries shied from signing the truncated articles, one pointing a finger at Nicolas Midi for testimony that had been deleted. A letter from the Bishop of Avranches, protesting that the whole matter should have been referred to Rome, was left out of the transcript. Manchon testified that Master Jean Lohier told him, "It seems that they are proceeding more on hatred than otherwise, and for this cause I shall stay no longer, for I want nothing to do with it."[61]

In her cell five ruffians guarded Jeanne in chains. She was fettered at the feet and further tethered to a huge block of wood. Jeanne was routinely mocked, which caused her anguish, as she feared that she would be molested. She stated that she preferred death to such conditions, and begged to be kept in ecclesiastical confinement with women, as was her right. Jeanne passed two months in prison in this manner. Two physicians testified who had attended Jeanne when she was violently vomiting in prison. Both told a similar story. One of them, Jean Tiphaine, related, "I took her pulse in order to discern the cause of her illness, and I asked her what she felt and where she hurt. She told me that a carp had been sent her by the Bishop of Beauvais, that she had eaten some of it, and that she thought it caused her illness." The other physician, Guillaume de la Chambre, added:

> I went to see her, as did Master Desjardins and the others. We palpated her on the right side and found her feverish. We therefore decided to bleed her. When we made our report to the Earl of Warwick, he said, "Be careful when bleeding her, for she is cunning and might kill herself." Nevertheless, she was bled, which gave her immediate relief.
>
> As soon as she was thus better, Master Jean d'Estivet

came, who exchanged insulting words with Jeanne and called her "wanton whore." She was so agitated by this that she became feverish and fell ill again. This came to the Earl's knowledge, who forbade d'Estivet to insult Jeanne anymore . . . I know, as far as one can know by the art of medicine, that she was a virgin and intact. For I saw her almost naked when I examined her.[62]

After Jeanne was threatened with torture on May 10, John of Luxembourg visited her in prison with an offer on May 13:

"Jeanne, I am come to ransom you, provided that you will promise that you will never take up arms against us."

She answered, *"En nom Dieu*, you are making sport of me, for I know well that you have neither the will nor the power."

And she repeated that several times because the count persisted. And then she said,

"I know that these English will put me to death, because they think afterward to win the kingdom of France. But were there a hundred thousand *goddons* more than they are now, they will never have this kingdom."

At these words the Earl of Stafford was angry and half drew his dagger to strike her, but the Earl of Warwick prevented him.[63]

After her recantation, when Jeanne resumed wearing men's clothes, the transcript of the Rouen trial stated that she said she had done it of her own volition, as she was continuously in the proximity to her harassing guards. Jeanne buttressed this reasoning to a Rouen townsman, Pierre Cusquel, who stated at the Reclamation trial it was "not to give herself to the soldiers whom she was with." Martin Ladvenu testified that Jeanne had told him an English lord had tried to rape her. Jean Massieu recalled that Jeanne said her guards had substituted men's clothes for her dress, not letting her go to the bathroom unless she changed.[64]

Ostensibly Jeanne was burned for this offense, although there were deeper theological and political reasons. Before her execution, Jean Massieu testified to a collective impatience. "I was pressed hard by the English, and even by one of their captains, to leave her in their hands the sooner to put her to death, saying to me, 'What, priest, will you make us dine here?'"[65]

The *Journal d'un Bourgeois de Paris* gave a graphically lurid account of Jeanne's fiery death:

> She perished soon, and her dress was all burned away, then the fire was drawn a little back that the people should not doubt. The people saw her stark naked with all the secrets a woman can and should have. When this sight had lasted long enough, the executioner replaced great fire under that poor carrion, which was soon charred and the bones reduced to ashes . . .

After her death Cauchon attempted to certify what he had not been able to obtain from Jeanne in life, a confession that her voices had lied to her. "Truly I see well that they have deceived me," one of several assessors was coerced to remember Jeanne confessing on her last morning. Notary Guillaume Manchon refused to add his signature to the record: "I was at the continuation of the trial until the end, except at some examinations of people who spoke to Cauchon aside, like private persons. Nevertheless, my lord of Beauvais tried to constrain me to sign them, which I would not do."[66]

After this cumulative review instigated by Charles VII, a copy of documents from the trial of Condemnation were ceremonially burned in 1456 by the public executioner in Rouen, where Jeanne had been put to the flames twenty-six years before.

Legends of Faux-Jeannes After Death

Jeanne d'Arc lives on of course, like King Arthur and Robin Hood, long after the Cauchons and kings and courts have been reduced to footnotes in her epic. In fact she popped up only five years later to the credulous. In one of several versions recorded in 1436, La Pucelle was seen again one day in Metz,

> calling herself Claude. On the same day, Jeanne's brothers came to see her. One was a knight named messire Pierre, and the other petit-Jean, esquire. And they thought that she had been burned, but when they saw her they recognized her, and she too recognized them . . . and she spoke most often in parables, and she told neither the substance nor the appearance of her intentions. She said that she would have no power before St. John the Baptist's Day . . . they gave her several jewels and they recognized that she was indeed Jeanne La Pucelle of France.

Jeanne d'Arc, you see, was never burned at the stake; it was some hapless nonentity who was substituted. Terminating her career as a *pucelle,* this former Maid of Orléans married one Robert des Armoises, to settle down in Metz, just up the road from Domremy. Or perhaps she had been raised up by God, as another pretender claimed, who then traveled around Germany for a while performing parlor tricks and dispensing theological advice. This Maid returned to France to join up with her former colleague Gilles de Rais, both being hanged and burned in 1440 for heinous crimes in Nantes.[67]

Today there are many other Jeannes who have been resurrected in literature, hundreds of years after her contradictory career and reputed martyrdom. Some are even more spotless, others more fearless, others remarkably intellectual—still others a farce—intentionally or inadvertently. As we shall discover, it is not easy to become both a confirmed saint and a literary kaleidoscope. Certainly the two Jeannes would never recognize each other, which clearly was what some along the way set out to accomplish. Have they succeeded? In the tortured process Jeanne d'Arc winds up belonging more to the world than to God.

3

Jeanne in the World Thereafter

Jeanne: *I am with child,* ye bloody homicides:
Murder not, then, the fruit within my womb,
Although ye hale me to a violent death . . .
York: She and the Dauphin have been *juggling.* . . .
Jeanne: You are deceiv'd; my child is none of his:
It was Alençon that enjoy'd my love.
York: Alençon! that notorious Machiavel!
Jeanne: O, give me leave, I have deluded you:
'Twas neither Charles nor yet the duke I nam'd,
But Reignier, King of Naples, that prevail'd.
Warwick: A married man! that's most intolerable.
York: Why, here's a girl—I think she knows not well,
There were *so many* whom she may accuse.

Shakespeare, *Henry VI, Part One, Act V, Scene IV,* 1591

And the greatest of rare exploits
Was to preserve her maidenhead for a whole year . . .
To love an ass, to give him her flower!
But oh heavens—*what an ass it was!*

Voltaire, *La Pucelle d'Orléans,* 1762

Clearly Jeanne the slut did not ascend at once into sainthood. As she had suffered ordeal by fire, her reputation underwent ordeal by derision. In the next century Shakespeare had sport with Jeanne the demon, the "high-minded strumpet"—

"Pucelle, that witch, that damned sorceress." Voltaire, over three hundred years after her death, made even viler sport of the pious legend, specifically lampooning the insipidly pompous epic poem *La Pucelle d'Orléans ou La France Délivrée,* written by Jean Chapelain in 1656. Chapelain's work almost singlehandedly killed off Jeanne as a serious literary subject for an entire century. In place of an invented magic horse, Voltaire substituted an impressively endowed winged jackass, which almost deflowered the frequently nude Jeanne—who instead gives her virginity up to the Bastard of Orléans. Voltaire pulled up short of carnal knowledge with a jackass—fortunately for his own ashes, which were relocated to the Panthéon in Paris during the French Revolution in the 1790s. His remains would not have been the first (or the last) to be hurled out of that tumultuous national shrine, which would later be decorated with glorious frescoes of Jeanne's life.

Voltaire and the eighteenth-century Enlightenment sensed too much of the Church and monarchy of the French *ancien régime* in Jeanne to treat her as anything but a symbol trussed up to buttress their authority. To the new French *philosophes,* the Middle Ages were wholly a time of gloom and outmoded superstitions, the remaining institutions of feudalism to be rebelled against. By 1793 and the dawning of the Romantic era, Englishman Robert Southey was outraged at Voltaire's bald attempt at humor. Southey transformed Jeanne into a child of the soil, a Rousseau-ennobled innocent, daughter of the family of man, yearning to breath free. After victory at Orléans she exclaims through Southey:

> . . . easier were it to hurl the rooted mountain from its
> base, than force the yoke of slavery upon men
> *Determin'd to be free*

Jeanne was also endowed by Southey with a companion named Lafayette, "name that freedom still shall love," to hit on a symbol of liberty in both the American and French revolutions. Even during renewed war between France and England, Jeanne's image appeared pristine above the battle. When a musical pantomime of her life was presented in London in 1795, the first rendition had her escorted to hell by demons—the persona of Shakespeare two hundred years before—her exit condemned to the flames: "Break thou in pieces and consume to ashes, thou accursed minister of hell!" But audience reaction was so outraged in the Covent Garden theater that the demons were quickly recostumed as angels on the way to heaven.[1]

The political secularization of Jeanne was on: Jeanne of nature, Jeanne of liberation, progressively anything but a dumbfounded adolescent hit on the head by Jehovah. Jeanne as patriot was a humane improvement over her first literary image as living Amazon. Neither portrayal, however, was surprising, given her virginity, transvestism, and military accomplishments. It was a tradition that began with the mythical Diana, Roman goddess of the hunt, and formerly the Greek goddess Artemis. She was man's worst nightmare, turning one hunter who had watched her bathing into a stag, so that his own dogs tore him to shreds. This chilly fusion merged into the legend of Penthesilea, Queen of the Amazons, a band of warrior women—and virgins—who were fearless in battle, who even burned off their right breasts in childhood, the better to shoot their arrows at men. In a variation of the central legend in which she is killed by Achilles (as the two poignantly exchange a first and last look of amour before her demise), it is Penthesilea who kills Achilles, and then herself, when she realizes—this is *her* Achilles' heel—that she has broken the Amazon code by falling in love with a man. Shakespeare included this fearsome aspect as well:

Jeanne: My courage try by combat, if thou dar'st,
And thou shalt find that I exceed my sex . . .
And while I live, I'll ne'er fly from a man.

. . . I must not yield to any rites of love,
For my profession's sacred from above;
When I have chasèd all thy foes from hence,
Then will I think upon a recompense.
Charles VII: Stay, stay thy hands! Thou art an Amazon . . .[2]

Over four hundred plays and musical works would be written about Jeanne by the late nineteenth century; the first biography was written around 1500. The Burgundian historian began with an apology: "My prayer is, please bear with me, the writer, and forgive me for the mistakes and inaccuracies you may find." The facts and the legend, however, appear amazingly intact: Jeanne's miraculous sword, her telling the king his secret prayer, his testing her over recognizing him, her military career, her trial, her condemnation as "an example of monstrous cruelty." Her ordeal was compared to Christ's and in the end she died a martyr. It is remarkable that so many essentials of Jeanne's life were commonplace to Shakespeare later in the same century, even if distorted for the pleasure of English groundlings at the Rose Theater in London. There are recognitions of her humble origin ("I am by birth a shepherd's daughter"), her voices ("which by a vision sent her from heaven"), her magical first recognition of the dauphin ("be not amazed, there's nothing hid from me"), his abandonment of her ("Is this thy cunning, thou deceitful dame?"), and her death as a heretic ("Bring forth that sorceress, condemn'd to burn").[3]

Otherwise Jeanne remained largely a cipher in the story of Charles VII. Until the nineteenth century the rare mentions of her on either side of the English Channel took occasional swipes at her virginity—or lack of it—and claimed that she had bedded down with Robert de Baudricourt, the Bastard of Orléans, or half of her army, as accounts mounted up. Jeanne languished for several hundred years as an Amazonian bit player among the *Neuf Preuses*, the Nine Female Worthies, a rotating cast of women taken from the Bible, antiquity, and history. But as Marina Warner minutely traces Jeanne's evolution in her great work, *Joan of Arc: The Image of Female Heroism,* the role of Amazon was a literary dead end:

> Joan of Arc would never have survived in memory as a figure of good if in history's eyes she had remained a faithful follower of Diana . . . Joan's Amazonian likeness had to be softened to be countenanced at all; her transvestism, her armour, her inviolability had to seem something that in the final conclusion was offered on the altar of male supremacy.[4]

Primitive feminism was emerging in Jeanne's own century. The famous poet Christine de Pisan, chronicler of the French court, wrote *Ditié de Jehanne d'Arc* after the victory of Orléans in 1429, in which Jeanne had pulled off more than thousands of men could have done: "Oh! what honor for the female sex! It is perfectly obvious that God has special regard for it." Christine was in positive raptures: "Neither Hector nor Achilles had such strength!" In 1647 a Jesuit named Pierre Lemoyne tried to theologically dampen this first sexual schism in his work, *A Gallery of Strong Women.* Heroic virtues, Lemoyne stressed, came from above impartially:

> It is certain that these faculties are not different where the sex is different. . . . The light that descends into the spirit of man is not purer nor does it come from a higher sphere than the light that descends into the spirit of a woman and this equal light, coming from the same source, can kindle an equal fire of equal strength in the heart of both.[5]

Jeanne Transformed by Nineteenth-Century Theater and Literature

It was in the nineteenth century that Jeanne began to emerge as a universal commodity, beyond an androgynous footnote in the world chronicle of men. With her spiritualism and supernatural persona, Jeanne had evoked nothing but derision to eighteenth-century Enlightened rationalism. The Romantic movement that followed, however, had another view entirely. Friedrich von Schiller started off in 1801 with his drama *Die Jungfrau von Orleans,* in which he flailed at Voltaire's insult: "Oh virgin, mockery has dragged you through the mire . . . but be without fear." But Schiller, for all his defense of this uncorrupted force of nature, still cast her in the Amazon tradition, invincible unless she falls in love:

> In rugged bronze thy body shall be laced
> In steel thou shalt enclose thy tender breast
> With man's love thou shall never be embraced
> Nor passion's sinful flame thy heart invest
> Thy hair shall not by bridal wreath be graced
> No lovely child may nestle at thy breast
> But with war's honors I will make thee great.

Jeanne tragically succumbs to love on the battlefield at the first sight of an English soldier named Lionel. Before Lionel, a poor fool named Montgomery is killed by her in battle:

> *Montgomery:* Dreadful is your speech, and yet your glance is soft
> You are not terrible to look at close at hand
> I feel my heart attracted to your lovely form
> O by the gentle nature of your tender sex
> I beg you and implore: Have mercy on my youth!
> *Jeanne:* Do not invoke my sex! *Do not call me a woman!*
> Like spirits incorporeal that do not woo
> In earthly wise, so I belong to no race of mankind
> Nor does this armor cover any heart.

Whack! Montgomery is dispatched. Reviving a theme from the Penthesilea and Achilles legends, Schiller has Jeanne about to finish off Lionel too, but unfortunately for her conflicted sexuality she looks into his face before cutting off his head. She is smitten. "What have I done?" Jeanne screams in anguish. "My vow is broken now!" She soon dies on the field, her body patriotically covered by battle standards. Schiller also continues her purity, and links it with the soil:

> Farewell, you mountains, you beloved pastures,
> Familiar quiet valleys, fare you well.
> Among you Joan will no longer wander,
> Forever Joan bids you now farewell.[6]

Some Frenchmen began chafing at the idea of a foreigner poaching on their heritage with such a "monstrous German drama." This annoyance would eventually become more visceral. By maintaining the pastoral ideal, however, Schiller's work continued a lyrical tradition that celebrated Jeanne's sanctified heritage amid the flora and fauna of Domremy. Verdi and Tchaikovsky would later incorporate this tradition into their operas. Jules Michelet, the renowned French historian, stressed Jeanne's soil-ful Gallic purity by 1844: "The Savior of France had to be a woman. France herself was a woman. She had the same fickleness, but also the same loveable sweetness, the same easy and charming compassion . . . she remained at heart closer to nature." Michelet asserted that Jeanne was the first visionary of French nationalism, which before her had been merely a vague idea, a country of fractured principalities. "May the French always remember," he wrote movingly, "that our *patrie* was born from a woman's heart, from her tenderness and her tears, from the blood she shed for us." Michelet perpetuated a virgin Maid to replace the post-rationalist Virgin Mary, sent to save France by suffering the passion of her son, Christ. "The Virgin was needed, a virgin descended upon earth in the guise of a maid from the common folk, young, fair, gentle, and bold. . . . Pity was so immense within her that she had no pity left for herself." Novelist Alexandre Dumas continued to touch the heart by transforming Michelet's Christ imagery:

> Joan of Arc is the Christ of France; she has redeemed the crimes of the monarchy, as Jesus redeemed the sins of the world. Like Jesus, she suffered her passion; like Jesus, she had her Golgotha and her Calvary.[7]

The cumulative effect continued a transition from heavenly inspiration toward a secularized Jeanne, sanitized of religious supernatural influences and inching toward a revolutionary democratic goddess, born from the forehead of Rousseau. The process was subtle and lovely. Romantic Nature replaced a biblical God, which nurtured Jeanne uncorrupted, like a plant. Her voices came not from antirational saints but rather from within Jeanne herself, by unpolluted instinct. "God-consciousness," the parallel nineteenth-century theology of Friedrich Schleiermacher, oozed from her chlorophyll-rich veins. And the secular Jeanne, like Eugène Delacroix's painting of Liberty, was always lurking in the bushes, ever ready to leap over a barricade and lead the people. *Allons, enfants de la patrie!* By midcentury, Alphonse de Lamartine continued Jeanne's transition: the ancient instincts of the Gauls were distilled into the soul of a woman. Explaining her voices, Lamartine continued to undercut theistic implications in 1852:

> Should one be amazed that such a concentration of thought in a poor, young, ignorant, and simple girl should finally produce a state of transport in her, that she should have heard with her own ears those *internal* voices which spoke unceasingly to her soul? . . . liberating her country was born from the Bible and folktales together. It was the poetry of village fireside vigils. Joan of Arc made it the religion of her fatherland.[8]

The Politically Correct Jeanne

Vive la France! The glorious apotheosis of Jeanne d'Arc was approaching completion, a vibrant synthesis of Romanticism and Nationalism on the march to enter the French psyche forever. Earlier in the nineteenth century the value of Jeanne as political commodity had not been lost on the pragmatic Napoleon Bonaparte: "United, the French nation has never been conquered," he said in 1803. "The illustriousness of Jeanne d'Arc has proved that there is no miracle that cannot be accomplished by the genius of the French people, when national independence is threatened." Jeanne was considered a precurser to Napoleon, rallying France to unity.

Napoleon tried to reconcile his new First Empire with the disenfranchised Catholic Church, which had been plundered of its medieval fortune during the French Revolution, a period that saw hundreds of priests and nuns executed under the Reign of Terror. Jeanne's image also had taken a beating during the Revolution because of her relationship with the Church and despised monarchy. Many of her relics and monuments had been destroyed in the frenzy. Her moth-eaten standard was publicly burned, along with an old hat. Her legendary sword disappeared in the confusion. Even the bronze from an old memorial in Orléans was transformed into new Revolutionary cannon. Jeanne's annual May celebration was banned, after over three centuries of veneration. Napoleon revived the cult of Jeanne as a postrevolutionary peace offering. In 1804 the emperor enthusiastically endorsed a new monument being erected in formerly royalist Orléans, and donated six thousand francs himself to its completion. The city's celebration of Jeanne's liberation on May 8 was also revived. The statue depicts her in full stride bearing militant sword and standard, skirts flowing and long hair blowing behind her, headlong toward any enemy of France. This included Britain and most of Europe in that fateful year, when Napoleon went on the offensive. Birth from the soil and the people—equating zealous *Patrie*—was manifest.[9]

After Napoleon's downfall at Waterloo in 1815, Jeanne went through a transient royalist revision in the 1820s. This better suited the tastes of restored monarchy, which had been returned to the throne in the persons of Louis XVIII and Charles X. In the theater she was usually recast in the amazonian mold of Schiller, where she firmly established the king after her victory at Orléans, where the happy story ended. One line in particular always prompted thunderous French applause: *Les Anglais sont de bien vilaines gens* ("The English are truly nasty people.") Sometimes Jeanne was more feminized along contemporary lines, in which she would flit around the stage on the verge of hysteria, dramatically counterpointed by motionless, trance-like poses, which reflected popular interest in sleepwalking, magnetism, and supernatural possession. The recently erected 1804 statue in Orléans, a direct product of the Napoleonic era, came under criticism as being too dated and provocative, expressing "*un mouvement trop violent,*" "a movement too violent, and too affected by the epoch from which it was made." By 1840 the statue was being compared to a foppish "sort of Murat in petticoat"—a reference to Napoleon's most visible general, known for outrageous titivation and splendid costumes. The statue was ultimately relocated to an obscure spot in Orléans and replaced by another.[10]

By the 1840s, Jeanne's life had resurfaced as real history through the monumental work of Jules Quicherat, a pupil of Jules Michelet, who labored nine years to edit and publish her two trial records in five definitive volumes in 1849. The process represented nineteenth-century efforts to establish history as an objective science, with references, footnotes, and other paraphernalia that began to separate "history" from prior centuries of unchallenged legend. Through Quicherat—and for the first time in over four hundred years— Jeanne existed in her own voice; her deeds became even more inspirational as witnessed by flesh-and-blood contemporaries. "I do not create the truth," Quicherat wrote to his mentor Michelet, "I free it, and once freed, I consider it as belonging to the world." By 1869 the work had prompted a group of French bishops, headed by Félix Dupanloup of Orléans, to petition the Vatican for

Jeanne's canonization. They maintained that she had not only saved France, but also obviated the heresy it might have fallen into, by following the will of God. "It would also constitute," Dupanloup stated, "a title of honor for the French people."

The following year, in 1870, history intervened in the form of a new invader—Germany. A Prussian count had already shamed France by trying to buy Jeanne's little home in 1815. The French owner had refused the generous offer of six thousand francs, which propelled him into fervent celebrity. Three years later the Département de Vosges purchased the house for 1,800 francs, to transform it into a national shrine. By 1871, after the crushing defeat of France in the Franco-Prussian War, much of Jeanne's former Lorraine was in German hands. Indeed various German writers had already tried to capture Jeanne herself, claiming she was really born on Teutonic soil. Quicherat's work had been propelled into birth because a German scholar had threatened to research Jeanne's trial records in 1835, causing Frenchmen to rush in to preserve their heritage from hostile takeover. French pilgrimages to Domremy doubled during the 1870s, and *Le Livre d'Or,* the guest book in Jeanne's house, was crammed with supplications to the people's unofficial saint, praying for liberation from the new conqueror.[11]

Jeanne d'Arc became much more visible in statuary after the Franco-Prussian War, as the crushed pride of France began to regroup behind militant equestrian Maids across the land. In 1874 a most visible golden one was erected in Paris, the work of Emmanuel Frémiet. It was placed in the Place des Pyramides, near the old St. Honoré gate where Jeanne was wounded in her failed attempt to take the city in 1429. For Frenchmen at the time it was an emblem of renewal, "that France can repossess herself, that she must resume." Significantly the site also faced the entrance to the Tuileries Palace, the former residence of French monarch Louis XVI, who was beheaded during the Revolution. The locale was inspired as a symbol of reconciliation; according to one formulation it was "the morrow of our past disasters and sadness, a statue of hope and resurrection." By 1878 the French government faced a schizophrenia of sorts when the centennial of Voltaire's death came up on May 30. This, awkwardly, happened to be the same day on which Jeanne had been burned at the stake. It was the Daughter of God and the defunct *ancien régime* versus the victorious *Liberté-Egualité-Fraternité,* pitting conservative religious against secular descendants of the Revolution. Both claimed Jeanne's icon—Jeanne with a red liberty cap—which might be torn asunder in the streets. Even if Voltaire was a beloved oracle of liberty, the devout had not forgotten his insult. Demonstrations, therefore, were banned.[12]

During the 1880s, a conservative politician, Joseph Fabre, proposed a national feast day in honor of Jeanne d'Arc, a coalition of "both believers and liberal thinkers." Like oil and water, the oxymoron further divided the French people. For example, some Catholics suggested that the new feast day should replace "the feast of the assassins"—Bastille Day. Conservatives had always considered the virginal, obedient Jeanne d'Arc to be a purer national symbol than Marianne, France's emblem of liberty born during the French Revolution. For them she was a bare-breasted harlot, reflecting their opinion of the sluttish Third Republic. Liberal thinkers in turn reacted by taking to the streets with a banner proclaiming, "To Jeanne d'Arc: abandoned by the royalty, by the priests, a victim of the clergy."

The trial of Alfred Dreyfus for treason in the 1890s, a convulsive aftermath of the Franco-Prussian War, also added fire to the flames. Jeanne was evoked in Dreyfus' defense, another individual who had been crushed by wrongful authority. Having been declared outside of society, she and Dreyfus, a Jew, shared much in their shameless treatment by the establishment. But again Jeanne was polymorphous, a talisman for both sides. To bitter complainers that Dreyfus got off easy (he was sentenced to Devil's Island and later acquitted as falsely accused), Jeanne was thrust forth as the symbol of national do-or-die, which she had done to assert monarchy through Charles VII—no matter what his shortcomings—and the unquestioned authority of the *Patrie*.[13]

The fault lines widened on the eve of the twentieth century: conservative versus liberal; reactionary monarchists still festering from the 1789 Revolution versus a century of revolutionary socialists; Old Church versus New State; the ultraconservative organization *Action Française*—outraged by the Dreyfus acquittal—agitating against the *Ligne des Droits de l'Homme,* founded by Dreyfus sympathizers. Liberals of the latter camp proceeded to divide France into an argument over separation of church and state, which included the cutting-off of funding for Catholic schools to form a mandatory free public secular education. It was not a pretty scene—and it would bitterly play out through two World Wars, the rise of fascism, the occupation of France under its Vichy collaborators with the Nazis, and a fresh wave of anti-Semitism. (At the time of the Dreyfus affair, French Bishop Pierre Cauchon was even accused of being a Jew.) Either way, both growing factions would claim Jeanne as *une sainte pour tous*—confusingly true—who sprang from the people while they sprang at each other.

Even the Nazis who occupied Paris in the 1940s used films about Jeanne d'Arc to try to whip up hatred for England. A foretaste of things to come was the 1935 German film *Das Mädchen Johanna,* with script input by Joseph Goebbels. Posters showing her ghost grieving over the burning ruins of Rouen decried the results of allied bombing. She was also used to hone chauvinistic xenophobia against England—which is never very difficult in France. In 1940 the Vichy propaganda machine cranked out a play for French youth in which *bonne* Jeanne of Lorraine proclaimed, "Poor *Goddons!* So sad really to have left behind their beer, their fog, and sea." *La bonne Lorraine* was constantly used as an icon for new moral purification of French youth under occupation. One version fostered her as a model to aspiring girls to be good providers for men. She was depicted in a flowing dress rather than her decadent transvestite pants: "If Joan inspires respect it is because she thinks of everything. And the soldiers like her because she cares for them, primarily by cooking." Women were instructed to "exercise the virtues of patience, persistence, and resignation. . . . It is in love that our future mothers will find the strength to practice those virtues which best befit their sex and their condition." Keep a clean house, cook and sew well, and above all be obedient to your husbands—having babies for the Fatherland. In 1942 the tottering eighty-six-year-old puppet head of the Vichy government, Marshal Philippe Pétain, made a national radio broadcast stressing the rebirth of France under new mastery, through the example of Jeanne d'Arc:

> Nevertheless, she did not experience success suddenly. Too much selfishness surrounded her. Too much cowardice, too much doubting, too many plots. . . . It is only after severe efforts that she had the joy of feeling followed. One understands at last the necessity of gathering behind the master and abandoning the paths of foreigners.[14]

Yet during these black years of occupation, which continue to haunt France, Nazi efforts to incorporate Jeanne into the Third Reich only backfired by keeping French nationalism alive among resistance fighters. Jeanne's very cross of Lorraine was chosen by Charles de Gaulle's underground forces as a symbol. The Vichy government fired away at de Gaulle in exile in London, comparing him to Pierre Cauchon, a traitor in league with the English. De Gaulle in turn compared the French armistice of 1940 to the Treaty of Troyes in 1420, a traitorous sellout to foreign powers. In 1941 he orchestrated in absentia a silent protest to the annual celebration of Jeanne in his homeland, instructing that the French people take to the streets, "to look each other straight in the eye, their glance sufficient to express their common will and brotherly hope."

At the triumphal end of the war, de Gaulle thought of Jeanne's example as he paraded down the Champs-Elysées of a liberated Paris in 1944. American President Franklin D. Roosevelt had repeatedly scoffed at de Gaulle for having "a Joan of Arc complex"; De Gaulle himself had announced by London radio that he was a reincarnated Joan of Arc in 1943. There was only one difference, he recalled: "she had an army, but I do not."

Given Jeanne's Promethean plasticity, it is scarcely surprising that Jeanne the revolutionary also has inspired Marxist interpretations of her meaning to society. These even made it across the Atlantic as inspiration for the 1960s Cuban revolutionary, Che Guevara. Since the turn of the twentieth century in France however, Jeanne has been more visibly an icon of the French political right, progressively alarmed over a loss of national identity and purpose, contrasted to that of Jeanne. The homage to former glory has been sanctified by the annual laying of lilies at Emmanuel Frémiet's equestrian statue on the Place des Pyramides. Beginning in the 1980s, the *Front National*, an ultraright descendant of *Action Française*, use Joanist iconography in an attempt to "purify" France of all foreign influences: African immigrants, Jews-as-usual, English beef, American hamburgers, whatever comes to mind as newly subversive. The party's leader, the xenophobic Jean-Marie Le Pen, surrounds himself with statues of Jeanne both at home and work. He is also fond of quoting her to rally the French against manifest invasion: "To battle. God will give us victory!" Many of his followers carry a baguette under one arm as a traditional symbol of French pride, proclaiming the party motto, "France for the French."[15]

The Long Church Transformation Into Saint Joan

While the secular Jeanne was being fractured into competing political icons, the Church was not idle. Popular pressure once more pushed to embrace her as its own saint, too, historical irony notwithstanding. The Church over the decades had lost much of its allure about both Jeanne and a good deal else among the *vox populi*. An anticlerical bent had been noticeable before the French Revolution, where it ignited into a holocaust that consummated the split between Church and State with the guillotine. After the French proposed sainthood for Jeanne beginning in 1869, pressure led Pope Leo XIII to declare her as Venerable in 1894, the first step toward Catholic sainthood. It was not coincidental that eight months before, the French people had voted in a socialist government, pushing France and the Vatican to the brink. Matters only worsened toward a total breakdown through the turn of the twentieth century, as political extremes hardened on both sides. By 1909, Pope Pius X had approved her advance to the next rung of Blessed. The First World War suspended the process, along with everything else in Europe.

In the years of formal religious investigation along the way, however, the old central question had to be addressed: Was Jeanne d'Arc virtuous to God alone, or was she only a secular national heroine, her renown dependent merely on military and temporal exploits? Beginning in 1893, the Devil's Advocate, an ancient position charged with finding holes in any case proposed for Catholic sainthood, had first compared Jeanne's petition with that of Christopher Columbus, a venerated achiever, but ultimately in the political realm alone. (Columbus had had his run at beatification in the 1870s, but the office of Devil's Advocate had prevailed over his many promoters—including the Italian pope.) Jeanne's military prowess and patriotic symbolism worked against her spiritual case. Catholic judges were looking for divine virtues, "which pertain to the eternal salvation of souls." Secular patriotism alone undercut the Church Triumphant, which "thrives without faith or religion and even provides an excuse for crimes." Restoring the monarch Charles VII was a political—not religious—achievement.[16]

Even in this worldly context, however, it was argued that Jeanne had not been a total success in her military goals, and therefore could not have been anointed uniquely by God. After her capture she had fallen apart in the face of death, as charged by the Devil's Advocate: "greatness of soul gave out, the splendor of divine revelations vanished, and grave faults are seen to have obscured her virtues, whatever they were finally." The main cardinal virtue missing by the time of Jeanne's fiery end was lack of heroic fortitude. Even before that the Maid of Orléans had often been boastful and defiant of the Church. She had immodestly flaunted her body for repeated examination, and carnally exposed her breasts. She also had a bad temper, and willfully did not always follow her voices. Ultimately she even denied them. This was not the pattern of traditional sainthood, which was defined as passive and long-suffering, with unflagging joy and faith in God in the face of extermination. Over the years three Devil's Advocates succeeded one another in the assignment of refuting the relentless assault of Jeanne's popular legend, which had been fueled by nationalistic politics. By 1902 the latest one, Alexander Verde, had even suggested that Jeanne's voices were a manifestation of hysteria.[17]

Jeanne's official advocates during this progressive Vatican process countered with her devout religious constancy and daily prayer. The Office of Defender argued that her military success—which was no less startling than Napoleon's—"can only be ascribed to the glory of God who, in His inscrutable wisdom, hath chosen the weak things in the world to confound the things of the mighty." Again the old scripture from 1 Corinthians, cited by theologians in Jeanne's time, was employed: God "may not confide such undertakings in anyone with whom He is not satisfied." Any partial failure on Jeanne's part was argued as more ascribable to the weakness of her contemporaries than to her. Like the beheaded John the Baptist, Jeanne had been prevented from fulfilling her full objectives only by the wickedness and lapses of others.[18]

By 1920 the defense had prevailed. Pope Benedict XV declared Jeanne officially Saint Jeanne d'Arc. There remained the dilemma that the Church had burned her as a heretic nearly five hundred years before. But the judges at Rouen in 1431 were not really the Church of Rome. Instead they were participants in a political schism—which was historically accurate, if not eternally confusing. Jeanne, after all, had appealed several times to be taken to Rome. The Church now leaned heavily on the witnesses at the Rehabilitation trial for support, and downplayed Jeanne's own words at her trial of Condemnation. The supernatural was reaffirmed both by miraculous cures and by signs at her death. Jeanne was not designated a Martyr of the Church for obvious reasons, because only a splinter wing of the Church had colluded to put her to death. Factually she herself had not sought death in God's name, and in the end had been terrified of it. She exists as a Virgin in the Catholic religious Calendar, a demi-saint perhaps, but no less confusing than the disputed meaning of her life. For that matter Jeanne's precious Saint Catherine and Saint Margaret had previously been removed from the Church Calendar of Saints for being too apocryphal. They had been only second-tier "auxiliary saints," existing out of regional legends that had sprung up over six hundred years before the first pontifical canonizations began at the end of the tenth century. Now Jeanne has two national days in France: May 8 for the State, and May 30 for the Church. To further compound confusion, the conservative *Front National* has opted to have its homage to her on May 1—the annual May Day holiday in Europe, with a socialist pedigree.[19]

Jeanne and Modern Literary Transition

Around the same time as Jeanne was being canonized—but antagonistic to the process—the rationalist works of Anatole France, Mark Twain, and George Bernard Shaw competed to expand the views of her being offered to modern minds. This process is thoroughly covered by William Searle in *The Saint and the Skeptics.* The most historically influential of these authors was Anatole France, an advocate of Naturalism, a nineteenth-century rationalist doctrine which held that nature is a self-regulating system, not dependent on supernatural forces. Only science verifies reality, and so-called miracles have rational explanations. France therefore explained Jeanne's apparent resurrection of the infant three days dead by arguing that the child was merely comatose. In this view it was the religious power of belief by those around Jeanne that made the act seem miraculous, an example of the creative power of myth. "Joan is made entirely of poetry," France stated. "She sprang from poetry, popular and Christian."

In *Vie de Jeanne d'Arc*, the great work on which he spent decades, France used his extensive knowledge of medieval superstition to explain away Jeanne's phenomena, in his own expansive manner. His research was greatly aided by the scholarship of Pierre Champion, who soon would overhaul the trial texts of Jules Quicherat published seventy years before, which added invaluable details and shored up certain academic deficiencies, adhering to more contemporary notions of scholarship. As consultant and proofreader of Anatole France's burgeoning text, Champion tended to do the spadework, while France cast his own literary spell. France's study led him to the conclusion that Saint Margaret and Saint Catherine were indeed imaginary; they probably never had lived as historical people. (A view with which the Church eventually agreed.) Shorn of the supernatural, Jeanne was a sort of army mascot. France argued that in an age when monarchs still listened to visionaries, the deluded Jeanne was probably directed by some unknown priest or Armagnac religious faction, "to give courage to the French, to terrify the English and to prove to everyone that God, Saint Michel, and Saint Catherine were Armagnacs." France conceded that he was in a race with the Catholic Church, "before the priests perch her on their altars. There is no time to lose. . . . If I excuse, if I admire the visions of the poor little shepherd girl, it does not follow that in writing her story I have given credence to the miraculous. Quite the contrary; I have continuously borne in mind that the duty of the intellectual is to explain all facts by relating them to natural causes."[20]

Anatole France believed that nothing is truly objective, certainly not history, including his own. Everything indeed is a hallucination. Through a distorted glass we can only "know" in part what we perceive: "Do we know anything whatever about the outside world?" France asserted, "reality or appearance, it is all one"—in which he was restating an especially French observation that spans from René Descartes in the sixteenth century to twentieth-century Existentialism: *cogito ergo sum*: I think, therefore I am. So it blossomed in his monumental biography, finished in 1908. France believed that Jeanne's "perpetual hallucinations made her more often than not incapable of distinguishing truth from falsehood." And her voices repeatedly played her false straight to the stake, leading her into messianic overconfidence, delusions of grandeur, error, and death. "Feeling both heaven and earth forsake her, she fell into a deep despair," France concluded. A half-century before, Jules Michelet also had addressed the tragic despair of abandonment by Jeanne's saints, which has never been properly answered: "Why was it, alas, that they came more rarely now, in the hours of greatest need? Why did the comforting faces of the saints no longer appear except in a dubious light, which grew dimmer day by day? She had been promised deliverance: why did it tarry?"[21]

Although Anatole France believed that Jeanne would be committed to an insane asylum in modern times, he did not think her any crazier than her Rouen judges in the fifteenth century, "who had an inflexible faith in demons. But whereas Jeanne's dreams were radiant and incited her to the noblest enterprises, those of her tormenters were disgusting, infamous, and monstrous. . . . Each of the doctors seated there in the chapel of the castle had burned ten, twenty, fifty witches, all of whom had confessed. Would it not have been foolish, in light of that fact, to doubt the existence of witches?" It was, after all, the Middle Ages: the judges "believed, most of them, that they were proceeding truthfully in a matter of faith . . . they wanted to judge well." (In fact mass trials and execution of witches became more common decades after Jeanne's time. Despite France's assertion, it is unlikely that any of the Rouen judges had taken part in multiple witch burnings). France maintained that Jeanne herself would have condemned others with the same superstitions. Toward the end of her brief, floundering career, she had been momentarily tempted to turn her crusade against a group of heretics called Hussites in far-off Bohemia, dictating a (disputed) letter full of threats "to extirpate the dreadful superstition with my blade of iron and to snatch you from heresy or from life itself."[22]

Although France the skeptic could not embrace Jeanne's uncompromising religious commitment, he conceded that this propelled her heroism in battle: "She performed better than the others, not because she knew more about it; she knew less. But she had more heart . . . she did not hold back in the slightest, having offered herself unreservedly in advance." But unlike Michelet and others, France did not believe that Jeanne was an inspired precursor of nationalism. Amid a time of feuding duchies, fiefs, and principalities, the romantic notion of *Patrie* was still hundreds of years away, far above the head and times of so simple a girl. "It must be great, the power of the Holy Ghost, to inspire so stupid a girl," France confided. "That's the way of it. The Holy Ghost does not inspire intelligent people." In general France voiced the lament of the modern soul brought low, fueled by his own contributions: "Along with faith and hope, we have lost charity. . . . We have eaten of the fruits of the tree of knowledge and a taste of ashes has remained in our mouths."[23]

France's attempt to produce a more rational and humanistic version of Jeanne, *Vie de Jeanne d'Arc,* was excoriated by conservatives. Historians lambasted the book's inaccuracies, which the author dismissed as "nitpicking by zealous inquisitors." The Catholic right and recalcitrant royalists began deriding him as Anatole *peu-France* (Anatole scarcely-France), whose cynicism bordered on national treason. Liberals, however, embraced his work, the very two-volume heft of it alone appearing canonical enough to recommend it for all future historical citation. Ideological fights literally spilled over into the halls of academia. In 1909 a Freemason professor named François Thalamas, who taught such rational skepticism about Jeanne at the prestigious Sorbonne in Paris, was dismissed. The ferment reached the French Parliament, resulting in Thalamas being reinstated. Despite police protection, violent protestors of the *Action Française* broke in to thrash Jeanne's tactless modern assailant. Anatole France's secretary, Jean-Jacques Brousson, turned on his mentor after his death in 1924 to publish his own conservative works on Jeanne, with kiss-and-tell revelations about what France had confided to him concerning France's palpable irreligion. In reviewing this backbiting deluge of ideology on the collective French psyche, spanning from Michelet to Anatole France, Joanastic scholar Nadia Margolis insightfully observes, "each author or artist conducts—and often simultaneously undergoes, *malgré lui*—his own personal trial, with its own verdict, not only about Joan but also about himself."[24]

Saint Joan According to Mark Twain and George Bernard Shaw

The passion over Jeanne's passion was not confined to France. At a parallel time in the 1890s, Mark Twain saw only Jeanne the uncorrupted child, a sacrificial lamb martyred by bigots in a world without God. To him she was one of a kind, perhaps the only entirely unselfish person who had ever lived. "All the rules fail in this girl's case," Twain declared in a triumph of despair. "In all the world's history she stands alone—quite alone." Like Anatole France, Twain was post-enlightenment and antagonistic to religion, but his approach to Jeanne was scarcely an exercise in rationalism. Unlike France, Twain was a Francophobe, in personal torment, desperately romantic in search of belief toward the end. Facing debt and ruin in later life, Twain considered *Personal Recollections of Joan of Arc* his most monumental work of faith. "Possibly the book may not sell," he wrote a benefactor in 1895, "but that is nothing—it was written for love." He assured his family that it was his most serious undertaking, to be published anonymously so as not to be pre-labeled as humorous. Twain enthusiastically began his work in Florence, Italy, with his family as critics, his favorite daughter Susy being the most active. By day the work leaped off Twain's pen, as nightly he read portions aloud. "Many of Joan's words and sayings are historically correct," Susy approved, "and Papa cries when he reads them. In fact he almost always fills up when reading any speech of hers." Susy herself was repeatedly overcome, asking her father to wait until she could get another handkerchief.[25]

Susy died of meningitis only months after *Personal Recollections of Joan of Arc* was completed. "How cruel it was," Twain wrote to a friend in anguish over a vengeful God, "how exactly and precisely it was planned, and how remorselessly every detail of the dispensation was carried out." In grief he decided that Susy had died at the right time, "the fortunate time of life, the happy age—twenty-four years old. At twenty-four, such a girl has seen the best of life—life as a happy dream. After that age the risks begin, responsibility comes, and with it the cares, the sorrows, and the inevitable tragedy." The last thing Twain read to Susy was *Joan of Arc*, "and the last words of that which I read were 'How rich was the world etc.' And to me these words have a personal meaning now." One shrinks from the double poignancy of certain passages in Twain's work: "Yes, she was gone from us: Joan of Arc! What little words they are, to tell of a rich world made empty and poor! . . . To know Joan of Arc was to know one who was wholly noble, pure, truthful, brave, compassionate, generous, pious, unselfish, modest, blameless as the very flowers of the fields."[26]

Remarkably, what had inspired thirteen-year-old Samuel Clemens into becoming a writer back in Hannibal, Missouri, was the chance finding of a page fragment on the life of Joan of Arc, literally blown into his life by the wind. The boy took it home to his family to inquire if she was a real person. Toward the end of his literary career, Twain learned French and took on the trial records, along with past French biographies, closely following Michelet for historical framework. After a dozen years he believed he done thorough enough research, progressively writing his own observations in book margins: "Her saints are merely idiots. They remind her of *nothing* that is valuable." Other revealing objections are "This is the nineteenth century," "How stupid!" "Slush!" and "Shucks."

Despite rejections of the more devout interpretations of Jeanne, Twain seemed impressed over past comparisons of her with Jesus. "Christ before the doctors again," he noted on one Catholic work's description of Jeanne at Poitiers. Her judges he called "mitred donkeys." After six false starts Twain decided to tell the story through the eyes of her page Louis de Conte, a sort of Huckleberry Finn wandering through Twain's preconceived fifteenth century. As the youth made his way to the inquisition in Rouen, the tone of shining good versus black evil is manifest:

> All the way, both going and coming, I plowed through chattering and rejoicing multitudes of English soldiery and English-hearted French citizens. But there was no talk but of the coming event. Many times I heard the remark, accompanied by a pitiless laugh—"The fat Bishop has got things as he wants them at last, and says he will lead the vile witch a merry dance and a short one."

Jeanne is brought before the fat Bishop Cauchon,

> puffing and wheezing there, his great belly distending and receding with each breath, and noted his three chins, fold above fold, and his knobby and knotty face, and his purple and splotchy complexion, and his repulsive cauliflower nose, and his cold and malignant eyes—a brute, every detail of him . . . far down the stone-paved corridors, one heard a vague slow sound approaching: clank . . . . . . clink . . clank—Joan of Arc, Deliverer of France, in chains!
>
> . . . .
>
> Half way to her bench she stopped, just where a wide shaft of light fell slanting from a window, and slowly lifted her face. Another thrill!—it was totally colourless, white as snow; a face of gleaming snow set in vivid contrast upon that slender statue of somber unmitigated black. It was smooth and pure and girlish, beautiful beyond belief, infinitely sad and sweet.[27]

Twain maintained the Victorian convention of a woman in distress, valiantly trying to ward off vile seducers. He unceasingly painted Cauchon as satanic, "born a devil . . . fanning himself in the world he belongs in." His very name was too close to *cochon*—pig—for Twain to miss an opportunity of a pun against this twisted being: "One wonders if he ever knew his mother or ever had a sister." Cauchon's minions were "scavengers . . . his breed of reptiles . . . a kennel of mastiffs and bloodhounds harassing a kitten!"

In his melodramatic reliving of the trial, Twain extended the theater of Jeanne's best answers, as when she was seemingly cornered over being in a state of grace. Judge Lefevre rises in protest, as described by Twain's de Conte:

> "It is a terrible question! The accused is not obliged to answer it!" Cauchon's face flushed black with anger to see

this plank flung to the perishing child, and he shouted: "Silence! and take your seat. The accused will answer the question!"

There was no hope, no way out of the dilemma . . . for the Scriptures had said one *cannot know* this thing. Think what hard hearts they were to set this fatal snare for that ignorant young girl and be proud of such work and happy in it. It was a memorable moment for me while we waited; it seemed a year. All the house showed excitement; and mainly it was glad excitement. Joan looked out upon these hungering faces with innocent untroubled eyes, and then humbly and gently she brought out that immortal answer which brushed the formidable snare away as it had been but a cobweb:

"If I be not in a State of Grace, I pray God place me in it. If I be in it, I pray God keep me so."

Ah, you will never see an effect like that; no, not while you live. For a space there was the silence of the grave. Men looked wondering into each other's faces, and some were awed and crossed themselves; and I heard Lefevre mutter, "It is beyond the wisdom of man to devise that answer. *Whence* come this child's amazing inspirations?"[28]

Except for a few trivial incidents that Twain invented for reasons known only to himself, his rendition was historically faithful, but relentlessly one-dimensional and platitudinous. One senses a fatigued and dispirited writer, worn down by personal tragedies, making a final attempt to reach out for something unattainable, unsullied, beyond this world, and beyond the emotional artistic balance that make Twain's earlier works enduring. "I like the Joan of Arc best of all my books," Twain wrote in 1908, "and it is the best; I know it perfectly well."

Despite his desperate floundering for some higher belief toward the last, Twain could never bring himself to believe in the belief of his unspotted heroine. Like Anatole France, Twain conceded that Jeanne's religious fervor propelled her achievements, despite the American's skepticism about formal religion—"yet nothing but this base superstition could lift her to that fearless height," he scribbled in the margin of one Catholic work. Twains's explanation for Jeanne's essential power was her childlike faith, full of "sublime ignorance," enhanced by an uncanny intuition that he could not account for, "that mysterious something that puts heart into soldiers, and turns mobs of cowards into armies of fighters that forget what fear is when they are in that presence." Like Michelet, Twain kept Jeanne a perpetual child unspotted by sexual maturity as well. In a parallel passage in Michelet's work concerning her never experiencing "the physical curse of women," Twain wrote approvingly, "The higher life absorbed her & suppressed her physical development."

With premeditation, Twain's Cauchon took advantage of Jeanne's childish faith, tricked her into signing a false confession, had her female clothes stolen to force her to relapse into heresy, and with a mocking laugh assigned her to the English and death. Facing death, she was finally true to herself: "She would sacrifice herself—and her best self; that is, her truthfulness—to save her cause; but only that; she would not buy her life at that cost . . . hell itself could not move her from that place." Twain ended with a searing lamentation, echoing Jeanne's last screams to Jesus: "Christ have pity! Saint Margaret have pity! Pray for her, all ye saints, archangels, and blessed martyrs, pray for her! Saints and angels intercede for her! From thy wrath, good Lord, deliver her! O Lord God, save her! Have mercy on her, we beseech Thee, good Lord!"

In Twain's youth he had written his sister over the death of their brother, Henry, in heartbreaking similar cadences: "Hardened, hopeless—aye, lost—lost—lost and ruined sinner as I am—I, even I, have humbled myself to the ground and prayed as never man prayed before, that the great God might let this cup pass from me—that he would strike me to the earth, but spare my brother—that he would pour out the fullness of his just wrath upon my wicked head, but have mercy, mercy, mercy upon that unoffending boy." [29]

In contrast to Mark Twain's visceral pathos, the style of George Bernard Shaw's play *Saint Joan* is detached, brittle, and comical:

Joan:	Who be old Gruff-and-Grum?
Charles VII:	He is the Duke de la Trémouille.
Joan:	What be his job?
Charles:	He pretends to command the army. And whenever I find a friend I can care for, he kills him.
Joan:	Why dost let him?
Charles:	How can I prevent it? He bullies me. They all bully me.
Joan:	Art afraid?
Charles:	Yes: I am afraid. It's no use preaching to me about it . . . I am quiet and sensible; and I don't want to kill people: I only want to be left alone to enjoy myself in my own way. I never asked to be king: it was pushed on me . . .
Joan:	Blethers! We are all like that to begin with. I shall put courage into thee.
Charles:	But I don't want to have courage put into me . . . put courage into the others, and let them have their bellyful of fighting, but let me alone.
Joan:	It's no use, Charlie: thou must face what God puts on thee. If thou fail to make thyself king, thoult be a beggar: what else are fit for? Come! Let me see thee sitting on the throne. I have looked forward to that.

Charles: . . . I don't want a message; but can you tell me any secrets? Can you do any cures? Can you turn lead into gold, or anything of that sort?[30]

Although as hostile to religious dogma as France or Twain, Shaw too was searching for new meaning through Joan, some form of peppy Deism warmed over from the eighteenth century. The Irishman believed in an impersonal Life Force, a will in the universe, an *élan vital.* "You cannot think of him as a person," Shaw stated in 1907, "you have to think of him as a great purpose, a great will, and furthermore you have to think of him as engaged in a continual struggle to produce something higher and higher." Individuals exist as the Life Force's only instruments in this evolutionary struggle. Christ did not die for man's sins, because such was an immoral proposition, invented by the Apostle Paul. For Shaw it was the height of irreligion to sit meekly on one's hands, ignoring poverty in the name of God's will, hypocritically praising the poor and weak, a precursor of the hands-on Social Gospel School that flowered in his time, along with the Salvation Army:

> If you don't do his work it won't be done. . . . But if you will stand by your God, if you will say, "My business is to do your will, my hands are your hands, my tongue is your tongue, my brain is your brain, I am here to do thy work, and I will do it," you will get rid of otherworldliness, you will get rid of all that religion which is made an excuse and a cloak for doing nothing.

Anthony S. Abbott has examined Shaw's evolution of beliefs in *Shaw and Christianity*. Not for Shaw the awe-ful God of fear from his stern, nineteenth-century Irish Protestant upbringing in Dublin: not for one who once pulled out his watch and challenged the Almighty to strike him dead in five minutes. But nineteenth-century Darwinism was not that Life Force for Shaw either, a devout Socialist on the way to Communism, who had been transformed by Karl Marx's theories on the roots of poverty. Shaw decried that social Darwinism only sanctified excesses of survival-of-the-fittest Capitalism, as he had experienced in operation by Protestants over Catholics in Ireland. He stated that the profit-mad nineteenth century was "the most desperately mean, sordid, selfish, rascally, dastardly century that anyone could wish to live in." If people of old seemed ridiculous in once believing the world was flat, now "modern science has convinced us that nothing that is obvious is true, and that everything that is magical, improbable, extraordinary, gigantic, microscopic, heartless, or outrageous is scientific."[31]

Rebelling against uncaring society and modern materialists, Shaw admired Joan because she embodied immaterial things, along with one of his favorite proverbs: Where there is a will, there is a way. As Joan had stated, *Aide toi, Dieu te aidera* ("Help yourself, and God will help you"). Joan embodied Shaw's "evolutionary appetite." Along with his other heroes like Socrates, Jesus, Martin Luther, and Issac Newton, she had goaded human history to a higher plane. Shaw believed that Joan's genius came from the holy ghost of his Life Force—the imagination—as captured in a clever turn of phrase in the play, when Joan first approaches Robert de Baudricourt.

> *Joan:* I hear voices telling me what to do. They come from God.
>
> *Robert:* They come from your imagination.
>
> *Joan:* Of course. That is how the messages of God come to us."[32]

It was not really Saint Catherine or Margaret, Shaw believed, but Joan's power of imagination fostered from childhood that created a "sane" hallucination for the better good. "Only the echoes of my own commonsense," Shaw has Joan state in his most grievous transgression of her own words. Aping Martin

Luther's famous declaration of personal faith during the Reformation, Shaw further has his protagonist declare to the Inquisitor about trusting her own judgment over the Church's: "What other judgement can I judge by but my *own*?"

Shaw had previously described his writing as a stream of hallucination, mystically springing into his imagination from a source beyond his comprehension. Long before writing *Saint Joan,* his description of how he wrestled with his work might serve as a prototype of Joan's own evolution with her saints: "At first, I hardly know the speakers, and cannot find names for them. Then they become more and more familiar, and I learn their names. Finally I come to know them very well, and discover what it is they are driving at, and why they have said and done the things I have been moved to set down."

In earlier years Shaw confessed, "Whether it be that I was born mad or a little too sane, my kingdom was not of this world: I was at home only in the realm of my imagination, and at my ease only with the mighty dead." Like Anatole France, Shaw believed that Joan's century had been pregnant for the acceptance of visionaries. After the horrors of World War I, which he vehemently opposed, Shaw saw this form of madness for the better, compared to modern insanity: "To Joan and her contemporaries, we should appear as a drove of Gadarene swine, possessed by all the unclean spirits cast out by the faith and civilization of the Middle Ages, running violently down a steep place into a hell of high explosives." In *Saint Joan* he has a character express, "We want a few mad people now. See where the sane ones have landed us!"[33]

Shaw's work is less focused on Joan herself than on authority's reaction to her, an ideal format for his pithy observations in *Saint Joan.* The Inquisitor warns of the insidious nature of heresy:

> Heresy begins with people who are to all appearances better than their neighbors. A gentle and pious girl,

> or a young man who has obeyed the command of our Lord by giving all of his riches to the poor, and putting on the garb of poverty, the life of austerity, and the rule of humility and charity, may be the founder of a heresy that will wreck both Church and Empire if not ruthlessly stamped out in time . . . they all began with saintly simpletons. . . . You must not fall into the common error of mistaking these simpletons for liars and hypocrites. They believe honestly and sincerely that their diabolical inspiration is divine. Therefore you must be on your guard against your natural compassion.[34]

Thus Shaw presented Joan as an earlier protestor against the established Church a century before Martin Luther. She herself had been preceded by Mohammed in the Eastern world, and Jesus before him. The character Warwick explains her threat to the stability of both Cauchon's Church and Warwick's feudal aristocracy: "It goes deep, my lord. It is the protest of the individual soul against the priest or peer between the private man and his God. I should call it Protestantism if I had to find a name for it." Cauchon has already stated the fear of the Church: "What will it be when every girl thinks herself a Joan and every man a Mahomet?" In historical irony, the real Protestants of the sixteenth century had largely ignored the legend of Jeanne. They had found her too tainted with Catholic idolatry, destroying representations of her at every opportunity.[35]

Shaw later went back and forth in denying that he was anti-Catholic as such. A conciliatory Catholic friend had talked him out of a first swipe in his preface to *Saint Joan:* "What is wrong with the Church is that the entrance to it is blocked up by superstitious rubbish." Shaw toned such passages down. But he still wound up typically combative in the finished version, skewering organized religion in both Catholic and Protestant form:

> The Reformation, which Joan had unconsciously anticipated, kept the questions which arose in her case burning up to our present day (you can see plenty of the burnt houses still in Ireland) with the result that Joan has remained the subject of anti-clerical lies, of specifically Protestant lies, and of the Roman Catholic evasions of her unconscious Protestantism. The truth sticks in our throats with all the sauces it is served with: it will never go down until we take it without any sauce at all.[36]

Shaw added his own strong sauces. "There are no villains in the piece," he declared, maintaining over and over that Joan's trial was imminently fair. It was her trial of Rehabilitation that was riddled with perjury, as Shaw mocked at the end of his play. "Joan got a fairer trial from the Church and the Inquisition than any prisoner of her type and in her situation gets nowadays in any official secular court." Twain would have howled at this statement, as did historians at the time, but Shaw has even Joan herself concede this when she returns as a ghost to discourse with King Charles. Were her judges corrupt? "Not they," she shrugs off. "They were as honest a lot of poor fools as ever burned their betters."

Charles: Are you really dead?
Joan: As dead as anybody ever is, laddie. I am out of the body.
Charles: Just fancy! Did it hurt much?
Joan: Did what hurt much?
Charles: Being burnt.
Joan: Oh, that! I cannot remember very well. I think it did at first; but then it all got mixed up; and I was not in my right mind until I was free of the body. But do not thou go handling fire and thinking it will not hurt thee.

Shaw soon has a twentieth-century clerical-looking gentleman enter the stage wearing a tall hat. First he is met with incredulous stares from the actors; then everyone bursts into uncontrollable laughter, according to Shaw's stage direction. As if fresh from Victoria Station, the unabashed gentleman officiously reads the news that Joan has just been declared a saint. "But I never made such a claim," she protests. The modern spokesman insists that it is official, and that statues of her in France are now so numerous that they block traffic. Once Jeanne has finally comprehended her own resurrection, the gentleman retires with the startled explanation, "I must return to Rome for *fresh* instructions."[37]

Despite such setups for caustic belly laughs, Shaw insisted his play was a tragedy of Promethean dimensions (although his own director had to bridle Shaw from playing up all the funny business in rehearsals). The Irishman certainly achieved a black comedy, full of intellectual and moral hooks, a stage not to trot out the preordained blackguards of Twain, but rather the universal banality of evil. "It is when men do their best, with good intentions," Shaw stated, "and what normal men and women find that they must and *will do* in spite of their intentions, that really concern us. The rascally bishop and the cruel inquisitor of Mark Twain . . . are as dull as pickpockets; and they reduce Joan to the level of the even less interesting person whose pocket is picked. I have represented both of them as capable and eloquent . . . because only by doing so can I maintain my drama on the level of high tragedy and save it from becoming a mere police court sensation."

In that approach Shaw was at least original, even if he repeatedly bent the recorded facts to make his theatrical point—which he explained in his preface:

> The tragedy of such murders is that they are not committed by murderers. They are judicious murders, pious murders; and this contradiction at once brings

> an element of comedy into the tragedy: the angels may weep at the murder, but the gods laugh at the murderers. . . . Joan was persecuted essentially as she would be persecuted today . . . the Church could not tolerate her pretensions without waiving its authority or giving her a place beside the Trinity during her lifetime and in her teens, which was unthinkable. Thus an irresistible force met an immovable obstacle, and developed the heat that consumed poor Joan.[38]

In skirting melodrama Shaw maintained his own knowing derision, slamming works like Twain's as idolatry, which presented "a credible human goody-goody . . . an unimpeachable American school teacher in armor." Twain and Shaw had met in England in 1906, and both hit it off personally. But Shaw was ruthless in his disparagement of his colleague's one-dimensional romance: "Mark Twain, the Innocent Abroad, who saw the lovely churches of the middle ages without a throb of emotion . . . was clearly out of court from the beginning." Twain had labeled Joan's century as "the brutalest, the wickedest, the rottenest in history since the darkest ages." Shaw accused Twain—"the Mississippi pilot"—of presenting Cauchon

> as an unconscionable scoundrel, and all the questions put to her as "traps" to ensnare and destroy her. . . . The tragic part of the trial was that Joan, like most prisoners tried for anything but the simplest breaches of the ten commandments, did not understand what they were accusing her of. She was much more like Mark Twain than Peter Cauchon. . . . Mark would have shared her innocence and her fate had he been dealt with by the Inquisition: that is why his account of the trial is as absurd as hers might have could she have written one.[39]

If Shaw's own interpretation of the powers-that-be from a half-millennium before seems strangely modern, brimming with insights of twentieth-century ideologues, he had his own rationalization: "It is the business of the stage to make its figures more intelligible to themselves than they would be in real life; for by no other means can they be made intelligible to the audience."

Though Twain could not concede it, Shaw and Anatole France appreciated that Joan was as absolutist as her judges, claiming absolute truth with an equal intolerance against those who did not share it. Shaw also included a dimension of Joan that Twain avoided: her willful pride. "The old Greek tragedy is rising among us," the archbishop states in *Saint Joan*, as he sees the end coming. "It is the chastisement of hubris." In a larger commonality, however, Shaw and Twain both treat Joan as a sacred individual opposed to all worldly institutions. If Twain has Joan bravely remaining steadfast to her self-truthfulness in the face of death, Shaw has Joan state a similar credo when she is abandoned by her own party:

> I see now that the loneliness of God is His strength: what would He be if He listened to your jealous little counsels? Well, my loneliness shall be my strength too: it is better to be alone with God: His friendship will not fail me, not His counsel, nor His love. In his strength I will dare, and dare, and dare, until I die. I will go out now to the common people, and let the love in their eyes comfort me for the hate in yours. You will all be glad to see me burnt; but if I go through the fire I shall go through it to their hearts for ever and ever. And so, God be with me!

It is Shaw's version of Gethsemane. William Searle argues that Shaw's declaration even here was subtly unorthodox. "In it, Joan not only presumes on the continued favor of God, but she even proposes to emulate his self-sufficiency." She is more interested in her own reputation than in Christian faith: "In short, Joan is a saint because she is a genius—or, in other words, an enlightened heretic." Shaw himself has a character carp that Joan "thinks she has God in her pocket." But facing death Joan feels betrayed by all, including her voices: "They have deceived me," she moans before recanting. "I have been mocked by devils: my faith is broken. I have dared and dared; but only a fool will walk into the fire: God, who gave me commonsense, cannot will me to do."[40]

In Shaw's first stage production of his play in New York, most of the spectators felt it far too long. In particular the jarring epilogue of Joan's resurrection had the audience leaving early to catch commuter trains. The starting time was moved up to 8:00 P.M., but still some critics felt the work deadly verbose, "groggy for want of a blue pencil," proof of "Mr. Shaw's gift for interminable rag-chewing." Others praised it as the play of the century, the finest in modern English language. But most felt the epilogue in particular was long, unnecessary, even disruptive in its glibness. Of course Shaw did not agree: Joan's afterlife to him was crucial in making her alive in the present and future. "Without it," he explained, "the play would be only a sensational tale of a girl who was burnt, leaving the spectators plunged in horror, despairing of humanity. The true tale of Saint Joan is a tale with a glorious ending; and any play that did not make this clear would be an insult to her memory."[41]

The first actress approached to play Joan was a twenty-four-year-old Frenchwoman, who disagreed so much with Shaw's interpretation of her national heroine that she refused the part, suggesting the play instead be named *Saint Bernard Shaw*—"since I felt it was Shaw speaking rather than Joan." The young actress who did accept the role was a triumph—which only reduced her to tears. Winifred Lenihan did not enjoy the experience. "Shaw is irritating," she complained. "Just as one begins to soar in a part he pulls a string, and brings her down with a bump." After 214 performances in New York, Lenihan declined to go on tour. Shaw was never pleased with aspects of the American production, chafing at continual requests to shorten the play.

Brian Tyson traced the evolution of the drama in *The Story of Shaw's Saint Joan.* When the production opened under Shaw's thumb in London, Sybil Thorndike played Joan, although she was in her mid-forties. Shaw had envisioned her in the role as he was writing. He combatively protected every line of his three-and-a-half-hour work on home soil. At the start of rehearsals he asked her if she had read any histories about Joan. All of them, Thorndike responded. "Then forget them," Shaw instructed. "I'll tell you what to think." Thorndike was forced to accede: "Feeling like a Russian Communist, I was content to be told what to do." She became Shaw's beast of burden for the rest of her life, playing the teen around the world through seven different productions until her last performance on the BBC in 1967—at the age of eighty-five.[42]

The play moved around the world in fits and starts, to Stockholm, Berlin, Vienna, Rome, Moscow, and Tokyo. Robert Benchley witnessed a Russian production in Vienna in 1925 and fell out of his seat in laughter. "The characters, with the exception of Joan, are clowns," the American humorist wrote. "The Dauphin, in actual clown make-up . . . giggles pleasantly while huge bulbous-nosed churchmen discuss the state of the realm. The soldiers wear flannel uniforms, with nominal tin fittings to suggest armor, and tomato can helmets. The Maid alone is immune from the devastating parody." When *Saint Joan* opened in Tokyo the following year, stiff Oriental actors wore red wigs. "When they were not speaking," one described, "their hands hung down, with the little finger precisely at the trouser seam, like soldiers on parade. All that I learned from the play was that Japan is half the circumference of the globe from France." A later production met its cultural problems in Florence, Italy. The central road cast performed there intact, but nonprofessionals were used as anonymous monks and spear carriers. Actress Siobhan McKenna recounted an emotional moment portraying Shaw's Joan:

> We came to the trial scene, and when the soldiers were ordered to take me off to be burned, they refused point blank. The Italians are terribly emotional and very Catholic and all that. They were totally involved and *no way* were they going to burn Joan. They all got terribly excited and started to speak in Italian, "No, no, no!" It's awful, I thought, how are we going to finish the play if they won't take me off? Eventually, doing a Marcel Marceau pantomime, I took them off, pretending they were taking me off, literally hissing my little bits of Italian and saying "I must go, *vamos, vamos.*"

In Paris, producers of the play held their breaths, fearful of what might follow Shaw's treatment of their national heroine. Shaw demanded use of his past French translator, Augustin Hamon, who was tone deaf in lyrical stagecraft, but conformed to Shaw's commitment to Socialism, even if the collaboration resulted in a civics lesson instead of theatrical fulfillment. Shaw's prior plays had tended toward box office poison in France, considered too pedantic and parochially British. Even his successful *Pygmalion* fell on its face in 1923. "What chance have we in Paris," he anticipated in paranoia, "which, like Jerusalem, strangles her prophets? . . . If Paris perishes in ignorance of my works, the loss will be for Paris and not for me." Shaw felt that the French knew very little about Joan anyhow, more blinded by her role to the *patrie* than as a life force to the world. "I have educated London," he wrote, "I have educated New York, Berlin and Vienna; Moscow and Stockholm are at my feet, but I am too old to educate Paris; it is too far behind and I am too far ahead." Anticipating Shaw's treatment, French critics feared he was incapable of translating Joan's mystique. Yet for decades French theater treatments of Joan had progressed little from the Schiller tradition in Napoleonic times, full of mystical versifying and wooden platitudes, devoid of recognizable human reality. Something was due to snap.

Enter Georges and Ludmilla Pitoëff, a theatrical couple in Paris in charge of the play. Appalled by the tin-ear translation of Hamon, the Pitoëffs conspired against Shaw's legal right to have the translation revised. Sets were also redesigned to achieve the singular goal of Georges Pitoëff. "I want the audience to feel only one thing," he stated, "that Joan is a saint." Theater critics were curried for weeks, and on opening night they were assigned seats near those guaranteed to make favorable remarks as *claqueurs*. But these devices were unneeded. The performance was a triumph. Ludmilla Pitoëff, the emotional savior of the play, portrayed Joan with a pathetically angelic quality that melted all hearts. Tears filled the eyes of the audience nightly, as Pitoëff's waifishness undercut Shaw's brittle text. The actress herself underwent a religious crisis which she attributed to playing Joan, overcome by a feeling of impurity, mollified by making religious pilgrimages. Shaw was later understandably annoyed when he learned of the ruses—Hamon was livid—yet neither backed off from the reflected glory of the French *coup de théâtre*. Still Shaw much preferred the feisty persona of his old warhorse, Sybil Thorndike, "who could take a soldier by the neck and throw him out the window," he explained to a Frenchman. By comparison, the tragic Pitoëff "would never have driven a single Englishman out of France." Shaw later wrote a friend, "Oh, these Joans! there is no end to them. It was from the Berlin one that I caught influenza."[43]

Winifred Lenihan even received a medal from a Catholic cardinal for her betrayal of Joan. If such overtures implied that Shaw might be turning religious, he riposted, "There's no room for *two* Popes in the Roman Catholic Church." He later howled when a Catholic censor took his blue pencil to *Saint Joan* after Shaw (pushing eighty years old) adapted the play for a film script in 1935. Shaw had been leery of cinema's gaucheries: Hollywood "will stick a patch of slovenly speakeasy California dialect upon a fine passage of English prose without seeing any difference, like a color-blind man sticking a patch of Highland tartan on his dress trousers." Negotiations had broken off before when Shaw insisted on total control of his material. He reeled at the first suggestion that Greta Garbo play Joan, comparing her to sexual siren Mae West portraying the Virgin Mary. Shaw predicted that for women actors the role would pose the same challenge that Hamlet does for men.[44]

For screen purposes, Shaw shortened many passages of speechifying, including the specific statement that Joan was a nationalistic Protestant. Instead he let her actions imply it. A Catholic censor further struck lines about her being mocked by devils. There were objections to her voices being from her imagination and to her trusting only her own judgment. Stricken too were remarks about having God in her pocket and to God "fighting only with the big battalions" (as Napoleon had once declared). Gone was any inference that Joan committed suicide, a mortal sin. Shaw had stated that "her death was *deliberately* chosen as an alternative to life without liberty." In the play he backed this up by Joan's lengthy Liberty or Death speech, which reflected Shaw's belief that state executions were more humane than cruel imprisonment:

> You promised me my life; but you lied. You think that life is nothing but not being stone dead . . . if only I could still hear the wind in the trees, the larks in the sunshine, the young lambs crying through the healthy frost, and the blessed church bells that send my angel voices floating to me on the wind. But without these things I cannot live; and for your wanting to take that away from me, or from any human creature, I know that your council is of the devil, and that mine is of God. . . . His ways are not your ways. He wills that I go through the fire to His bosom; for I am His child, and you are not fit that I should live among you. That is my last word to you.[45]

The censor struck out the arrogant "you are not fit" passage and much that preceded it, suggesting the substitution that Joan should appeal to God and the pope. Shaw angrily responded that his play "was hailed by all *instructed* Catholics as a very unexpected first installment of justice to the Church from Protestant quarters, and in effect, a vindication of the good faith of the famous trial at Rouen." Of course the historical Catholic position was that the Rouen trial had been in schismatic error. Shaw argued that ninety-nine percent of Catholics were not informed enough to judge his work—yet even his "instructed" Catholic adviser, Father Joseph Leonard, had disagreed with his friend on the trial's fairness before Shaw wrote the play. Shaw anonymously quoted Father Leonard in his preface when the priest suited his purpose. On this point, however, Leonard maintained to Shaw that Joan's trial was "illegal and unjust. Cauchon was clearly out for her death." Shaw ignored the advice and left out any suggestion that Joan had pleaded to be taken to Rome, inferring the result would have been the same.[46]

For other technical reasons the film never came to pass in Shaw's lifetime. In 1957 a film version of Shaw's *Saint Joan* did appear, with a new screenplay by Graham Greene, a Catholic, who made clear that the trial was on the heads of the judges at Rouen, not the Church at large. Otherwise the Shavian spirit was left generally intact—including the ghostly epilogue and a flippant, high-pitched Jean Seberg as the Maid, who referred to the dauphin (Richard Widmark) as "Charlie." Charlie twitched around scenes like one of the Marx brothers, while Seberg tried to display depth with vapid stares. The film was savaged by critics, while audiences shunned it in droves. The director, Otto Preminger, referred to the box office dud as his "most distinguished flop." He was unaware of Shaw's own film adaptation until ten years after his production. Unlike some ghastly Hollywood bombs, this Joanastic disaster has not even managed to collect a retro-cult that cherishes unintended campiness and guilty pleasures. Tragically, Jean Seberg, originally plucked from Iowa in a national search for the role of Joan, had no professional acting background. After a tumultuous new life in France, she committed suicide at age forty.

Another major Hollywood film, starring Ingrid Bergman as the Maid, was also a critical and commercial disappointment. The Swedish actress had yearned to play the part since childhood, even retracing Jeanne's steps from Domremy to Rouen in rigorous preparation for her portrayal. Bergman honed her performance in a theatrical production. She met Shaw in 1948 and admitted to him that she disagreed with his play. "Your words are marvelous," Bergman told him, "but they are Shaw's words, not Joan's. She had no education and only her inborn common sense to give her courage. You made her far too clever."[47]

In this century, legions worldwide know more about Joan of Arc through Shaw's brilliant if dyspeptic interpretation than from history books. He brought her to life once again, rife with human complexities that she in fact demonstrated. But between his preface and his play, Shaw ends up trying to have too many things both ways, and no way. He tries to draw a distinction between the two, the play to be the proof of the pudding. But this is ultimately disingenuous, since both are his deeply felt thoughts on the same subject, the forty-page preface edited many times to seem more spontaneous (reminiscent of Twain's own *bon mot* that it took the American months to work up "a few good impromptu remarks").

As in past lengthy prefaces to his plays, Shaw presented not an off-the-cuff introduction but a master thesis, hitting hard or harder than the play in the painful debate over Joan's meaning. His bifid disclaimers notwithstanding, Shaw cumulatively must be held accountable for presenting Joan as a first Protestant, but somehow a legitimate Catholic saint, fully expecting Catholics to agree with his historical presentation turned on its head. Catholic or Protestant, Shaw's Joan is not a Christian despite her own stated beliefs, but instead an "evolutionary appetite"—directed not by God, but her own "commonsense." Shaw's genius is inspired by the imagination of his imaginary Life Force, a dynamic appealing to modern minds shorn of belief, but it is not fairly historical, nor fair to his subject. His stagecraft is magnificent, but it repeatedly cheats at the religious heart of the matter, which is the unflagging religion that Shaw consistently denies Joan to have lived and died for.

Shaw's double-layered contradiction is still with us. On the one hand the Church, full of "superstitious rubbish," was typically opposed to such freedom of thought and individual genius and burned it. On the other hand Shaw claimed that the Church was quite right—indeed "exceptionally merciful"—in its trial and execution of Joan by Cauchon, whom Shaw consciously whitewashed. Shaw fiercely stated that "the law of God is a law of change, and when the Churches set themselves against change as such, they are setting themselves against the law of God." The assertion is central to his evolving vision of the Life Force and his own belief in human evolution. But just when one concludes that Shaw is pronouncing the status quo dead, he simultaneously, and incomprehensibly, decrees a counterpoint in his preface: "Society must always draw a line somewhere between allowable conduct and insanity or crime, in spite of the risk of mistaking sages for lunatics and saviors for blasphemers. We must prosecute, even to the death."

Why this last and greatest moral contradiction, especially when Shaw conceded that Joan's burning was a horror, and that "any historian who would defend it would defend anything"? Arnold Silver, in an aptly titled study—*Saint Joan: Playing With Fire*—takes on Shaw's convolutions directly, and declares Shaw's teeming political arena fair game. Silver probes the Irishman's inner conflict with the "younger," more rebellious Shaw, before the Russian Revolution, and the "older" Shaw who became an apologist for the growing atrocities both of Lenin and Stalin after him. After his visit to Russia, Shaw openly endorsed the shooting of anarchists and members of the bourgeoisie who opposed the state; "parasitism," he then wrote, "is the sin against the Holy Ghost, and . . . though all other sins may be forgiven, to it there is only one reaction: bang!"

How can this be? Silver sees the horrific schism already at war in *Saint Joan:*

> Suddenly in the soul of George Bernard Shaw there were two people—on the one side the old rebel and individualist, the champion of private judgement, and on the other the new defender of law and order, of the duty of dictatorial governments to exterminate all dissidents . . . the big train of history was now moving fast, and mere individuals had better get out of the way.[48]

Though provocative and bristling with flinty observation for all, Shaw's play as he intended it is an intellectual joyride that substitutes cosmic humor for passion and polemics for pathos. It clearly works as theater, roundly disproving J. M. Robertson, Shaw's most rabid critic in his day, who predicted that the play would be forgotten within thirty years. Shaw was awarded the Nobel Prize, and *Saint Joan* remains a staple of worldwide theater.

Nevertheless there is an aftertaste, a nagging buzz of polemicists flying around a mildly ludicrous young thing shorn of her spiritual armor. T. S. Eliot called Shaw's work "the greatest sacrilege of all Joans: for instead of the saint or the strumpet of the legends to which he objects, he turned her into a great middle-class reformer." Eliot saw Shaw's ersatz-revolutionary Joan as a disciple of Schleiermacher and Nietzsche, among other pantheistic spokesmen of "every chaotic, immature intellectual enthusiasm of the later nineteenth century . . . deluding the numberless crowd of sentimentally religious people who are incapable of following any argument to a conclusion." Eliot dismissed the Life Force as so much "potent ju ju." But apparently Shaw's play prompted him to come up with his own, *Murder in the Cathedral,* as the counterpoint of a Christian believer. As for his own Shavian moments in the work, Eliot conceded that "I may, for aught I know, have been slightly under the influence of *Saint Joan.*"[49]

In his 1996 study, *Joan of Arc at the University*, Professor John D. McCabe of Marquette protested against modern interpreters like Twain and Shaw, "a curious collection of emphatic public atheists and skeptics, united in their common cause of celebrating Joan as a symbol of something or other, but always something secular." McCabe stated that, in human terms, Jeanne has been celebrated for her audacity and spunk. "But if we read the words of Joan that have come down to us, and try to discern therein her own understanding of herself, we do not find her claiming her authority in her spunkiness—we find her always claiming only the authority of the counsel that had come to her. She is a saint not because she was audacious but because she was prudent. . . . Prudence is simply doing what God asks one to do; prudence is surrendering oneself entirely to God. . . . And that is what Joan did. And how do we know it? By reading the record, by hearing Joan's own voice."

Others have maintained that Shaw's play missed the Promethean tragic figure he claimed to present, because Joan is not really the central focus of the work, but only a matchbook to strike off flaming ideas. But so what if Joan is only a conduit, the Irishman might have conceded, since he dealt most comfortably in the world of thought—audience be damned. In his preface he wrote that most spectators "go to the theater as many others go to church, to display their best clothes and compare them with other people. . . . But I can take no more notice of it than Einstein of the people who are incapable of mathematics." At the end of the first act of one work, Shaw has an actor address the audience: "The play is now virtually over, but the characters will discuss it at great length for two acts more."[50]

JEANNE AND CURRENT FEMINISM

Jeanne d'Arc's standard has not been embraced by modern feminists. Around the turn of the twentieth century, suffragettes sporadically paraded her image around as an armored emblem of militancy (which Shaw instructed Thorndike to emulate for a feisty posture). By the end of her feminist work published in 1981, Marina Warner does not attempt such political stereotypes, stating sublimely that such categorization is the problem of all past historical efforts, in the end the failure of language and symbol, "the vanity of our widespread refusal to accept that it is impossible to trap the idea of virtue within boundaries that will not alter."

Warner, however, provided her insight into why La Pucelle appeared dangerously uppity to more than just churchmen: "Joan is the personification of mobility: she accepted neither her peasant birth, nor her female condition, none of the limitations society had provided for her circumscription. Instead, in an age of chivalry, she assumed its most successful guise and dressed herself and comported herself like a knight born to the role." Shaw agreed: Joan "could coax and she could hustle, her tongue having a soft side and a sharp edge. She was very capable: a born boss." He, too, challenged traditional male historians of his day as incapable of historical understanding of Joan. He also noted that they "must be capable of throwing off sex partialities and their romance, and regard woman as the female of the human species, and not as a different kind of animal with specific charms and specific imbecilities."

Feminist historian Anne Llewellyn Barstow observed in 1986—not without irony—"that two obstacles to a feminist approach to Joan, her mystical experiences and her role as military leader, may have discouraged feminist historians. There is the further point that she was burned at the stake, and feminists have not been looking for martyrs." The Maid appears too mystical, religious, and sycophantic for modern tastes: "The self-direction that Joan established through the medium of her voices is threatening to contemplate; we may well ask if we want that kind of radical autonomy. And the fact that she was punished for her independence by death is appalling to women who are understandably angry at the price they are paying to live their own truth."

Ronald Zupko observed in *Joan of Arc at the University* that "Joan is frequently made out to be the foremost medieval freedom fighter, leading the charge for women's liberation in a rigidly fundamentalist, male-dominated society. She is a medieval Betty Friedan encouraging her sisters to do their own thing. There is nothing whatsoever in the historical record, especially in the many trial records and among Joan's personal documents, to suggest that women's liberation was ever part of her agenda. Besides, most writers advancing this position never mention Joan's many predecessors, among whom just one, Eleanor of Aquitaine, would make a much better candidate."

Feminist theologian Charlotte Allen noted earlier trends in modern feminist scholarship that betrayed a prejudice against women religious figures, starting with the Virgin Mary:

> The first wave of the women's movement tended to take a disparaging stance toward the nuns, lay spinsters, wives, mothers, queens, widows, repentant courtesans, and martyrs whom the official Church had canonized, deeming them if not downright neurotic, then at the very least daddy's girls of the religious power structure, rewarded with halos for their passivity and deference to their male betters.[51]

Militant feminist Andrea Dworkin has not shied from the subject of Jeanne. In her 1987 book, *Intercourse,* which roundly denounced women for having any intercourse with men as the beginning of dominance, Dworkin praised in particular Jeanne's virginity. "She did not have to run the gauntlet of male desire; and so she was free, a rare and remarkable quality and kind of freedom—commonplace for men, virtually unattainable for women." Free at last, Jeanne was able to kick butt just like men:

> Being female meant tiny boundaries and degraded possibilities; social inferiority and sexual subordination; obedience to men; surrender to male force or violence; sexual accessibility to men or withdrawal from the world; and civil insignificance . . . low civil status and being fucked as indistinguishable one from the other. She refused to be fucked and she refused civil insignificance: and it was one refusal; a rejection of the social meaning of being female in its entirety, no part of the feminine exempted and saved. . . . She refused to be female. As she put it at her trial, not nicely: "And as for womanly duties, she said there were enough other women to do them."

To avoid men altogether Ms. Dworkin, the modern goddess Diana, might agree with French theologian Jean Gerson, who discussed fourteenth-century prescriptions on "Ways of Overcoming Sexual Desire: Think about death; wound oneself; talk to oneself; talk to someone else; spit; throw cold water on oneself; get up suddenly; think about the pains of hell or the suffering of this world; make a sacrifice such as giving up wine; do without money and nice clothes; say three Pater Nosters."[52]

Jeanne recently has been sent her draft notice to join the lesbian ranks by Dr. Elizabeth Stuart, in her new work, *Religion is a Queer Thing.* As reported in the publication *Lesbian News* in 1998, Stuart was smartly (if not exclusively) described as "Britain's top lesbian Catholic theologian," who stated her logic for recruiting Jeanne. "One of the most important tasks of queer theology has been rescuing people from heterosexual history." Jeanne is suspected to be in the closet, along with Ruth and Naomi in the Bible and a handful of other saints among the ten thousand or so in the Catholic Church. But to earn this new honorary membership, one need not come out of the closet. "I describe them not as lesbian or gay but 'queer'," Stuart convolutedly explained, "by which I mean people who stood outside of the dominant social and sexual structures of their day. In this sense we who do define ourselves as lesbian, gay, bisexual, and transgendered today can recognize a family resemblance with these people. We need to root ourselves in a tradition." Even medieval Scholasticism was rarely so byzantine in conclusion, but welcome aboard Jeanne's long train of grappling ideologues.[53]

There is finally this to be said about Jeanne by a woman, expressed at the 2000 graduation ceremony of Agnes Scott College in Atlanta. Marsha Norman, a Pulitzer Prize and Tony Award recipient, contemplated:

> When did Joan of Arc really become a saint? What is a real moment of transformation, how do you know you've had one, and what do you do about it? When did Joan morph, cross the line, become a saint? When the Pope said so? No, she was already a saint by then, that's what made him think of calling her one. Was it when they lit the fire? Certainly not. They lit the fire because that's what we do to saints. We torture them. No. I'm sure the real moment of transformation was some very quiet moment, some moment only Joan was aware of, when Joan herself realized that things were different now, that she had changed. Maybe it had been going on for a while, so quietly that even Joan didn't notice. But then something happened and Joan saw her greatness, her sainthood, out of the corner of her eye, and knew it was not just an opinion or idea, but an identity. In that moment of transformation, Joan saw the truth at the center of her known world, and nothing was ever the same. But it wasn't the truth itself that transformed Joan; truth is everywhere. It was seeing it and admitting what she had seen.[54]

The words of Norman appeal to all beings, regardless of gender and belief, recalling the final agonizing question that

Pontius Pilate asked the condemned Jesus before washing his hands: "And what is truth?" But in the modern division of truth, God appears long since banished to yokels like Jeanne d'Arc—and even she has been purged of her own belief in protracted secular morphing.

Yes or no: martyr, mystic, mascot, witch, liar, lunatic, simpleton, tool, military genius, life force, patriot, fascist, socialist, prophet, Protestant, Amazon, crypto-queer, proto-feminist—heretic or saint? Whichever combination you select, you would not be far wrong. Or was Jeanne d'Arc in fact married to the biblical Noah, as identified by ten percent of the American public in a 1990's survey? Heretic and saint are official declarations by the Church. Historical and human opinion can agree on little else, including this. Jeanne has been compartmentalized by each generation, historian, and ideologue, continually a reflection of our own ethos, sticking her in some box that soon becomes dated and ultimately useless.

The search continues into the world of science. Surely we can corner Jeanne at last.

4

Madness: Jeanne Among the Doctors

Where is the Life we have lost in living?
Where is the wisdom we have lost in knowledge?
Where is the knowledge we have lost in information?
The cycles of Heaven in twenty centuries
Bring us farther from GOD *and nearer to the Dust.*
T. S. Eliot

Occasionally the modern age has strained to explain Jeanne medically. Certainly the most bizarre quick-fix of scientific bravura was offered by an American endocrinologist, Dr. Robert Greenblatt, who asserted that she was a man, suffering from a hormonal feminizing defect that caused him "to look and think like females"—whatever that implies for females. One feminist historian, Anne Barstow, found the exercise prurient. "Just how Greenblatt knows how 'females think' must remain as much a mystery as he knows how Joan had no pubic hair," Barstow retorted.

But this medical fondle, even if it could be verified, explains nothing at all, male or female. There is still the deeper cosmic mystery to address, Jeanne's voices. Were they from God or only from her imagination? Or today would they be considered from neither, the product of a psychotic mind? Anatole France confided to his secretary, "Do you know what the fate of Jeanne d'Arc would be today? Prison or the madhouse—the snake pit." A typical nineteenth-century scientific reaction to Jeanne's revelations was expressed by William Ireland, a Scottish physician in 1875, who worked in the Home and School for Imbeciles, near Edinburgh. "It is clear anyone making such pretentions at the present time would get her case considered by doctors of medicine instead of doctors of divinity; nor need it be said what would be their decision."[1]

Was Jeanne—in a word—crazy? Although Shaw did not believe so, he covered the possibility with his own dramatic touch:

> Dunois: Joan, you make me uneasy when you talk about your voices: I should think you were a bit cracked if I hadn't noticed that you give me very sensible reasons for what you do, though I hear you telling others you are only obeying Madame Saint Catherine.
>
> Joan (crossly): Well, I have to find *reasons* for you, because you do not believe in my voices. But the voices come first; and I find the reasons after: whatever you may choose to believe.[2]

In the fifteenth century, what was it to be considered cracked? As systematically cataloged by Karl Menninger in *The Vital Balance,* mental disturbances as early as Hippocrates in the fourth century B.C. began as descriptive conditions, with and without explanation—usually without. For the Greeks it was acceptable to be temporarily out of one's head when receiving messages from the gods. Plato even considered it a divine blessing to be the conduit of such messages for prophecy (from Apollo), religion (from Dionysus), poetry (from the Muses), and eroticism (from Aphrodite and Eros). But almost anything not in those realms was considered madness, arising from some physical disease (Hippocrates had split this into disease with or without fever; fever can be one cause of hallucination today). By Roman times in the first century A.D., elements such as excessive black bile entered the picture, causing "melancholia" in the opinion of one physician, Cornelius Celsus. This was separate, he wrote in *De Medicina,* from delirium due to fright, or yet an unnamed third condition, which consisted of being out of one's senses, with or without hallucinations. That third type has remained elusive until present times. Senile dementia soon was recognized as separate, along with dementia due to alcohol, drugs, and hydrophobia (rabies).

By the fifth century A.D. a decent description of what today would pass for manic-depressive psychosis was present in the plethora of *manias,* characterized by violent swings of unreasonable merriment and sadness. Later the idea of excessive humors became refined to those forms of melancholia due to yellow bile (agitation, anger) or to black bile (sadness, fear, delusions). Other subgroups of chronic excessive behavior came and went over the centuries, such as *Satyriasis* (excessive sexual desire), *Incubus* (nightmares), *Amor Insanus* (lovesickness), *Mollities* (passive homosexuality), *Oblivio* (loss of memory), *Fatuitas, Stultitia,* or *Amentia* (feeble-mindedness spanning to stupidity), *Lethargus* (excessive sleep leading to coma), *Demonomania* (possession by evil spirits), and even *Lycanthropy,* the delusion of being turned into a wolf—particularly during the month of February. This one hung around through Jeanne's time, along with many others. Various postulates on causation still kept traces of imbalances due to bile, but they also began to incorporate imbalances in the psyche by three souls, vegetative, animal, and rational in nature. The rational soul, *anima rationalis,* could have either a deficiency, causing loss of interest, or an excess, leading to excessive thought and melancholia. Although this concept of souls originated during the Dark Ages in the Middle East, Thomas Aquinas maintained imbalances of the three souls during the thirteenth century. Nevertheless Aquinas also maintained a category of insanity with hallucinations due to demons, separate from that still undefined "third type" that had originated from Celsus over a thousand years before. By Jeanne's time the Church had assigned many symptoms of depression to *accidia,* the sin of sloth. Since some concept of anatomy had entered over this long period, various excessive substances like bile or phlegma might cause problems in various parts of the brain; the most dire cases occurred when they collided in combustion (*Adu-ſtation*). Remarkably the brain was accurately divided into three compartments: the back portion relating to memory, the middle portion to imagination, and the front portion to reason. Nothing could be done for the patient. The only therapeutic decision was whether to put the deranged one away, administer last rites, or maintain a safe distance.[3]

Of all the things the Rouen judges accused Jeanne of, "mania" in its diverse manifestations was not one of them. Paris theologian Jean Gerson had warned of previous aberrations in women who were considered out of their minds, and rather uncomfortably close to Jeanne: "What if someone of the female sex were reckoned to talk in the great and marvelous things above herself, to add daily vision upon vision, to report abnormalities of the brain through epilepsy, or petrification, or some kind of melancholy as a miracle, etc., to say nothing unless in the place of God, without any medication." However this line of insanity might have appealed to the judges at Rouen, there were also dangers. Marguerite la Touroulde, who had shared her bed with Jeanne for three weeks before her capture, found her pious and unlettered, "but I never saw or noticed anything *uncanny* about her." Several priests also stated that Jeanne was of sound mind on the last day of her life, as they repeatedly tried to make her deny her voices and visions. By law, to put someone not of sound mind to death was illegal, although such a determination was fraught with inconsistency and argumentation. So it continues today.[4]

By contrast the dauphin's father, Charles VI, had periodic fits of mania, believing himself made of glass, living in terror of being shattered: cracked indeed. He even had iron rods placed in his clothing to prevent his disintegration. Poor Charles, known as "the Much Beloved," had been thoroughly normal until his early twenties, but after a febrile illness he began running down the palace halls howling like a wolf—lycanthropy? Once he snapped while riding in a forest, slaying several of his own entourage. On such occasions he was incapable of recognizing his own family. When lucid, Charles would plead for forgiveness, begging that his dagger be hidden from him when he felt his brain was clouding again. Doctors even considered cutting several holes in his scalp after incantations and application of a liquid made from powdered pearls failed to bring the king around. Praying before the shroud of Jesus only induced a three-day remission. Exorcism also failed to rid him of his torment, while he cried out to whomever was casting this spell "to torture me no longer, and let me die." Doctors from the University of Paris called for the expulsion of evil sorcerers in the king's court.

One of Jeanne's most faithful young followers, Gilles de Laval, Lord of Rais, became a psychopath after her death. Through his vast wealth he was a main agent in starting Jeanne's annual remembrance on May 8 in Orléans. After that he returned to his Breton estates to engage in sorcery and alchemy. Gilles de Rais was hanged and his body burned in 1440 for sexually abusing and murdering more than one hundred peasant children—committing sodomy on them before, during, and after death—then carving up their bodies for a final perversion. He once offered the eyes, heart, and sexual organs of a young boy to conjure up Satan. Even without torture de Rais confessed to more than all, attempting to achieve final salvation as the chief of sinners.[5]

By contrast, visionaries and prophets were considered sanely acceptable. Like monarchs before him, Charles VII avidly kept astrologers in his court. Astronomy, the movement of the heavens, was considered the prince of sciences. When mixed with magic and predictions, it became astrology, *divinatio per astra,* which was acceptable—but only within theological bounds. Biblically the star of Bethlehem had guided three astrologers to the birthplace of Jesus. But even though Christ had encouraged followers to watch for coming signs, when hocus-pocus predictions lapsed into the realm of threatening God's Will, astrology became suspect. Man's doctrine of Free Will came into play, in a roll of the dice. If one bet on a prediction and won, it must have been by celestial signs. If one lost it might be first fruits of sorcery, *superstitio*. Little superstitions had existed since the time of Saint Augustine, like curing hiccups by holding the left thumb in the right hand, avoiding a sneeze when putting on shoes, not stepping on the threshold of one's door, and the bad omen of having one's clothes chewed on by mice. Never allow a child or dog to pass between two people while walking! These little foibles might ruin one's day, or at worst threaten crops, but did not bring on the end of the whole world. One might plan future ventures on the promising dance of the stars, but one must accept the outcome as God's Will. Not to do so would invoke human manipulations of God's divine script of history.

This duality was confusing to maintain, even for theologians like Augustine and Aquinas, not to mention the common man. Everyone, high and low, lived in an age both of good or "white" magic and of bad magic, *maleficia*, the type that cast evil spells, as on Charles VI. Except for the final result, the distinction in the popular mind was not always clear. If a sick cow got well, the weather cleared up, or a dynasty thrived, this was white magic. The reverse was *maleficia*, the dark realm of casting spells through various conduits, like wax or leaden images of the one being cursed, the use of incantations in unearthly tongues, or the capturing of spirits in vessels and crystals to use like magic wands. Conjuring up heaven through angels, or hell through demons, were two sides of the same coin. Potions of love or hate were the same *maleficia*, and against natural law. The Church was suspicious of both types because they threatened the magic of *mysteria Christi* and the exclusive right of the clergy to dispense it, principally through the Eucharist. It was well and good for an orthodox cardinal, like Pierre d'Ailly in Jeanne's time, to draw up a nativity horoscope of Jesus, calculated to predict the end of Time, measured by the twenty-year conjunctions of Jupiter and Saturn. But Charles VII was considered on the edge of heresy, because of his enthusiasm for prophets and astrologers. The equivalent of court prophets for common folk were village wise people, *magi,* usually women with paranormal powers, adept at minor healings and finding lost objects. Most considered this to be "natural" good magic, although here too the Church had reservations. Jeanne herself was asked if she could perform such little feats, and was accused of having divined the location of a pair of lost gloves, which she denied. Asked about locating a lost cup, she said emphatically, "I know nothing of all that." She also denied that one of her godmothers was a village wise woman.[6]

Jeanne as Deluded Liar

One explanation for Jeanne's voices is that she perpetuated a grand hoax. There is an acceptable opening for this possibility in that she dissembled at length about the sign given through her to Charles. It has never been historically certain exactly what the sign was that so convinced the dauphin when Jeanne first talked with him alone, though it has been suggested that she revealed his prayers to him. Pressed into a corner at the trial, Jeanne exaggerated and became progressively unbelievable. She had never wanted to discuss the matter at all. When the subject was first broached, she declined: "Forgive me, *passez outre.*" When asked five days later if she had seen an angel above the dauphin's head, she emphatically said no: "By Saint Mary, if there *were* any, I did not know, nor did I see one." Two days later she again declined to talk about a magical crown because she might perjure herself.[7]

There is evidence, however, that Jeanne did perjure herself, as several priests testified who interviewed her on the last day of her life. According to the Rouen transcript, four clerics stated one week after her execution that Jeanne confessed that she had fabricated the whole episode about the crown and angel. In the same session she also denounced her voices as evil. She herself had been the angel and no other, according to statements from Pierre Maurice, Jean Toutmouillé, and Nicolas Loiselleur. As Martin Ladvenu testified: "Without being constrained to do it, she said and confessed that, whatever she had said and boasted about this angel, there had been no angel who had brought the crown, but rather Jeanne herself had been the angel who had said and promised to him whom she calls her king that, if he put her to work, she would have him crowned at Reims."[8]

Virtually all chroniclers of Jeanne have denounced these confessions as counterfeits, invented for the Rouen record to feebly buttress the general sham. But their presence does open a door for logical investigators to take a new, harder look at Jeanne's prior statements. In *Fresh Verdicts on Joan of Arc,* Karen Sullivan reexamined the Rouen trial transcripts, to explore the possibility that Jeanne might have been badgered into answering particulars about her revelations, particulars that she had no prior reason to contemplate. Is it possible that she often simply fabricated answers to fit the demands of her judges? Their relentless suggestions—on saintly hair, height, manner of dress, scented crowns—forced Jeanne, Sullivan stated, to "depict her experience of the voices with a degree of detail that she does not appear to have perceived, and thus translate her vague, vernacular perception of her voices into a precise, learned discourse." Deborah Fraioli expressed a similar suspicion in *Joan of Arc: The Early Debate*, which examined not the format of the Rouen trial but rather contemporary documents related to Jeanne's first trial at Poitiers. On the subject of the more protracted questioning afterward at

Rouen, however, Fraioli speculated that "under the constant pressure of the trial, and because Joan did not know what the prelates wanted from her when they posed their questions, it appears that, by any fair estimate, Joan sometimes changed her tune when she provided them with answers." Other investigators, noting similar inconsistencies, have drawn the same logical conclusion. Even the respectful Jules Michelet conceded a "white lie" or two in 1853: "Some may strive to throw a veil over these things, to conceal this human, fallible aspect in a figure they desire to be altogether holy; but her fluctuations are none the less apparent. It is unjustified to claim that the judges managed to mislead her in those questions."[9]

Jeanne's trial at Rouen was littered with details about Saints Catherine, Margaret, and Michel that are almost comic in their minutiae. By contrast, in the second examination after her death, general recollection was that Jeanne had sternly maintained that she was sent directly from God, *Dieu, a Deo,* without reference to saintly intermediaries. Testimony on the third day of her Rouen trial also buttressed this contradiction, in the opinion of Karen Sullivan:

> Asked whether it were an angel coming directly from God *(de Dieu, a Dio)*, or if it were a saint, she answered it came from God *(ex parte Dei)*, and added, "I believe that I do not tell you perfectly all that I know, and I have a greater fear of saying something that displeases *them* than I have in responding to you. And, as for this question, I ask for a delay."
>
> Asked if she believed that God would be displeased if she told the truth, she answered my lord of Beauvais that the *voices* had told her to say some things to the King (Charles), and not to him.[10]

Asked again three days later, on February 27, Jeanne was given three clear options for the source of her voice: an angel, a saint, or God direct? She answered clearly, "They are the voices of Saint Catherine and Saint Margaret . . . to tell you this, I have leave from Our Lord (Christ)." But before conceding that Jeanne probably made up her saints, why is there often a very confusing mixture of the singular and plural when Jeanne explained her inspirations? Note that God, Christ, "them" singular and plural voices, Saint Catherine, and Saint Margaret are all in a theological mélange in the same testimony above. In the first three days before Jeanne's specific saints emerged at Rouen, there remains an enduring puzzle for those who analyze the transcripts in those first critical sessions. Jeanne was asked over a dozen times about her heavenly voice in the singular. Ignorant, inattentive, confused, or slyly (take your pick), she responded over half the time to this *singular* form of the question by switching her answer to the *plural* form of voices.

To believe in plural intermediaries from one God is not to confuse them as to ultimate singular authority, nor did Jeanne ever do so during her draining months at Rouen. And who were *they*, one is left to ponder, if not plural voices conveying the will of a singular God? Jeanne variously referred to God as *Dieu, mon Créatur*, or my Lord, the King of Heaven, *le Roi du ciel.* Other designations were *notre Seigneur*, or even *Messire*, a secular term of respect for a feudal seigneur (which evolved in the French language into *monsieur*). During her Rouen testimony the name of Christ is interchangeable with my Lord—"the Lord who redeemed us from hell," as she specified. It was common in her age to consider the Son as God per se. This emphasized the belief, principally after the example of Saint Francis of Assisi, of Christ as the Passion, God having been utterly—completely—transformed into suffering flesh for mankind's salvation. In this new, more passionate belief in the ultimate meaning of the crucifixion, God the Father was altered beautifully, but also confusingly so for church Trinitarians, as well as for ordinary believers, like Jeanne. *Je suis cy envoiée de par Dieu, le Roi du ciel!* she repeatedly declared.

Both Father and Son were inseparable to Jeanne, one transformed entity, one being, not two or three. Although Jeanne certainly cherished her saints, her *Conseil*, ascribing to them sweet voices and warm attributes, she never worshiped them in themselves. They were always lower intermediaries from God/Christ, and could even be argued with and disobeyed.[11]

In and out during Rouen, angels and saints came in flocks of heavenly hosts, or singly (Michel), or in a duo (Catherine and Margaret), or one without the other, or occasionally as a voice with indeterminate identity. It is historically accurate that the saintly identities of Catherine, Margaret, and Michel were not specifically named by witnesses at her later rehabilitation exam, although descriptions of Jeanne's intermediary voice or voices were provided by several. As Bertrand de Poulengy testified, "I myself was much stimulated by her voices, for it seemed to me that she was sent by God." Although frequently evoking God's name, she never claimed to hear from God directly.[12]

The practical importance of Jeanne's daily expression supersedes labyrinthine dissection of Trinitarian doctrine, then or now. She surely was blissfully ignorant of the whole subject, her expression instead being a result of *direct*, personal revelation, not derived from reams of Latin text and the dogma of her day. It is amusing to contemplate her mother translating from Thomas Aquinas while teaching her the most rudimentary three church credos, memorized by virtually all illiterates, without one whit of scholastic theology. Considering Jeanne's lack of such distant erudition, it becomes even more compelling that she was telling the truth about her saints from the first, not inventing them in retrospect. At the least it clearly shows that her *Conseil* worked as plural manifestations from a singular above, always. It started before the trial at Rouen. One does not even have to accept Jeanne's own words there: "I have told you often enough that it is Saint Catherine and Saint Margaret. *Believe me if you will.*" The reason one does not have to believe only Jeanne is that her voices were described by others before Rouen, others who never laid eyes on her.

How did this plural ambiguity, instead of a singular *Dieu,* even get started if not from Jeanne's first responses two years before at Poitiers? Nearly two years before the Rouen trial, Alain Chartier, a poet in Charles's court, wrote to some distant prince describing the heaven-sent *puella* who was miraculously saving "decaying France," and who had mentioned her voices since childhood. Of course it was second-hand information, at the very earliest stages of Jeanne's legend. But every legend has to start from something concrete, or something heard—even if falsely reported or perceived. What was the *origin* of this detail about Jeanne's voices? What was the corpus of inchoate knowledge about this then obscure sixteen-year-old, who might as well have arrived at Chinon from the moon? Also significantly before Rouen, an anonymous author spread a popular broadside across Europe entitled *De mirabili victoria*, with a portion precisely fitting the formula of Jeanne's own words to an uncanny degree:

> unquestionable signs prove that she has been chosen by the King of Heaven as His standard bearer . . . to overthrow by the hand of a woman, a young girl, a virgin, the powerful weapons of iniquity; this Maid, finally surrounded by *helpful angels* with whom her virginity forms a link of friendship and relationship, as Saint Jerome says and as it is frequently seen in the history of saints, where they appear with crowns of lilies and roses. (italics added)[13]

Here again at a significant stage before Rouen is restated the biblical format of a singular God, choosing a servant to do His bidding on earth through intermediaries—"surrounded by helpful angels"—who progressively in Jeanne's case revealed specific identities, identities that she herself repeatedly said she was both fearful and slow to finally recognize as Saints Michel, Catherine, and Margaret. Regardless of the authorship and motivation of *De mirabili victoria* (splendidly examined in Deborah Fraioli's fine work), from what other inspiration might the disputed writer have found to compose such a testament, if not from Jeanne's prior responses at Poitiers? She certainly maintained these same essentials throughout her later Rouen ordeal, as if one who could not read had somehow memorized her Latin script from the previous *De mirabili victoria*.

It is more logical that the reverse took place: that the religious tract resulted from Jeanne's prior statements, which were eventually lost in the Poitiers records. Note the same formula that she maintained about the holy status of being La Pucelle (beyond merely being a sexually inexperienced French *vierge*), as recorded in the Rouen transcript on March 12. Note again Jeanne's repeated natural expression concerning plural manifestations from God:

> Asked whether, when she promised Our Lord to keep her virginity, she had spoken to Him, she answered, "It ought to be sufficient to promise to those *who were sent* by Him, that is to Saint Catherine and Saint Margaret." . . . She said that the first time she heard her voice, she vowed her virginity as long as it should be pleasing to God. She was then of the age of thirteen years or thereabouts. . . . Asked if *her voices* had ever called her "Daughter of God, Daughter of the Church, Great-Hearted Maid," she answered that, both before raising the siege of Orléans and afterwards, every day *they* spoke to her they often called her "Jeanne the Pucelle, Daughter of God." (italics added)[14]

After Jeanne did hesitantly accept the authenticity of her voices, her first pledge of faith was her virginity, something not asked of her, an act one can only assume was her own humble offering of spiritual purity. The spiritual aspect of virginity in Jeanne's day could be redeemed, even after the physical aspect had been lost in surrender to carnality. According to no less an authority than Jean Gerson, if non-virginal women should stop, "repent, and confess of their wrong will with a good heart, they recover their virginity." Furthermore, if a woman lost her virginity against her will, "her merit does not increase or decrease." Jeanne still had not been told to go fight for France, and her spontaneous offering of virginity remains profoundly moving in its commitment.

Again, in terms of dwelling in realms beyond Jeanne's own natural comprehension, compare her answer one day later at Rouen with the identical rationale from *De mirabili victoria* concerning the central way in which God chose to work, "to overthrow by the hand of a woman, a young girl, a virgin, the powerful weapons of iniquity." Why was Jeanne chosen as God's instrument? "Why she, sooner than another," as the question was honed to a fine point. "She answered, 'It pleased God to do so, by means of a simple maid, to drive back the King's enemies.'"

This is the *leitmotif* of *De mirabili victoria*, paraphrasing 1 Corinthians 1:27: "But God chose what is foolish in the world to shame the wise. God chose what is weak in the world to shame the strong." This very verse was cited repeatedly at the time to justify Jeanne's holy mission. It was as if some mutually reenforcing agent were about, something in the air *before* and during her trial.[15]

Jeanne's subsequent jumbled testimony concerning the crown and sign to Charles has been left at the phantasmagorical level by her most assiduous defenders, and there it must remain. Jeanne had warned that she might not always tell the truth, and most concede that here is a shining example of a tall tale, or *pseudologia fantastica*, the psychiatric term defining the inability to discern which parts of one's storytelling are true and false. But Jeanne does not have to be judged a psychotic in post-Freudian terms merely because at times she embellished her revelations when she became fed up:

"As to some things I shall tell the truth—as to others—not!"

But the possibility that clever Jeanne lived a total lie for six years is untenable to common sense. Anatole France's interpretation that she was a deluded simpleton used by anonymous Armagnac priests to spread a hoax—scaring the English into believing that God was French—is equally preposterous over the long run. Short of declaring Jeanne crazy or a liar, however, such is the only beginning-to-end theory that can withstand the pressure of current rationalist understanding. A hoax theory is too facile, too tenuous to sustain the considerable weight of contrary evidence. A British biographer of Jeanne, Andrew Lang, leapt to her defense in 1908, attacking the priestly conspiracy theory of Anatole France along with much else the Frenchman stated—even to the extent of questioning the soundness of France's scholarship. "I know not how to understand," Lang wrote in *The Maid of France*, "the method of making very strange statements, and supporting them by references to books and pages in which I can find no such matter." Concerning France's priest hoax, utilizing Jeanne as puppet, Lang stated: "This theory is unthinkable. . . . No priest could possibly have taught her, through her Voices, that only an ignorant peaceful peasant girl, herself in male costume, could drive the English out of France. Much less could a supposed series of clerical impostors have . . . unanimously insisted on a course which, to human common sense, seemed the quintessence of crazy folly."[16]

The most popular secular attempt to reconcile Jeanne to "normalcy" is to interpret her voices as manifestations of her own will, that her voices said only what she wanted them to say. "The voices come first; and I find reasons after," as Shaw put it. He believed the voices were an earthbound extension of her imagination, filtered through her judgment, executed through her will. Shaw mentioned the works of psychologist Francis Galton in attempting to explain the source of Jeanne's voices. To Shaw she was a Galtonic visualizer.

Francis Galton was a contemporary of Carl Jung and Sigmund Freud, in hot pursuit of unlocking the unconscious mind around the turn of the twentieth century. Galton first conceived of the famous word association test, noting that words were not haphazardly chosen in free association. (This would soon evolve into the more familiar Freudian slip of the tongue.) Such associations revealed the subconscious, which lay otherwise invisible beneath conscious thought, where, in Galton's formulation, "one portion of the mind communicates with another portion as with a different person." Jung extended these word associations to expand his own theories of archetypes and the collective unconscious. Early in his career Galton had pursued the trail blazed by Franz Mesmer in the late eighteenth century, who had used magnetism and magnetic "looks in the eye" to hypnotize—or mesmerize—patients into a state of subconscious trances. At first Galton fiercely tried to concentrate, to project his own thoughts in telepathy with his patients' thoughts. It proved fatiguing for him—and unnecessary, he discovered. "At last I succeeded in letting my mind ramble freely while I maintained the same owl like demeanor. This acted just as well." It became clear that only the *appearance* of authority to the hypnotized subject mattered in the end.[17]

Galton maintained that many mentally healthy people have extreme visualizing facility—Shaw's Life Force of imagination would be an instance—sufficient to hallucinate without being considered insane. As Shaw believed, concerning Jeanne's visualizing ability to see imaginary saints, "the street is full of normally sane people who have hallucinations of all sorts which they believe to be part of the normal permanent equipment of all human beings." Galton thought that gifted children often passed in and out of the real and visionary world of fancy with little or no distinction. In 1908 this ability to recall visions more intensely than reality was termed "eidetic imagery," from the Greek word *eidos*, that which is seen.

E. R. Jaensch found this voluntary ability in sixty percent of children, but it disappeared after age twelve under normal circumstances. If such hallucinatory imagination were encouraged instead of repressed, Galton believed the child perhaps would mature as a visionary. The unconscious mind might eventually project a "fancy picture" over external reality in a sort of visual blur, based on past images stored away. Thus Shaw embraced Galton to explain the source of Jeanne's voices, which emerged in a time aswirl with visions, saints, demons, and unquestioned Christian symbolism. "If Joan was mad," Shaw stated in his preface to *Saint Joan*, "all Christendom was mad too, for people who believe devoutly in the existence of celestial personages are every whit as mad in that sense as the people who think they see them."[18]

But if so—if the voices were subjectively internal and controlled by Jeanne's volition alone—then she had progressive internal conflicts with her own mind, including her imagination, judgment, and will. Shaw and most others skirt this central conflict through an inconsistent argument that her voices originated only from within her faculties. Indeed the factual course of events suggests the opposite interpretation: Jeanne began to have doubts, conflicts, and ultimately disobeyed forces entirely external to her own volition. She had a two-phased career with her voices. The first portion—obedience and agreement with them—met with unbroken success. After Charles was crowned at Reims, the pattern reversed. Jeanne progressively struck out on her own, following her own judgment and will more than her voices. She had not been told by her voices to attack Paris. Mounting failure set in, she was captured, and—against the direct counsel of her voices—she attempted what should have proved a fatal plunge to escape from a tower. She miraculously survived; her voices forgave her. Jeanne's twentieth-century biographer, Vita Sackville-West, took up this overlooked point against mainstream rationalizers:

> It disposes, almost *ipso facto,* of the argument, again so often advanced, that her voices were merely the subjective expression of her own inward desires. It proves that, on occasion, her saints could go against her, and that she could go against her saints. What are we to make of this? . . . The entirely credulous mentality will accept it as a final proof of the objective nature of Jeanne's inspiration. The more skeptical mentality will ponder over the psychological questions aroused, and will fail to come to any decision. For myself, being neither credulous nor skeptical . . . the whole story appears as one of the strongest arguments that can be advanced in favour of an objective rather than a subjective influence working on Jeanne.[19]

One must come to a crossroads at this point, to choose one path or the other—and they are mutually exclusive. Either a given young woman, Joan of Arc, who physically existed in history, progressively was told what to do by some *external*, objective, independent source, a distant power that rewarded obedience and punished its opposite; or her inspiration came from *within*, a subjective inspiration either from her "normal" imagination or from what today is defined as an abnormal source, psychotic hallucinations. The answer cannot be both: either it is external or it is internal. If one subscribes to the notion that Jeanne's voices only reflect her internal conscious will, it is noteworthy that she on occasion admitted to having difficulty hearing or understanding those voices, that is, her own thoughts. The voices usually appeared on their own, though on occasion she could call them to appear. When she was deathly ill in prison, her saints once appeared in miniature: *quantitate minima, sub specie, minimus rebus.* Or they awoke her, perhaps mingling the dream world with consciousness:

> Questioned as to what she was doing yesterday morning when she heard the voice, she answered she was asleep, and that the voice awoke her . . .

> Asked if she did not thank the voice, and kneel down, she answered, "I did thank it, but I was sitting on my bed. I clasped my hands, begging and praying that it might help and *advise me* in what I had to do. The voice told me to answer boldly."
>
> Question: "Did the voice not say certain things to you, before you prayed to it?"
>
> Jeanne: "Yes, but I did not *understand* them all. But when I was aroused from sleep it told me to answer boldly." (italics added)[20]

Finally Jeanne herself relentlessly maintained a dichotomy between her own actions and her voices, admitting that she herself repeatedly had stumbled and erred—but never her voices. When her judges accused her of only following everything that her voices told her to do, Jeanne angrily corrected them: "everything *good* that I did." Like Sackville-West, biographer Marina Warner also believed that this extraordinary girl "had placed her council firmly outside herself; there is never the slightest hint that she heard an inner voice advising her. On one side, there was Joan with her own views, and on the other, there were her voices. Their identities never merge."

When asked at her trial about the commands of her voices, Jeanne clearly stated more than once, "she did not answer whatever came into her head, but what she answered was by *their* command." Additionally there appeared to be nothing infallible about Jeanne's human gullibility, as if she possessed some psychic extrasensory perception. During her imprisonment she was rather easily duped by a sly priest, Nicolas Loiseleur, who lied to her about being from her region, extracting personal testimony in private, only to repeat it to the court, while other judges eavesdropped through a hole in the wall.[21]

Ultimately it was also the judges at Rouen, who condemned the mortal Jeanne to be burned, who buttressed their own fear of her extracorporal voices. The most valuable last "confession" added to their transcript (one that the body of history believes Jeanne never made) was her personal rejection of her voices. To quote their official record about her *soi-disant* last words: "She understood and knew that she had been tricked by them. . . . It was true that she had been deceived. Since they had deceived her so, she believed they were no longer good voices or good things. 'I do not wish to add any further faith to these voices.'" Perhaps Jeanne said this in terminal despair. Yet why did they have such a heavy-handed dread of fantasies, if Pierre Cauchon and his minions believed that a country girl's voices existed only in her imagination?[22]

JEANNE AND MODERN PSYCHIATRY

Jeanne maintained two identities—her own volition and that of her voices—with a moral distinction between them, without being confused or tripped up by months of probing. But can one person possess different identities, inhabiting the same mind and body? Could Jeanne have had a split personality, what today is categorized as Multiple Personality Disorder? The validity of this disorder is not embraced by all psychiatrists (especially in Britain as compared to America), who are now in disarray as the great pyramid of Freudian theory topples before a new world of drug solutions for specific chemical imbalances in the brain. Nevertheless in Multiple Personality Disorder two or more distinct personalities—and sometimes dozens—inhabit the same person, who is typically a withdrawn but otherwise ordinary woman taken over periodically by a darker, profane, aggressive other. The conscious "self" is usually unaware of the division, a staple of fascination from the fictional Jekyll and Hyde to the controversial *Three Faces of Eve*. Uncomprehending, the "good" personality may experience blackouts or trances, told afterward of another quite different self, with a different name and behavior. Or the individual may hear voices from within, directing their actions, arguing with one another, sometimes commanding self-destruction.[23]

Dr. Morton Prince recognized a famous case in 1906 involving Sally Beauchamp, a fastidious and well-educated young woman who suffered from what was thought to be hysteria. Around this time, hysteria was a catchall term for ailments mental, physical, or both, that resulted in unexplainable paralysis not neurologically related to prior trauma. With young neurologist Sigmund Freud in the vanguard, hysteria became the modern starting point for psychological theories about the subconscious in rebellion with the conscious.

Sally Beauchamp was highly impressionable and full of physical complaints. Her parents had experienced an unhappy marriage; her father had a violent temper. Her mother had died when Sally was thirteen. Sally ran away from home when she was sixteen, the conflicts with her father having sent her into trancelike states. Her submissive personality gradually changed. Dr. Prince began treating her with hypnosis, which revealed a second personality. This person was bold, adventurous, and amoral. She loved playing tricks on Miss Beauchamp, telling lies, causing embarrassing contortions and mannerisms, taking her on long walks to exhaust her. A year later a third personality emerged, more outgoing than Miss Beauchamp, more confident and full of courage. Nearly a century ago Dr. Prince described the three as "the saint, the woman, and the devil." Almost four centuries before, Jeanne had gone through the same theological evaluation at Poitiers to discern by *discretio spirituum* whether she was really human, guided by God, or a creature of the devil.[24]

The saint (Superego), the woman (Ego), and the devil (Id). According to Freud, we all have different voices that tug at our daily attempt to maintain acceptable behavior. There is the pleasure-seeking voice of the infantile Id, full of libido. The word is sexually charged, derived from Freud's bedrock theory of the Oedipal complex and infant sexuality. Carl Jung preferred the term "psychic energy" to libido, skirting Freud's hypersexual preoccupation with the past. Jung ultimately split with Freud in search of a more forward-thinking dynamic that explored experiences after infancy, seeking universal symbols. Both libido and psychic energy would correspond to Shaw's Life Force, the primal psychic identity that propels the Ego through existence. Later Freud postulated another voice, a countering parental policeman, which he called the Superego. This voice seeks perfection, not pleasure. The Ego listens to the Id and Superego in conflict, making executive decisions based in daily reality.

Have you ever heard something like this yourself? "Touch that woman's breast. It feels good . . . go on . . . she wants you to," the Id impulsively goads the Ego. Or, "You know you loath him—hit him!" But the Superego counters: "Unthinkable! Nice people don't do that." Caught in the middle of the dialogue, the Ego sides with one or the other, usually the civil Superego: "Of course not—what would people say!" Yet we still *feel* these impulses, think them daily, literally can hear them in our heads, perhaps each minute, on the brink of acting them out. POW!

> Id: Gee, that *did* feel good.
> Superego: But you should be ashamed of yourself. Apologize immediately!
> Ego: I'm very sorry.
> Id: (not really)
> Ego: Oh, shut up. I was really a bad person. The Superego just told me so.
> Id: Don't kid yourself . . . do it again . . .

And so on, as we wrestle with those forces within us, caught between primal impulse and conscience. These voices are at least consciously "heard." They can be fully articulated to a friend over coffee, with shared familiarity ("haven't you always wanted to punch out that pompous ass too?"). The voices are normal, the fuel of literature and theater, of gab and gossip. How many other times has someone offered a penny for your thoughts? You look up as if returning from a trance, to realize to your own amazement that you have just been having a vibrant discourse with Humphrey Bogart or George Washington, or continuing a bitter argument with a dead relative—who talks back. In sum we are constantly talking with people not physically present, by volume more often than talking with people who *are* present. Whether we enjoy it or not, we are always conscious and in dialogue, even if alone in the middle of the Gobi Desert. And when we are talking only to ourselves—who is talking and *who* is listening?

It is the identical question asked by St. Augustine in *Dialogue with Myself,* written fifteen hundred years ago. "Myself reflecting with myself for some time on various things, and persistently for many days quizzing myself over what I should seek, and what to avoid, I suddenly addressed myself—*or someone did*—outside me or inside I could not tell, though I am deeply concerned to find out."

Augustine called these startling moments *soliloquia,* "lone speakings." More than ever this phenomenon of who is who intrigues both modern philosophers and neuroscientists. Not that these two schools have ever been on cordial terms; the split between science and philosophy began hundreds of years before Jeanne's day. Now a battle for this frontier of consciousness is upon us. Are we one, or several, or in dialogue with someone outside of our own invention? Both disciplines believe that the other is using the wrong tools to find the ghost in the machine.

Philosophy evolved from ancient theology and metaphysics to the theory that precise words, combined into infallible concepts, define something, *a priori.* Substituting one simple word, like *not,* changes things significantly. Science, the stepchild of philosophy, evolved from poking into material realities to show that the same thing will happen over and over—the bedrock of reproducible proof by the scientific method, *a posteriori.* Science obeys infallible mathematics, beginning with the fundamental observation that two plus two equals a neanderthal four . . . unless one multiplies four by zero. Poof—now you see four, now you do not, like hitting the delete key on a computer. Where did four go? Is it still somewhere inside the computer, or did it go off to a distant dimension? Depending on semantics, four went to one of two polar opposites: nothing or infinity. Is four a semantic or a scientific proposition? The Hottentot culture in South Africa solved this dilemma to their own satisfaction; any thing over five is "many." The mysterious concept of zero—nothing which is an active agent of *everything*—switched over to metaphysics long ago. What a metaphysical paradox that something which is physically "solid," like a table, factually consists of more blank space than real matter. Could a table ever literally transmigrate through a wall? Scientific theory believes that it can: metaphysics indeed.

For physicists, dabbling in philosophy is seen as a debacle of the unintelligible in pursuit of the undeterminable. Recently some scientists have been forced to ask philosophers for help in trying to capture that most elemental staple—time—into some core formula of Einstein's space-time continuum, because the little *t* keeps disappearing. "To tell you the truth," confessed one physicist, "I think most of my colleagues are terrified of talking to philosophers—like being caught coming out of a pornographic cinema."[25]

In scientific terms the process of self-dialogue is called inner speech, expressed in language and thoughts to oneself, which can be easily elaborated to others on request. But within this world there is a more distant sort of subterranean self-mumbling, called subvocal speech, that form we are not aware of when we read, or even concentrate. Experiments show that subtle electrical "voice" mechanisms are occurring in the primary speaking organs, the larynx or mouth, little muscular movements that do not reach our consciousness. In reading, this process slows down speed, but improves comprehension; the more difficult the text, the more subvocal speech occurs.

Since the late nineteenth century, scientists have speculated whether this subvocal speech is the fodder for hallucinations, termed "verbal pseudohallucination." Experiments have shown a high incidence of subvocal activity during hallucinations. A few studies suggest that the unscrambled subvocal murmurings are the same as what is said in hallucinations, typically brief orders in the third person. But any scientific conclusion remains inconclusive, and must go begging at the door of metaphysics. To wit, are subjects *initiating* hallucinations with their own subvocal speech, or subvocally *responding* to voices from elsewhere?[26]

The conscious self may sleep, but the unconscious, through dreams, apparently never rests. As Freud stated, "The voice of the intellect is a soft one, but it does not rest until it has gained a hearing." Plato thought dreams were a divine route to truth, whereas Aristotle considered them a mere jumble of fragments from wakefulness. These differ little from conflicting interpretations today. Carl Jung thought Morton Prince's fragmented personalities to be manifestations of psychic complexes with an independent existence. Perhaps too they are the actors in dreams that hold us powerless, the impish complexes that play daily tricks. "They slip just the wrong word into one's mouth," Jung thought. "They make one forget the name of the person one is about to introduce. They cause a tickle in the throat, just when the softest passage is being played on the piano at a concert. They make the tiptoeing latecomer trip over a chair with a resounding crash. They bid us congratulate the mourners at a burial instead of condoling them." Does the brain have something, or some place, that houses free will, even a soul, as the Greek Dualists believed? Or in the scientific view, is it an evolutionary computer only capable of receiving sensory input, reacting in a preordained Darwinian manner to neurochemical squirts?[27]

When it comes to Jeanne's possible possession by pathological multiple personalities, a few parallels with young Sally

Beauchamp's experience are apparent, but for the most part we see vast differences. There appeared to be no devil directing Jeanne's actions, although some judges at Rouen might have believed this theologically and culturally, and were motivated politically to prove it. As in Sally's case, Multiple Personality Disorder usually has a background of prolonged childhood trauma, including physical or sexual abuse. Although this cannot be known of Jeanne's background, it is not readily inferable. As recounted in her own words at her trial in 1431:

> Questioned about her father's dreams, she replied that when she was still with her father and mother, she was often told by her mother that her father had said that he dreamed his daughter would go off with the soldiers, and that her mother and father took great care to keep her safely, that they were very strict with her, and that she was always obedient to them. . . . She said further that she had heard her mother say that her father had said to her brothers, "If I thought that such a thing could happen as I dreamed, I should want you to drown her, and if you did not, I would drown her myself." And Jeanne greatly feared that they would lose their minds when she left to go to Vaucouleurs. Asked if her father's thoughts and dreams had come to him after she had her visions, she replied, "Yes, more than two years after she first heard the voices."[28]

Her father's recurrent dreams about her leaving home, along with his threat to drown her if she did so, are traditionally explained as his fear that she would join the army to wind up a whore. Although some might have a Freudian field day with this nugget, one can theorize no further with what little else is known. In strong contrast to Jeanne, however, sufferers from Multiple Personality Disorder are usually so incapacitated by past demons that they are incapable of the kind of leadership that Jeanne so abundantly displayed.

It is interesting to speculate about what might have occurred centuries ago concerning demonic possession. Colin Ross did so in his book on Multiple Personality Disorders. The first psychiatrists must have been shamans, literally sucking out demons through a hollow tube, or bargaining to exorcize them away in rituals. Next came the Church, which had its hands full of prospects. The possessed tended to be women, which has led certain feminists to speculate about attempts to dramatize inner forces in past times of extreme female repression, using as examples medieval women rife with visions in Jeanne's day, or occasionally, Jeanne herself. In the centuries that followed, contagious outbreaks would dramatically increase, like the seventeenth-century witches in Salem, Massachusetts. Consider this encounter in 1714, from Dr. Ross's book, in which a Christian minister described two possessed women, one of whom was seized in a physical paroxysm:

> Satan abruptly hurled his invective at me by her mouth. *"Silly fool, what are you doing here in this workhouse? You will get lice."*
>
> I made him this answer. "By the blood, the wounds and martyrdom of Jesus Christ, thou shalt be vanquished and expelled!"
>
> Thereupon he foamed with rage and shouted, *"If we had the devil's power we would turn the earth and heaven upside down. . . . What God does not want is ours!"*

The minister coaxed the unwilling woman into a church. From the pulpit he read portions from the Gospel of St. Mark regarding Jesus' banishing of demons. The current demon protested, *"Will not you soon have done?"*

> After I had replied, "When it is enough for God, it will be enough for thee, demon!" Satan broke into complaints against me.
>
> *"How dost thou oppress, how dost thou torment me! If*

only I had been wise enough not to enter thy church!" As he cried out impudently, *"My creature must now suffer as an example!"*

I closed his mouth with these words. "Demon! The creature is not thine but God's! That which is thine is filth and unclean things, hell, and damnation to all eternity."

When at last I addressed to him the most violent exhortations in the name of Jesus, he cried out, *"Oh, I burn, I burn! Oh, what torture! What torture!"* or loaded me with furious invectives: *"What ails thee to jabber in this fashion?"*

During all these prayers, clamourings, and disputes, Satan tortured the poor creature horribly, howled through her mouth in a frightful manner and threw her to the ground so rigid, so insensible that she became as cold as ice and lay as dead, at which time we could not perceive the slightest breath, until at last with God's help she came to herself."[29]

Dr. Ross was among those who believe that, like hypnotism, such possessions respond to suggestions from someone in authority, or who evoke authority from a higher source. This central principle of religious exorcism has not changed for centuries. In the biblical passage when Jesus transferred demons into a herd of swine, he asked the possessed one's name: "My name is Legion, for we are many." In terms of autosuggestion, note the parallel physical behavior of the possessed woman in 1714, after this passage from the ninth chapter of the Gospel of St. Mark was read to her:

When Jesus saw that a crowd came running together, he rebuked the unclean spirit, saying to it, "You dumb and deaf spirit, I command you, come out of him, and never enter him again." And after crying out and convulsing him terribly, it came out, and the boy was like a corpse, so that most of them said, "He is dead." But Jesus took him by the hand and lifted up, and he arose.

By the nineteenth century, possession had begun to pass from priests to physicians, from biblical demons to demonic possession from the dead. As the source of the demons changed with the times, so inexplicably did physical responses to hypnosis change over the years. In Mesmer's first days of magnetic hypnosis in the 1780s, the subjects contorted themselves and writhed about. A few decades later they had ceased such gyrations. No one knows why. By the early nineteenth century patients first began to forget what had happened during the trance. Around 1825 they began to spontaneously diagnose their own ailments. None of this had been reported before. By the mid-nineteenth century phrenology enjoyed a psychic vogue, rendering hypnosis a temporary handmaiden. Pressure on the scalp over preconceived zones elicited a parallel response: push on the spot assigned for speech, for example, and the hypnotized subject was struck dumb. Rub the area over the area for "veneration" and the person fell to his knees in prayer. Then followed others like the French physician Jean Charcot, who first rendered various parts of the body paralyzed by command. This was unprecedented behavior.

Again the hypnotic power of suggestion from one in authority was no different from the treatment of an aboriginal shaman, or present practitioners of voodoo in the Caribbean. By the late nineteenth century Freud believed that demonic possession issued from the inner unconscious of psychic forces, a manifestation of hysteria. "What in those days were thought to be evil spirits to us are base and evil wishes," he stated, "the derivatives of impulses which have been rejected and suppressed." Compared to medieval times, "we have abandoned the projection of them into the outer world, attributing their origin instead to the inner life of the patient in whom they manifest themselves."[30]

Toward the inner life the field of psychiatry relentlessly followed Freud and his contemporaries, armed with dark primal theories, ink blobs, and the new talking cure, seeking to release traumatic repressions that oozed from the fissures of neurosis, or exploded in volcanoes of psychosis. Inner demons were released through the new religion, psychoanalysis. By now those who repeatedly hear, see, and experience phenomena such as Jeanne d'Arc are considered abnormal. They are diagnosed as delusional or even psychotic, accused of experiencing hallucinations, the false perception of things not based in reality. By today's standards Jeanne would be considered a serious candidate.

A psychiatric text lists hallucinations in a variety of manifestations: auditory messages over two words in length; visions (not defined as abnormal if the eyes are closed); "twilight" visions when half-asleep or awakening (also not psychotic); unexplainable smells, tastes, and tactile sensations, such as insects crawling over one's skin. If one merely feels such sensations but recognizes them as not real, this is defined as temporary and normal. Pink elephants after a drinking binge are acceptable—but not if they start hanging around and telling you how to run your life.

Sensations of voices are the most common hallucination among psychotics. A few who initially hear their own thoughts spoken aloud (*écho de pensée*) may progress to a state in which the voices come from without, conducting a running commentary on the person. Visual hallucinations may accompany the voices, but this is usually in acute delirious states, such as those induced by psychedelic drugs or alcohol. Normal grief and depression may give rise to visions of a dead relative, or seeing oneself in a coffin. These, too, are temporary.

Jeanne and Physical Brain Theories

A minority may have a physical or organic cause for such hallucinations, diagnosable as temporal lobe epilepsy. Located along the sides toward the back of the brain, the temporal lobes subserve hearing, speech, smell, taste, emotion, and are the warehouses of memory. An abnormal electrical discharge may induce a small seizure that in some cases spills over to the back occipital lobe, the clearinghouse of sight, causing both auditory and visual hallucinations. Jeanne once described her visions as appearing in miniature, and on one occasion in her campaign she appeared to be seeing what her colleague Jean d'Aulon clearly did not. Her attendant spotted her nearly alone during a retreat. He was very alarmed: "But Jeanne answered me that she was not alone, and that she still had in her company fifty thousand of her men, and she would not leave there until she had taken the town. At that time, whatever she might say, she had not with her more than four or five men, and this I know certainly, along with many others who likewise saw her."[31]

Jeanne never had a fraction of fifty thousand soldiers in her company at any time. In her anguish of the heated moment, she was either overreacting, or momentarily delusional. In either case her zeal carried that particular day beyond all bounds of reason, and the town of St.-Pierre-les-Moutiers was taken by storm. If such aberrations had maintained a continuous pattern, Jeanne might now be a candidate for manic-depressive psychosis or bipolar disorder, on a rollercoaster of delusions of grandeur, mysteriously counterpointed by downward black defeats of the soul. But assuming that Aulon's description is credible, no one else witnessed Jeanne so completely out of contact with reality. Over the years her nature was not one of such violent mood swings. She was quick to both temper and tears, certainly always adamant and impatient, but never depressed without reason.

This come-and-go nature of her loss of perception might nevertheless be consistent with something transient, like a temporal lobe seizure. A first case of religious experience related to epilepsy was scientifically recorded in the late nineteenth century, invoking continued study today. Although usually arising in the late twenties, the condition may begin in childhood or adolescence, with attacks of sudden fear and a rising sensation in the stomach or chest. There may be headaches, vertigo, and an aura of *déjà vu.* According to which side of the brain the seizure starts in, the opposite side of the body is affected, and leads to bizarre and involuntary movements of the eyes, face, or limbs. Brain trauma at birth is a common cause, along with childhood febrile illnesses, or past head injury. A broad personality profile may include humorlessness, fixation, sanctimoniousness, religiosity, aggressiveness, with a desire to punish offenders. One British study found a significant increase of associated psychosis in young, left-handed females. Around half of the sufferers betray repressed sexuality on sensitive questioning, with total loss of sexual interest among female patients. "They were aware that they were different," an investigator learned at the Johns Hopkins Medical Center, "and expressed their amazement—and sometimes disdain—at their fellowman's preoccupation with sex."[32]

In 1986 in Britain it was postulated that Jeanne had a rare form of tuberculosis in her temporal lobe that caused such temporal episodes, possibly caught from the cattle she tended. Though unlikely—other symptoms of the disease are totally absent in her physically active life—this guess is as good as any, assuming one can answer her total experience by assigning some physical, anatomical lesion inside her brain. But even in this latest theory, examples of over one hundred tuberculous tumors in the brain—referred to as buttressing this possibility—blatantly negate the premise. The vast majority of lesions occurred everywhere *but* in the temporal lobe, and *none* caused temporal lobe epilepsy. The idea is not new, having been put forth in 1958, locating the tuberculous lesion precisely "in the region of the left temporo-sphenoidal lobe of Joan's brain," in the opinion of John and Isobel-Ann Butterfield. The Butterfields assigned a systematic complex of medical maladies that may be caused by tuberculosis, including lack of menstruation, disseminated abdominal infection, and even kidney failure, all rare complications. Riddled from top to bottom with tuberculosis, Jeanne indeed would have been deathly ill for nearly six years, while she galloped around saving France.[33]

Concerning temporal lobe epilepsy, there is too much else to reconcile medically, with or without the presence of bovine tuberculosis. Specifically Jeanne had no epilepsy, no physical seizures. Except to voluntarily raise her eyes ecstatically to heaven when once describing her voices, nothing else could suggest even a *petit mal*, or mild seizure. Auditory hallucinations in temporal lobe epilepsy are vague to incoherent, short, and generally unpleasant. There is no record in Jeanne's life of loss of consciousness, no sudden and uncontrollable expressions of panic when a seizure was pending, no involuntary smacking of the lips, lolling of the eyes or tongue, spastic limb contortions, loss of bladder control, biting of the tongue. Temporal lobe epilepsy is largely a physical manifestation; the minority who do experience brief hallucinations have the manifestations during the aura that *precedes* a seizure. Nothing fits at all, yet this explanation of a temporal lobe "problem" is on the ascendancy. But this hits at the very heart of all scientific explanations. On the one hand, rather ingenious–even plausible—theories are offered to precisely place some lesion inside Jeanne's brain, which would then induce the pathological symptoms required to "diagnose" the cause of her total experience. But all such theories select only the symptoms needed to make a very narrow case—ignoring a whole complex of related symptoms that would render the latest explanation implausible to impossible. What is dreadful is that at least some scientists must be fully aware of the game they are playing, off on a historical holiday. Certainly they would never play by this double standard in dealing with their own live patients, or would only tolerate such ersatz "science" during an amusing after-dinner talk, before sobering up to return to the hospital the next morning. Clearly the subject of Jeanne d'Arc brings out the beast in everyone, past and present.

In 1991 Elizabeth Foote-Smith and Lydia Bayne, two neurologists at the University of California in San Francisco, proposed a provocative theory that might apply to young Jeanne: musicogenic epilepsy. The entity appears to be a rare but valid manifestation of temporal lobe epilepsy, causing momentary ictal aura and ecstacy induced by music. There are not always associated psychomotor physical seizures. Perhaps the Russian novelist Fyodor Dostoyevski had this condition (or perhaps he didn't), in which he was induced by bells to spasms of religious ecstacy. Yes—bells—the mechanism that George Bernard Shaw dramatically used in *Saint Joan*. Instead of bells going ding-dong-ding to the ordinary ear, Shaw in his play has Jeanne hear Dear-child-of-God, Be-brave-go-on, I-am-thy-Help, God-will-save-France . . . ding-dong-ding. "Then Joan," says the character Dunois with a sigh, "we shall hear whatever we *fancy* in the booming of the bell." Certainly in childhood Jeanne had an association with bells. She fell to her knees in the fields whenever she heard them, and even scolded a local priest when he failed to ring them on time. During her trail at Rouen, on February 24, 1431, Jeanne was asked by interrogator Jean Beaupère at what time she had heard her voice the day before: "She answered that she had heard it three times, once in the morning, again at the hour of Vespers, and yet again at the hour of the Ave Maria. Sometimes she heard it more often than this, she said. Questioned as to what she was doing yesterday morning when she heard this voice, she answered that she was asleep, and that the voice awoke her."

Early on there is a reasonable association between voices and bells, but even in the above statement there is no uniformity. On the last day of Jeanne's life, a priest named Pierre Maurice suggested to her that her voices were exclusively caused by bells, since she previously had brought up the association.

"When men hear bells," Maurice suggested, "they imagine they hear and catch certain words." Unfortunately her response was neither yes or no: "Jeanne said and confessed that she had had apparitions come to her, sometimes in a great multitude, sometimes in small number, or in minute things. She did not otherwise describe their form and figure." Poor Jeanne had too many other discourses with her voices not associated with the ringing of bells for this appealing theory to become comprehensive. Yet if one throws in a bit of childhood eidetic imagery, a dollop of Shaw's Galtonic visualizer, a strong dose of obsessive neurosis and affective disorder, rounded out with just a pinch of temporal lobe epilepsy (but without epilepsy itself), the resulting concoction might satisfy scientific tastes, even though the chances that these conditions might conjoin would be medically infinitesimal, nor would any single entity encompass Jeanne's total experience.[34]

Some have proposed Saint Paul as a candidate for temporal lobe epilepsy as well. He started with a flashing light like Jeanne's, which was followed by a voice and a vision of Christ during his famous conversion on the road to Damascus. Paul later described one of his religious ecstasies in 2 Corinthians:

> I know a man in Christ who fourteen years ago was caught up to the third heaven—whether in the body or out of the body I do not know, God knows. And I know that this man was caught up into Paradise—whether in the body or out of the body I do not know, God knows—and he heard things that cannot be told, which man may not utter. On behalf of this man I will boast, but on my own behalf I will not boast, except for my weaknesses. . . . And to keep me from being too elated by the abundance of revelations, a thorn was given me in the flesh, a messenger of Satan, to harass me, to keep me from being too elated. Three times I besought the Lord about this, that it should leave me, but He said to

> me, "My grace is sufficient for you, for my power is made perfect in weakness."[35]

In addition to Dostoyevski and Saint Paul, others in the medical literature suspected of having had religious temporal lobe episodes include the Islamic founder Mohammed; Margery Kempe, a Christian mystic of Jeanne's time; Emanuel Swedenborg, founder of the New Jerusalem Church; Mormon founder Joseph Smith; and even the artist Vincent van Gogh, who suffered numerous religious auras in his mid-thirties. All would be prime fodder for the theories of Sigmund Freud, who considered any form of religion to be an expression of neurosis; the more devout, the deeper the pathology. According to Freud, Dostoyevski was probably an example of hysterical neurosis. His seizures were a manifestation of repressed guilt over the death wishes he harbored for his father. The fact that Dostoyevski's father in fact was murdered by someone else only enhanced this repression. Thus Dostoyevski overidentified with the suffering of Christ as self-punishment for his own guilt.

This fit into Freud's general formula of the Oedipal complex as the genesis of religious belief throughout the ages. "God," the father figure for all fathers, was a source of fear because of the threat of castration. Instead of loving "God," mankind has always feared him, really wanting to kill him. By the time of Christ this had evolved into "original sin," which Paul admonished his fellow Jews to confess to, extending back to the book of Genesis. The Father had found the "first Adam" in criminal congress with Eve, a symbol for the Freudian mother. This set up an Oedipal conflict, which led to a wish for the father's death, causing guilt and conflict. In Freudian terms the only solution was to sacrifice Paul's "second Adam," Christ, the son of the Father. After that atonement (with a welcome release of Freudian guilt), Christianity became a "son-religion" instead of a "father-religion." For devout Freudians the bread and wine of the Eucharist are only replacements for more ancient animal sacrifices, culminating in the "totem meal," the devouring of flesh sacred to the tribe in spiritual communion.[36]

Sudden and intense religious conversions have been a rare manifestation of temporal lobe epilepsy. A 1970 study in England closely examined their content in six patients, reviewing dozens of other cases in past medical literature, also noting that over eighty percent of all religious conversions occur before the age of twenty. Of the six patients who developed incapacitating seizures, three had no prior interest in religion. By contrast three others, one of them an orthodox Jew, had been raised in strong religious backgrounds. After their conversions, four of the patients remained intensely religious, often neurotically so. The other two lost their new faith over time. One of the latter, a bus conductor, had his sudden conversion at age forty-seven. While collecting fares on the bus, he felt himself in heaven. He told all the passengers, and he laughed to himself constantly for the next two days in religious ecstasy. He remained very devout for three years, then just as suddenly became an atheist, stating, "I used to believe in heaven and hell, but after this experience I do not believe there is a hereafter." After a portion of his temporal lobe was removed, his epilepsy ended, but he remained in a depressed state.

The Jewish patient suddenly had a vision that he was in an airplane over France, which climbed until it arrived in a different peaceful land, where the power of God enveloped him. "I became intensely interested in following the teachings of Jesus Christ," he stated. He then joined the Pentecostal church, switching later to Methodism, turning every conversation toward a belief in Christ. More than two years after his conversion experience, he began walking the streets like an apocalyptic prophet, carrying a banner proclaiming, "Be prepared to meet thy God." One nonreligious Scottish farmer had an onset of seizures after forty, and became paranoid that the Russians were in a race to find the truth about God. "I was fanatical," he said, "terrified that I would not be able to carry out my belief that the greatest power is the love of God. Somehow I had to find a way to prove it because the Russians had found another."

One thirty-three-year-old English clerk, who also had had no past interest in religion, became seized with the idea that he was the son of God while walking through the Strand in London: "It was a beautiful morning and God was with me and I was thanking God, I was talking to God. . . . God isn't something hard looking down on us, God is trees and flowers and beauty and love. . . . God was telling me, 'at last you have found someone who can help you,' and He was talking about you, doctor, He was talking about you."[37]

Do any of these religious profiles remotely resemble the profound experience of Jeanne d'Arc? Well before this current focus on the mysterious temporal lobes, Anatole France's lengthy work on Jeanne at the turn of the twentieth century included the opinion of Dr. Georges Dumas, a neuropathologist at the Sorbonne in Paris. Dumas believed that her voices were part of some organic pathology, her hallucinations perhaps induced by constant fasting or lack of menstruation. The latter condition was implied by Jeanne's squire, Jean d'Aulon, at her trial of Rehabilitation. Jeanne's unconscious thought (*pensée obscure*) was often at variance with her conscious thought (*pensée claire*), although her experiences to Dumas seemed objective. Perhaps she was suffering from some pathology in the right side of her brain. But Dumas could go no further toward a more precise diagnosis, and therefore he returned to the nineteenth-century catchall of hysteria. "If hysteria did affect her," he bowed out quite romantically, "it was only to permit the most secret emotions of her heart to objectify themselves in the form of visions and celestial voices . . . it fortified her faith, consecrated her mission but, in her intelligence, in her will, she remained healthy and upright.

Nervous pathology can scarcely throw a feeble glimmer of light on this part of the soul."

Decades before Dumas, Jules Michelet had offered a mixed scientific and pre-Shavian diagnosis: Jeanne embodied a concentrated vital force—perhaps her voices fueled by incomplete sexual development—which combined with her spark of common sense: "Joan's eminent originality was her common sense. . . . Unawares, the young girl created, so to speak, her own ideas, turned them into realities, made them entities, powers, imparted to them, from the treasure of her virginal life, an existence so splendid, so compelling that the paltry realities of this world grew faint by comparison."[38]

Until the early twentieth century, it was believed that the major component of female hysteria was sexual frustration, mollified by proper marriage, sex, and childbirth. "Well of course, darling, Joan never had a period, you see," actress Sybil Thorndike explained to a later portrayer of the stage Saint Joan, Joan Plowright. "And if you don't have a period, you do get these kinds of visions." Thorndike expressed this belief of female hysteria in the 1960s, an apparent carryover of her nineteenth-century formative years. Nearly three thousand years before that, physicians believed that the uterus became periodically engorged with some form of seed—wandering in consternation upward in the body from the pelvis—to choke its host in a miasma of fluttering physical symptoms, extending from breathlessness to drooling private parts below. Hippocrates' classification of hysteria was confined to fits by women suffering from periodic gasping for breath, pain, and convulsions. By the seventh century A.D., this was assigned to "uterine suffocation." Talk about raging hormones: as early as the fifth century, treatment for this complex consisted of manually stimulating the external genitalia to induce a healing crisis of "hysterical paroxysm," which would return the contrite uterus to the pelvis. With an extended officialdom of thrusting loins and ecstatic moans, little seemed changed conceptually by 1913, judging from an advertisement for a neanderthal electric vibrator, with this assurance: "All the pleasures of youth will throb within you." In fact the vibrator, which had been invented in the 1880s, was considered naively scientific: "gynecological massage" was prescribed by earnest physicians to writhing hysterics, carried out in portentous "vibratory operating theaters." Sessions sometimes lasted up to a full hour, and all in good faith. Patients and doctors took the prescriptions very seriously . . . until the 1920s, when early risqué movies began exploiting the obvious modern understanding of vibrators. This epiphany harkened back to the 1780s in France, when an official scientific committee, which included Benjamin Franklin, reported back to King Louis XVI that Franz Mesmer's illicit Parisian experiments were *too* mesmerizing. Women were overly susceptible to his strange energies, leading to occult eroticism, as the official report darkly stated: "Touch them in one point and you touch them everywhere."[39]

Jeanne and Schizophrenic Hallucinations

Wandering and predatory uteruses aside, if there appears to be no specific anatomical lesion or physical imbalance to account for Jeanne's voices, there remain the voices of schizophrenia, the dark central well of madness. It is the retreat of the psyche inward, leaving a fragile outer shell. In the early twentieth century the condition derived its name from Swiss psychiatrist Eugen Bleuler, who described it in the hallmark term, "divorce from reality"—the splitting of consciousness. The condition surely must have existed before, but its ephemeral nature defies earlier identification, despite claims that the Egyptians, and later Hippocrates, recognized it distinctly from other forms of mental deterioration. Perhaps schizophrenia is that "third type" of mania, lingering around undefined since ancient Greece. In present times psychiatrists still cannot all agree on schizophrenia's many faces.

There can be endless emotional poverty (*anhedonia*), touched on by Shakespeare's Hamlet: "How weary, stale, flat, and unprofitable seem to me all the uses of this world." A sort of negative aura may repel empathy; indeed patients have a dearth of empathy, in the sense that they cannot comprehend another's relationship to themselves or the world. Abstract thought becomes difficult, emotional expression limited or absent, resulting in a humorless "flat affect." Or a horrific idea may invoke inappropriate laughter. Bleuler feared that in chronic cases the sufferers would never return completely to this world. Instead they would be haunted permanently by delusions and unknown demons, who read their minds, spied on them, hated them, and plotted against them.

Voices are the most common manifestation, issuing from the radio, or the walls, or a microphone placed inside one's organs by an alien force. Whole organizations may be involved in trying to do the individual in. Paranoia can be incapacitating. Whereas the voices of Multiple Personality Disorder are confined to within the head, schizophrenics usually hear the voices speaking from outside themselves. With the patient under hypnosis, Colin Ross maintains that a therapist can typically converse and bargain with the voices in the former disorder, but not in schizophrenia. Neither can the patients themselves—although a few may try to respond to them by remarks or gestures. The voices in schizophrenia can command, mock, shout, whisper, or mumble dreamily, be single or multiple. The messages tend to be short, with little variation. Some command voices speak of suicide and antisocial acts. For those with a pious religious upbringing, the messages may be religious, from angels, demons, or God. Images of heavenly raptures may accompany the voices, which often speak from an external fixed location in each patient.[40]

Voices may appear only under certain provocations, and a few patients may allay them with distractions, but there is no ultimate escape. Some patients deaf from birth can somehow still "hear" them. One study from the Harvard Medical School in 1987 found that opening the mouth widely can interrupt the voices, leading some to speculate that they are self-generated by the patient's own subvocal speech, which in fact repeats their own thoughts. Schizophrenics in the study, however, seemed indifferent to using this simple solution to stop them—even if they were terrified by the voices they themselves initiated. Does this imply a degree of self-imposed madness? The authors cautioned against applying this technique universally, "lest one thereby deprive the patient of a helpful compensatory device." Colin Ross expressed the same caution in unroofing various personalities in Multiple Personality Disorder, concluding that a socially unacceptable one is always "bad," to be exorcized hypnotically without considering what supportive role it might play in the patient's total dynamic. If both are true, there would be an implication that even on the other side of the psychiatric looking glass, there still might be a psychic balance of morality—a soul concerned with good and evil—instead of a physical brain only battered around by impersonal neurochemicals.[41]

Unlike Colin Ross and others, maverick psychologist Wilson Van Dusen maintained that he has had repeated discourse with the voices of hundreds of schizophrenics, without hypnosis. Van Dusen was a disciple of the eighteenth-century Swiss mystic Emanuel Swendenborg, whose views on religion reflect his own. Swendenborg, also admired by Bernard Shaw, believed that all of life is united by a hierarchy of beings, from God down through angels to man, who is also subject to counteracting influences from hell. This moral structure is classic, having evolved centuries before. Thomas Aquinas codified it in the thirteenth century. Good and evil tussle it out inside the unconscious mind of man's dual experience, whose ego stands in a free space between them, choosing both with a degree of free will, like a pre-Freudian trinity.

Mixing some science with a huge dose of metaphysics,

Van Dusen believed that schizophrenics offer us a glimpse into everyman's struggle. "One consistent finding was that patients felt they had contact with another world, or order of beings. Most thought these other persons were living persons. . . . Most were frightened, and adjusted with difficulty to this new experience." The voices tended to group themselves into a negative lower order or a less common positive higher order. "Lower order voices," Van Dusen stated, "are as though one is dealing with drunken bums at a bar who like to tease and torment just for the fun of it. They will suggest lewd acts and then scold the patient for considering them. They find a weak point of conscience and work on it interminably." Van Dusen found these voices bent on destruction:

> The most devastating experience of all is to be shouted at by dozens of voices. When this occurred the patient had to be sedated. The vocabulary and range of ideas of the lower order is limited, but they have a persistent will to destroy. They invade every nook and cranny of privacy, work on every weakness and credibility, claim awesome powers, lie, make promises and then undermine the patient's will. They never have a personal identity, though they accept most names or identities given them. . . . All of the lower order are irreligious or anti-religious. Some actively interfered with the patient's religious practices.

As in medieval possession, the lower order occasionally claimed to be from hell, and spoke through the patient with a different voice from his own. On one occasion Van Dusen was even able to administer a Rorschach inkblot test to a voice, eliciting a different response from the patient's. "Sometimes they acted through the patient. One of my female patients was found going out the hospital gate, arguing loudly with her male voice that she didn't want to leave, but he was insisting. Like many, this particular hallucination claimed to be

Jesus Christ, but his bragging and argumentativeness rather gave him away as the lower order."

By contrast Van Dusen found the less vocal higher order to be benevolent, "helpful, instructive, supportive, highly symbolic and religious. It looks most like Carl Jung's archetypes, whereas the lower order looks like Freud's Id. In contrast to the lower order, it thinks in something like universal ideas in ways that are richer and more complex than the patient's own mode of thought. It can be very powerful emotionally and carry with it an almost inexpressible ring of truth. The higher order tends to enlarge a patient's values, something like a very wise and considerate instructor." Such higher order manifestations made up less than twenty percent of Van Dusen's encounters, and did not seem able to offset the lower order enough to comfort the patient: "I am relatively certain that religious faith alone doesn't prevent hallucinations, because many patients try to save themselves by their faith." Van Dusen felt he was confronting Swendenborg's polarity of good and evil played out in the human psyche. He conceded that such conclusions are beyond present scientific verification.

A 1994 study in Birmingham, England, also examined the nature of voices in schizophrenia. The psychologists concluded that all the voices were omnipotent in knowing and dominating the patient's thoughts. Voices with evil intent were twice as common as benevolent ones. Evil voices originated from the devil, witches, space travelers, Russians, a former employer, a dead friend, and an ex-girlfriend who had achieved goddess status. The latter's messages were contradictory: "kill yourself/quit smoking/don't go to church today." Even ones assigned to presumably benevolent sources like God often commanded malevolent acts.[42]

Besides voices inducing paranoia, most schizophrenics experience thought itself becoming scrambled—a form of soul murder, as one patient poignantly described. Though divorced from normal social intercourse, schizophrenics are not unaware: some maintain they are *too* aware. Indeed there is possible sensory overload, with resultant disintegration of self. They may be overly aware, thus fragmented by stimuli that "normal" people are oblivious to. But conditions are much more pervasive than a "nervous breakdown" in chronic schizophrenia. Some repeat statements stressing I-am, in a desperate attempt to avoid becoming I-am-not. Even their bodies may not belong to them, as if every action were performed by some automaton, not the patient, in danger of physical fragmentation before their very eyes—much as Charles VI believed himself made of glass. Drawings of human figures often show a fractured nature. Severe victims may try to escape to a catatonic refuge, but they will allow their frozen poses to be altered like mannequins. This condition is termed waxy flexibility, and patients can maintain the new posture for remarkable periods without fatigue, as if through a supernatural strength.

Bleuler believed the central problem of schizophrenia to be "loose associations," in which thoughts have no connection. The patient rambles on with no discrimination between particles of information (over inclusion), or draws bizarre conclusions: "I am a man. Napoleon was a man. Therefore I am Napoleon." Having another Napoleon confined across the hall does not confound such a belief. The patient may not even recognize a photograph of himself. Carl Jung, a disciple of Bleuler, expressed his frustration over trying to treat schizophrenics with psychoanalysis. "I felt hopelessly unscientific at treating them at all," he confessed. But Jung maintained a resigned benevolence:

> Even if I am not very hopeful about a patient, I try to give him as much psychology as he can stand, because I have seen plenty of cases where the later attacks were less severe, and the prognosis was better, as a result of increased psychological understanding. To make a correct

> diagnosis, and to nod your head gravely at a bad prognosis, is the less important aspect of the medical art. It can even cripple your enthusiasm, and in psychotherapy enthusiasm is the secret of success.[43]

What separates our normally fluctuating moods and mental lapses from schizophrenia? Most of us on occasion become addled, ramble on inappropriately, feel paranoid, appear introverted, flat, and depressed. But we do not repeatedly hallucinate, and more often than not we are logical, coherent, extroverted, even full of wit and verve, as Jeanne was. Hallucinations aside, the schizophrenic profile that separates a withdrawn, eccentric individual with a "schizoid" personality from a psychotic is a matter of degree, depth, duration, and even interpretation. Charles VII had a flat, schizoid manner, but not a schizophrenic psychosis. If thrust on the psychiatrist's couch, Hamlet himself would not qualify as a metaphor for schizophrenia because he could reason and moralize, in his case too tragically. But if some psychic oversensitivity does indeed serve as the spring for schizophrenia, Hamlet would be prime fodder: the man who knew too much.

Yet most investigators maintain that the schizophrenic's central problem is that they are not thinking too much—but *less* than normal. As Bleuler believed from the beginning, thinking stops in the middle of a thought, and may cease altogether for periods, resulting in rambling incoherence and what he termed "clang associations," disgracing the ego. Consider this discourse recorded from one schizophrenic in 1969: "Don't they drink water, two gulps, five gulps, two gulps. Cigarettes are the most important thing. Cigarettes. And then the others have to give me medicine by the way. That's the perfectly logical place to put them. Paul says here and here. In the muscles I think would be better."[44]

Jeanne and Primal Voices From the Gods

Alluding to Jeanne d'Arc as a past example of the human mind in schism, Julian Jaynes of Princeton University explored fantastic explanations for hallucinations in *The Origin of Consciousness in the Breakdown of the Bicameral Mind.* Jaynes submitted that thinking, reason, even consciousness itself was a rather recent acquisition of the brain, beginning to appear only around five thousand years ago, a mere blink in evolutionary time. What did early man do for all those aeons before he began thinking? He listened to voices. And then he acted without question, without introspection or thought per se. Instead of muddling around with stressful ideas, what preconscious man acted on instead were the unquestioned voices of the gods.[45]

Jaynes assigned the probable anatomical origin of the hallucinatory voices, Wernicke's zone of speech. It is the vital area in the brain for assimilating vocabulary, syntax, meaning, and understanding. Coordinating with another speech area nearby named Broca's area, Wernicke's zone is located on the posterior aspect of the temporal lobe, and fully functions on only one side of the brain. Together these areas dominate speech on the left side in right-handed people, who compose over ninety percent of the population. But even in left-handed people the majority still have their speech center on the left side of the brain. Most of the body is controlled by the opposite side of the brain, because the nerve pathways to the body cross over from the brain proper: a left-sided stroke causes right-sided paralysis of the body, and vice versa. What we see in our right eye is interpreted on the left side of the brain, and so on. Destroying or removing portions of the left hemisphere result in the loss of speech—but not the ability to *understand* instructions by the right side. Both sides of the brain are capable of memory and understanding, but only the dominant side can produce coherent verbal verification that it *does* understand. In the vast majority of us, the right side of the brain—corresponding to the speech area on the left—appears to lie dormant. Some maintain that this area is not even conscious, silently or otherwise.[46]

Why? Was it always thus? Teleologically evolution appears never to create something for nothing. Jaynes argued that in preconscious times, the right side told the left side what to do. And it was done—without thought, reflection, rationalization, justification, conceptualization, introspection, moralization, criticism, verbalization, articulation, discourse, dialogue, debate—the stuff of consciousness itself. As Jaynes speculated, "Before the second millennium BC, *everyone* was schizophrenic." (italics added)[47]

Quite an idea: or more precisely a non-idea, in an age when man had no capacity to formulate ideas with language and word-concepts, themselves faint fingerprints indicating to Jaynes the existence of the split or bicameral mind. For examples he delved into earliest literature, like the *Iliad* and portions of the Old Testament. As Jaynes cumulatively saw it, there is no concept of will in the Homeric writings, "the concept developing curiously late in Greek thought. Thus, Iliadic men have no will of their own and certainly no notion of free will . . . no one is moral among the god-controlled puppets of the *Iliad.* Good and evil do not exit." Therefore, according to Jaynes, right-brained Greek gods spoke to physical automatons, who obeyed without thought or tension between body and mind. That started with Dualism, the split of the spiritual psyche and divine *logos* from the temporal body or *soma,* which had developed more clearly around 500 B.C. Jaynes maintained that those with strictly prophetic bicameral minds were systematically nudged out by those with more conscious minds, or eliminated outright, as described in Zechariah 13:3–4: "If anyone again appears as a prophet, his mother and father who bore him will say to him, 'You shall not live, for you speak lies in the name of the Lord'; and his father and his mother who bore him shall pierce him through when he prophesies. . . . On that day every prophet will be ashamed of his vision when he prophesies."

Jeanne's indictment by her judges at Rouen can be encapsulated in one verse above: "You shall not live, for you speak lies in the name of the Lord." The same could be said in the case of Jesus. Addressing Christ's split consciousness over the first Christian centuries, Greek theologians thought themselves into knots. For them Christ was incomprehensibly both man and God, thus finite and infinite, mortal and immortal. By A.D. 325, the question of whether he was only of like substance with God the Father Yahweh (*homoousous*), or indeed the same substance as Yahweh (*homoousious*) led to the great "one iota" debate (iota being the letter "i" in the Greek alphabet). This became the wellspring for the Nicene Creed, which declared that Jesus was *homoousIous*—the same substance as God—the divine *Logos* become flesh incarnate. But the primal question still lingered in the finite minds of church thinkers. Was Jesus then of two natures or one, impossibly a fallible man and an infallible God? How could this be? How then could mankind identify with Jesus the Christ as somehow of his own earthly experience, sweating, hungry, thirsty, happy, angry, weeping, truly suffering human pain in the end to save all humanity?

Dualistic thought through the Gnostics had always maintained that Christ was totally divine, only *appearing* to be human. He was docetic: an apparition, apart from human carnality and physical sensation. This led to the first (and lingering) orthodox heresy. By A.D. 451 the Council of Chalcedon reconsidered that Christ was of two natures, man and God, all within one being—yet "without confusion, conversion, division, or separation." But of course much confusion and division still remained, as the question was later honed: if Christ is of two natures, does it not follow that He has two wills, a jointly human and divine mind? Precisely what did Jesus know—and when did *Christ* pre-know it? When was Jesus responding like a human being in the Bible, and when was Christ not responding at all as we would, because He was omniscient God beyond human empathy? Theologically this question began to split Christianity into Eastern Orthodox and Western Roman camps. The thinkers at Constantinople opted for one will in one being, while Rome progressively codified a dual-will formula. Despite competing creeds and formulae, the mystical question of split-consciousness in Jesus the Christ has never been resolved, because to this day we cannot yet comprehend its magnitude, much less define it, resulting in Trinitarian syllogisms, as if the Godhead were like the Three Musketeers: one for all and all for one. Human reason can do no better. "For now we see in a mirror dimly," Saint Paul expressed, "but then face to face."

It is inevitable that those outside the theological realm should rush in to fill the mystical void with psychiatric explanation. Albert Schweitzer reviewed such attempts in *The Psychiatric Study of Jesus*. Beginning in 1835, David Friedrich Strauss published his life of Jesus, *Das Leben Jesu*, exploring a self-deluded individual who madly thought the end of the world was coming in his own lifetime. Others followed who believed that Jesus was a benevolent Jewish teacher, and that his messianic expressions were added after his death by his followers. By 1905 Dr. Georg Lomer (writing under the pseudonym George de Loosten) concluded that Jesus had such an aberrant childhood that he became self-delusional and messianic about fulfilling Old Testament prophesies. He suffered bouts of depression, was highly agitated, and prone to outbursts of temper, as against defenseless fig trees and hapless money changers at the temple in Jerusalem. Jesus suffered from repeated hallucinations, both visual and auditory, hearing voices from outside of his body. Additionally he had a weak sexual identity and no sense of family loyalty, all of which were considered manifestations of psychic degeneration. By 1912 Dr. William Hirsch had diagnosed the symptoms of a chronic paranoid, a child obsessed with Old Testament scripture, dwelling on fantasies that he was a descendant of

King David. Jesus was pushed over the edge from latent to active paranoia by another paranoid, John the Baptist. Such delusions continued to build until Jesus had repeated hallucinations, beginning with his baptism, where he actually heard a voice that said he was the son of God. He further cemented his condition by going off into the wilderness to engage in forty more days of hallucination. From there he progressed to megalomania, with his sermons culminating in the single concept of "I AM," believing that all prophesy related to him. Charles Binet-Sanglé in his 1911 publication, *La Folie de Jésus,* concurred that Christ was a hallucinating religious paranoid, evasive and secretive, seized by "theomanic possession."[48]

As will be explored later, a similar psychiatric profile has been applied to Jeanne, with even more Freudian sexual convolutions. But concerning abnormally "normal" theories, Julian Jaynes explored ancient cultures and early symbols of man and his relationships with the gods, suggesting that there was a progressive transition from the right unconscious to the left conscious side of the brain. But this division of mind over matter was obtained at the cumulative expense of stress, caused by making decisions. Consciousness had a cumulative cost, a loss of unthought action dictated from the right side, taken over by the worrisome, progressively *angst*-ridden left side. Jaynes speculated whether current schizophrenia might be one of the residues of ancient voices trying to speak out.

Jaynes's bicameral physical mechanism is heretical. Indeed he tends to strain with spotty or selective proofs, occasionally rising to towering nonsequiturs. But as a dualistic explanation for insanity—the breakdown of consciousness—it would operate no differently from Freud or Jung's, in which the repressed subconscious is in rebellion with the I-am conscious, producing neurosis and psychosis. According to Jung:

> Insanity is possession by an unconscious content which, as such, is not assimilated to consciousness; nor

> can it be assimilated, since the conscious mind has denied the existence of such contents. Expressed in terms of religion, the attitude is equivalent to saying: "We no longer have any fear of God and believe that everything is to be judged by human standards." This hubris, this narrowness of consciousness, is always the shortest way to the insane asylum.[49]

Nor, as a few modern psychiatrists suggest, should hallucinatory voices always be labeled harmful. Some schizophrenics behave as if their voices were their only friend, even if scolding. If this seems inconsolably sad, Jung famously exclaimed over certain patients, "Thank God they became neurotic!"—which meant to him that something primal was nagging them, that all was not psychically balanced in their own mechanistic journey through existence. Jung and Freud themselves went through years of what they termed "creative illness" before emerging with their own novel theories. But some with "liberating" schizophrenia might get a bit carried away from social norms, at least according to a long-term patient interviewed on National Public Radio in 2002:

> Schizophrenia is a very individual and devious condition. I always have to make sure that I'm one step ahead of it, and take action when I see trouble coming. There's an awful price to pay if I don't. Having said that, it is also true to say that schizophrenia is like a two-edged coin. That is, there are positive and negative aspects. The trick is to extricate the one from the other. For instance, believing that you are Joan of Arc, or better still, Jesus Christ—as I have done—are extremely powerful and life-enhancing experiences. They are not just "rubbish," as one ignorant psychiatrist had commented to me. . . . Because of my delusions and hallucinations, I have done some things that I may not otherwise have done, like having outrageous affairs, taking my children on adven-

tures, coming out very publically as a bisexual lesbian, and becoming a poet and creative thinker.[50]

Neuroscientists now believe that the two hemispheres of the brain are split concerning perceptions of reality. Beyond the left dominant side being the "conscious" verbal articulator and the "silent" right side the mediator of spatial relationships, the right side also is more adept at grasping the gestalt of situations than the left side. In addition to—or is it apart from?—the dominant hemisphere's role of logical analysis, the right side is more facile at gauging perception. Put in psychological terms, if the left side is more coherent or "conscious," the right side seems more instinctual or "preconscious." One side sizes up what is said, the other silently decodes the body language behind the words.[51]

The right and left sides of the brain even appear to manifest different personae under adverse conditions. In 1977 tests were performed at the National Institutes of Health at Bethesda, Maryland, on over two dozen patients with temporal lobe epilepsy. They were divided into one group with seizures caused by pathological stimuli from the right temporal lobe, the other group with seizures initiated from the left temporal lobe. The majority of patients were not psychotic. Extensive profile tests were given, replete with tripwires to detect overt lying (yes or no: "I read every editorial in the newspaper"; "At elections, I never vote for anyone about whom I know very little"). Those with left-sided epilepsy tended to dwell on more cerebral preoccupations, such as religious matters and a sense of personal destiny ("I believe the Bible has special meaning which I can understand"). Those with right-sided epilepsy had a more primal emotional profile, dwelling on moods of elation and sadness. Left-sided patients tended toward paranoia, whereas right-sided patients were more inclined to manic-depression.

Additional support is given this implied split of consciousness and perception by experiments performed on patients who have had the main pathway of communication between the two hemispheres severed in an operation to correct epilepsy. In 1967 Dr. Roger Sperry of the California Institute of Technology marveled at the result: "Instead of the normally unified single stream of consciousness, these patients behave in many ways as if they have two *independent* streams of conscious awareness, one in each hemisphere, each of which is cut off from and out of contact with the mental experiences of the other."[52]

What might all of this have to do with Jeanne, a messianic teen in the fifteenth century? Could she possibly have heard voices of prophecy from the right side of the brain, speaking through the left? Julian Jaynes brought up the example of the Greek oracles, chosen from "young and simple persons," according to one description from the third century A.D. The unquestioned voices of the *Iliad* were by then an echo from over a thousand years before, in a largely conscious world struggling to retrieve them. Uneducated country adolescents became ideal mediums to train for priestesses at Delphi. Jaynes maintained that training was needed to bring the voices back more spontaneously, in a world by then awash in dialectics and early Christian theology—that is, conscious thought and reason.

At the legendary site at Delphi, a simple farmer's daughter would stand before the most learned of her day on a stone *omphalos* or navel, at the reputed center of the earth. Induced into a trance, the writhing oracle would speak of past and future things directly from the gods—*plena deo*: "from her frenzied mouth and with various contortions of her body," as one ancient described it: a description that reminded Jaynes of the symptoms of a temporal lobe seizure. No one doubted that the oracle was momentarily possessed, "for prophecy is a madness," Plato stated, "and the prophetess at Delphi and the priestesses at Dodona when out of their senses have conferred great benefits . . . but when in their senses few or none." Plato called such insanity "a divine gift, the source of the chief blessings granted to men." For him the word for the prophetic, *mantike*, and for madness, *manike*, were too close to form a clear distinction. During his famous trial ending in suicide, Socrates talked of his "demon" or voice that had been with him since childhood, telling him what to do, considering mental illness to be "the noble art." Aristotle wrote that creative types tended toward the *manike*: they were full of melancholia, which began to lead to a stigma. By Roman times individuals with such psychic powers progressively were viewed as evil. Degrees of epilepsy began the long transition from a gift of the ancient gods to the medieval curse of demonic possession.[53]

Although Jeanne was prone to raptures while in prayer, there is no evidence that she ever went into induced trances, spoke in tongues of things she knew not of, then popped back into consciousness. That role was assumed by shamans in Jeanne's time, and our own. But in strict scientific terms, what if the right side of the brain could be explored, made literally to speak? If Jeanne's brain could be opened and an electrode could stimulate her temporal lobes, who might appear? Saint Margaret and Saint Catherine? Yahweh or Greek gods?

Jeanne and Modern Brain Research

In 1963 Doctors Wilder Penfield and Phanor Perot published the results of such an experience, during operations to remove portions of the temporal lobe to correct temporal lobe epilepsy. Before surgical removal of the diseased portion, the area was stimulated with a mild electrical shock. "I was incredulous," Penfield exclaimed when he had first tried it thirty years before: there was a human response. "How could it be? This had to do with the mind! I called such responses 'experiential' and waited for more evidence." [54]

Over the decades more than six hundred patients had

similar stimulations over numerous areas of the brain, without voices or visions being evoked. Not one Jungian dream, Freudian nightmare, or Delphic prophecy appeared. "It is fair to say," Penfield observed, "that over the years every accessible part of the cortical mantle of the two hemispheres has been subjected to stimulation at one time or the other." Silence.

But when over five hundred patients had their outer temporal lobes stimulated, what appeared? Nothing at all in the majority. In forty patients, however, stimulating the temporal lobes incited combinations of voices and visions, set in dreamlike scenes with overtures of past experiences. One thirty-seven-year-old woman saw herself being born. A thirty-one-year-old stenographer exclaimed, "God said I am going to die." A fully conscious forty-six-year-old looked over at a male anaesthetist, who suddenly seemed like a female. "I almost spiritually spoke to that woman," the patient volunteered. This is not an ordinary figure of speech. A twenty-four-year-old woman heard voices calling her name before her seizures, usually from a man standing behind her, telling her to bend down. She also saw a small white cross moving in front of her eyes and was very frightened. When different sites in her temporal lobe were stimulated upon operation, she heard buzzing and murmurs at first, then perhaps a man murmuring, though she could not understand him. On restimulation she cried, "That man's voice again!" and began to sob. "The only thing I know is that my father frightens me a lot."

This study, selectively drawn upon by Jaynes, confuses more than buttresses his theory of the bicameral mind, although voices were over twice as likely to come from the right temporal lobe as the left. But the above experiences that I selectively picked occurred when the left—not the right—temporal lobe was stimulated. Indeed there was no discernible difference in the mystical profundity of such induced hallucinations from either side. Usually the voices and visions were prosaic and unfocused, and childhood memories predominated. A few visions were frightening. "There they go—yelling at me—stop them!" a fourteen-year-old girl begged when her posterior temporal lobe was stimulated. The angry voices lasted a full twenty-one seconds after stimulation stopped.

Anyone searching for some coherent pattern might conclude that the gods are musically inclined, indeed perhaps musicogenic. Fifteen patients heard tunes and melodies, distant but usually familiar: lullabies sung by their mothers, old radio theme songs, and the like. This occurred over four times more often when the right side was stimulated, conforming to the notion that musical abilities reside largely in the less verbal right hemisphere, the domain of spatial relationships, where musical and visual artistic abilities supposedly reside. A twenty-five-year-old French Canadian heard a tune from *The Life of Luigi,* and sang a portion for the operating staff. A nineteen-year-old male heard a song from *Guys and Dolls*. Before the operation his seizures were often brought on by music, especially modern jazz. A thirty-two-year-old had heard noises in the walls before her operation and seen visions of Rembrandt's painting, *The Night Watch,* as well as Christ coming down from the sky. When stimulated three different times in her right temporal lobe, she was treated to three renditions of "White Christmas." As was typical of such recitals, there was only the melody, without words, or perhaps with lyrics that the patient could not quite recall. They were just out of reach, as were most details on further inquiry."[54]

Despite that provocative start, subsequent studies provided less than meets the ear. At McGill University in Canada, probing-around both temporal lobes with electrodes induced mostly sensations of fear, discomfort, dizziness, nausea, changes in pulse and breathing, or alarming sensations in the chest, head, or abdomen—symptoms common to the patients just before an onset of seizure. Around half expressed a generally unpleasant spectrum of grimaces that registered distress, surprise, panic, anger, and sadness. Some hummed, whined, or cursed. Only two of seventy-five patients heard voices, neither profound. A minority had flashbacks and dream-like instances of *déjà vu.* One twenty-two-year-old man had repeated flashbacks regarding the fear of water, the first from when he was a child, and was held under water by someone bigger. When restimulated he recalled being in a strange place. "It was very spooky, but it was so far away. It was out by the sea and high up on a cliff, a feeling as if I were going to fall." On later stimulation he responded,"Yep, yep, yep, I am balancing on the edge of a fountain. I have often experienced this in *petit mals*. It is like I am in an old storybook. I am afraid to fall in the fountain."[55]

A comparable study at UCLA medical center in Los Angeles was also a rather silent experience, except for noises of clicking, buzzing, popping, and rare snippets of music. It did include more induced fear, dread, palpitations, pain, headaches, confusion, *déjà vu*, and occasional amnesia. After dozens of patients were stimulated over three thousand times in both temporal lobes, barely seven percent of the challenges evoked anything resembling a mental phenomenon—which curiously was the same percentage found by Penfield and Perot. One patient recalled a soap opera and some program about astronauts, which seemed "like a dream, a weird dream." More stimuli evoked a past trip to Yosemite National Park, lying on the couch watching television, a telephone conversation, her son's first day in school, and drinking a soft drink once in a small town: not very Olympian experiences. A twenty-four-year-old woman heard something said in Spanish. When probed with progressively stronger electricity in her right temporal lobe, she remarked that she felt bad, then felt like crying. When repeated nausea followed a clicking noise after thirty more stimuli, she finally displayed anger. Small wonder. To the doctors in California, emotions like fear or anger were more a reflection of the subject's previous personality, not some new manifestation induced by pushing mysterious old buttons common to all humanity.[56]

In a Japanese study, doctors stimulated the surface and deeper portions of the temporal lobe in chronic schizophrenic patients. Around half rendered up vocal or visual responses—all different from the hallucinations they already had experienced—although some of the responses suffer from translation across East-West cultures. Before stimulation one oriental schizophrenic heard a persistent voice announcing, "Formosa is bombed. Chiang Kai-Chek is killed by the women's army." When the temporal cortex was stimulated this message disappeared, only to return anew after the operation. During the experiment the vision of a man with a rice bag appeared, wearing an apron. Another heard his old voice scolding, "You are the worst schizophrenic. You shall be sent to a syphilis village!" Stimulation induced a new voice: "Isn't it so strange? Splendid, splendid." After the operation the new message was, "See? Go and talk to the dead." Most experienced a temporary diminishment of such disjointed experiences for a few weeks after operation, perhaps a minireplication of the effects of convulsive electro-shock therapy, still beneficial in extreme cases of psychosis.[57]

Despite this worldwide evidence following the experiments of Penfield and Perot, Julian Jaynes still disagreed with the collective conclusion that such nebulae are merely flashbacks to earlier days. Instead he drew his own conclusion to fit his sweeping theory: "The important thing about almost all these stimulation-caused experiences is their *otherness,* their opposition from the self, rather than the self's own actions, or own words. With a few exceptions, the patients never experienced eating, talking, sex, running, or playing. In almost all instances, the subject was passive and being acted upon, exactly as a bicameral man was acted upon by his voices."[58]

Was Jeanne acted upon? Yes, from voices outside of her own volition, she repeatedly maintained, despite skeptical modern interpreters who theorize that she only made them up to fit her purpose. Her voices were supreme, entities apart from her self, which she by her own will disagreed with, argued with, and disobeyed when the occasion demanded. Schizophrenics cannot do that: they are submissive and resigned for a multitude of theoretical reasons. A whole clinic full of them could not combine to get through one week of Jeanne's documented career.

If the voices did not come to Jeanne from an outside source, as they biblically came to Abraham and Moses, could they still have originated from somewhere inside her brain, but beyond her will and control? One must return to the untenable diagnosis of schizophrenia to ponder this possibility in modern times. Six patients were studied in 1995 using P.E.T. scans, which track blood flow in different areas of the brain when they are in animation. The patients were told to press a button when they heard their voices. "How horrible," "Don't act stupid," was the recurring message that haunted two patients. P.E.T. scans were recorded multiple times during such episodes, producing a form of color photograph of the brain in action. Even pushing the button caused the appropriate motor-controlling area on the left dominant hemisphere to brighten; all six pressed the button with the right thumb. When non-schizophrenics hear actual voices, only the auditory areas are activated along the outside of the temporal lobes—those same areas that light up on hearing a car horn. But in the schizophrenic subjects the zone that lit up when their voices spoke were areas deeper in the temporal lobe, structures related to the midbrain—as if *initiated* from there—not from an outside source. Similar studies have shown minor variations in brain geography, but they nevertheless support the central point that voices of hallucination begin from inside the brain, not outside.

What did not *normally* light up also intrigued the investigators: the prefrontal lobes, located just before the lobes at the very front of the brain that represent the highest integrative areas, that finally define the conscious person as individuals.

It is that area which receives information and then decides to act, like jumping back on hearing a taxi horn, or quitting one's job after due deliberation. One might decide not to quit the job. For personal reasons one might *choose*—decide—not to get out of the way of a taxi. But the vital prefrontal areas appear to monitor input sent forward from the temporal areas and midbrain to make this decision, serving as a reality check, before perception is cleared to the executive branch in the frontal lobes proper.

Perhaps absence of prefrontal lobe censorship makes schizophrenics confuse internal voices with real, physical stimuli. Perhaps we all are bombarded with the same internal demons of schizophrenia, but normally censor them out before they reach the "reality" of our conscious frontal lobes. Perhaps the schizophrenic is actively creating the "external" voices through normal subvocal speech, but cannot tune it out. Perhaps. Regardless, the result is the same: "The brain is creating its *own* reality," concluded David Silbersweig, one of the international investigators in a cooperative study between New York and London. "If I could design the perfect experiment," Jay Ingram, a Canadian science journalist, wrote on the subject of Jeanne, "I'd persuade Saint Joan of Arc to sit for a P.E.T. scan. . . . Maybe those images would come up with a single 'hot' area in her brain that is not visibly active in brains that are not hallucinating. Perhaps that site would be in the temporal lobe. . . . A fine-resolution brain scan might just reveal circuits for saints' voices burned into Saint Joan's brain."[59]

Perhaps, maybe, which is as far as science can go to date. Creating one's own reality returns to the core of divorce from reality, where Freud's libido and Jung's psychic energy create a world of nonreality, for no clear reason. But does this explain anything in Jeanne's world? Apparently not. Her visions were more vivid, continuous, and complex, more profound than a voice merely repeating "don't act stupid," or even some recurrent voice thundering "Obey God!" And if a fictional Hamlet would not qualify as a schizophrenic today, much less so would the real Jeanne. She might prick initial concern as a schizophrenic because of her visions; and even her judges—in an age of visions—were beside themselves in wanting to know more in that regard. Beneath the tricks and traps of their inquiries lay abject curiosity. In the unremitting day-to-day testimony they revealed their begoggled humanity in the presence of someone truly extraordinary, not of this world. Simultaneously Jeanne unrelentingly revealed herself as someone fallibly human—normal—quite of this world in and of herself, possessing no other gifts than the gift of her voices. She could think on her feet, reason, question, remember, retort, give as good as she got, feel and express emotions to the core. Schizophrenics are incapable of this. They are flat, confused, and helpless, fractured from reality.

Jeanne Ravaged on the Freudian Couch

At least one modern therapist has flatfootedly diagnosed Jeanne as a chronic paranoid schizophrenic, putting his main conclusion in italics:

> Often these patients have a clear-cut delusional system which is not open to argument, and their hallucinations reinforce their false ideas. *They know they are right in what they say and do, and have divine messages to prove it.* . . . This sort of obstinate belief that there is no question of doubt that she had heard the voices and that they were from saints with divine instructions clearly indicate that she was deluded.[60]

Biblical prophets—forewarned! Generally ignored by others who also edge up to this psychotic finality are small but significant details concerning the reaction of the bedeviled subject, when reacting with what are defined today as psychotic hallucinations. Compared to Jeanne, few patients experience voices as pleasant. Compared to Jeanne, few psychotics talk back to their voices. Compared to Jeanne and the private intimacy of her voices, over ninety-percent of schizophrenics hear their voices even when others are around. Most also have insomnia—never noted in Jeanne who, if anything, would be considered sleepyheaded on several occasions. For one example, she overslept the main assault of Orléans.[61]

Jeanne's unflagging characteristics are not those of schizophrenia, nor of temporal lobe epilepsy, nor do they fit any other modern classification of sustained mental illness. Psychiatrist Fred Henker of the University of Arkansas Hospital intellectually put her through the hoops using the *1980 Diagnostic and Statistical Manual of the American Psychiatric Association.* Concerning manic-depressive disease, criteria needed to make a diagnosis are: over one week of hyperactivity, talkativeness, flight of ideas, inflated self-esteem, decreased need for sleep, distractibility, or excessive dangerous activity (Jeanne would only seriously qualify on the last score). Concerning transsexual or psychosexual disorders, she would not qualify because she was not so uncomfortable with her own sex that she tried to physically eliminate it. To her death she was defiantly La Pucelle, daughter of God. As for qualifying as a transvestite, the modern criterion defines this designation as applying only to males.[62]

Not that such would explain anything if it were accurate. The question of lesbianism has been proffered before, based on Jeanne's asexual or androgynous character, her preference for sleeping with young girls over older women, her intense childhood friendship with Hauviette before leaving Domremy. In fact Jeanne received the full-drill Freudian treatment by a British psychoanalyst in the good old days of 1933, who diagnosed her as going through a strong homosexual stage full of masculine acting-out—probably an unconscious manifestation of penis envy. Allow Dr. Roger Money-Kyrle to explain, even though, as he excuses us from understanding, "those who have not been analyzed cannot expect to have any direct insight into the truth of Freud's conclusions."

> The visions themselves seem to have begun, when we might expect them, at the age of puberty—at the time when those early sexual impulses, which are regularly repressed by the Oedipus complex, are re-animated in the unconscious by the imperative demands of endocrine development. . . . Psycho-analysts are familiar with such conditions, and they know that when a religious patient is unable to remove the sense of sin by innumerable confessions, this sin is to be found in their old friend the Oedipus complex. . . . The super-ego is not content that the ego should sin no more; it demands that restitution should be made for past sins which cannot be undone . . . all deep analyses show clearly that the [Alfred] Adlerian "masculine protest" is only the semi-conscious expression of the Freudian "penis envy." . . . Jeanne, in her infancy, had a negative Oedipus complex. Like many little girls she coveted the phallus of her brothers or her father, but repressed this desire and reacted against it with guilt. Therefore her super-ego imposed upon her the task of restoring what she had wished to take. This task she symbolically fulfilled; for she it was alone who caused her Dauphin to be crowned. All analysts must have had patients with almost identical ideas.[63]

So there! For Dr. Money-Kyrle the crown is a phallic symbol—not a cigar, as you were previously led to believe. Beyond this ersatz-comic assessment befitting a Woody Allen parody, even considering a cluster of borderline personality disorders not characterized by visions, Jeanne does not fit multiple pyschotic criteria: maladaptivity, antisocial behavior, inappropriate anger, boredom, apathy, fear of loneliness, histrionic tendencies, narcissism, egocentricity, exhibitionism, vanity, shallowness, exploitativeness, lack of empathy, tendency to be crushed by criticism or defeat, proneness to manipulative suicidal threats. In understatement, Dr. Henker did assess her as "somewhat obsessive," messianic, and religiously driven.

Neuroscience is progressing on an uncharted frontier, far beyond post-Freudian theories. Electrical sensations are reaching toward God, or at least parlor tricks that push subjects past mundane normalcy into something resembling religious abnormalcy. The Internet brims with sites expounding the "parapsychology of God," replete with something called psi factor, implying that all humans have untapped extrasensory perception. Real scientists are probing subjects to locate some "God module" in the brain. Chasing consciousness to its highest source has been the obsession of the 1990s, bounding into the twenty-first century. Brain scans of Buddhist monks in meditation are being studied to watch the brain's electrical travels (clue: they turn off areas related to normal orientation in space). A few—precisely three—patients with temporal lobe epilepsy have been given word association tests to demonstrate religious hypersensitivity, compared to normal subjects, who respond more strongly to the subject of sex: score one for Freud. In Canada a psychologist has devised a magnetic helmet that can send avid subjects on out-of-body temporal lobe trips. The stock of Julian Jaynes is on the rise with each outburst of "Otherness." Franz Mesmer must be smiling somewhere over the continuum of his eighteenth-century magnetic swoons.

Edgy theologians are becoming quotable in the press. The Vatican is contemplating a conference to consider the implications of brain research. A turf war for the elusive soul is brewing. "A modern neuroscientist has no need for the religious concept of a soul to explain the behavior of humans and animals," stated Nobel laureate Francis Crick, codiscoverer of the molecular structure of DNA. "Not all neuroscientists believe the concept of the soul is a myth—but the majority do." Not all neuroscientists agree. "Most of my colleagues basically see religion as a sort of pathological state," noted neuropsychiatrist Angela Hegarty of New York University. "That is terrible thinking." Until 1994, "strong religious belief" was listed as a mental disorder in orthodox psychiatric manuals.[64]

CONCLUSION

The search will continue, and ever more revealing brain nebulae will lead to ever more intriguing questions. But the nonmaterial answer will always remain just out of scientific reach, as it did for Aristotle and Aquinas: Did God create the brain—or did the brain create God? Which prime mover is playing the music to the dance of existence? A child could predict the future accommodation. Instead of wailing and vitriol for coming decades, there will be growing harmony between science and religion, routinely reported in the popular press. The definition of God will become progressively acceptable to scientists, because they will provide the definition: See, it's all in your head. Theology will return to the nineteenth century, sighing that—after all—God was only the internal expression of mankind's highest aspirations. There will be universal happy talk. Long live God, because God is us. But then some old-time theologian, like another teutonic Karl Barth from the twentieth century, will come along and spoil the dance. He or she will raise a fiery finger to heaven and declare that God is an *external* force, sort of (but never really) of our comprehension, and that we must accept this *a posteriori,* or not at all. If anyone is still listening, we will return to the old miasma of debate and mystery. The death of God will no longer be an issue, but the terms of His nature will always be tossed around, which is never a bad thing.

Civilization has been captivated by the final answer, invariably filling in one that works in the meantime. One thus returns to the same groping for rational explanation of Jeanne d'Arc's voices in the early twentieth century, among dissenting if intrigued searchers like George Bernard Shaw:

> What then is the modern view of Joan's voices and visions and messages from God? The nineteenth century said that they were delusions, and it must be assumed that she was the innocent dupe of such delusions. The twentieth century finds this explanation too vapidly commonplace, and demands something *more mystic*. I think the twentieth century is right, because an explanation which amounts to Joan being mentally defective instead of, as she obviously was, mentally excessive, will not wash. (italics added)[65]

Something more mystic? The modern schism for Shaw and most of us is that the mystical explanation lies not in the physical, but the metaphysical, a realm that science *de facto* has declared does not exist. Jeanne's religious defenders believe that this realm does exist. With a few middling exceptions, neither side concedes much to the other, particularly science, whose certainties border on blind arrogance. Anatole France, Mark Twain, and George Bernard Shaw articulate the only rational explanations for Jeanne's experience. It has proven disappointing, for them and for us. A minority of scholars believe that Jeanne had a metaphysical experience, like Régine Pernoud, her awesome synthesizer who founded the Centre Jeanne d'Arc in Orléans. Other searchers like Vita Sackville-West and Marina Warner stop short of this, but have enough common sense to maintain, *ipso facto,* that Jeanne's voices came from outside of herself. This is a pie in the face to Shaw's inner "commonsense" that he ascribed to Jeanne—for him the only acceptable source of her inspirations. Yet too many scientists and the psychiatrically inclined muddle on in the school of Shaw, although at least some of them provide unintentional comic relief. Witness the "diagnosis" of Dr. Roger Money-Kyrle: Jeanne d'Arc as hapless tool of penis envy.

How prophetic are the words of the biblical Paul: "Claiming to be wise, they became fools, and exchanged the glory of the immortal God for images resembling mortal man or birds or animals or reptiles."

The central problem for the modern age is that we believe that we are too sophisticated—too enlightened—to believe, to truly accept what France, Twain, and Shaw equally dismissed as religious mumbo-jumbo. Most willingly tolerate religion as a form of style, practice it themselves, literally by over a billion Christians worldwide, and still more billions who are not Christian. But style is not the issue; substance is. Post-Enlightenment dogma will not accept intrusion of the metaphysical into the so-called *de facto* substance of the physical world. In a disdain that masks primal fears, we ignore it, pervert it, or try to explain it away with shoddy science, or *a priori* intellectual hocus-pocus. But it is in this *combined* realm where Jeanne d'Arc dwelled: physically normal in this world, but magnificently directed by something metaphysical beyond this world, resulting in her tragic death that we cannot tolerate. I am no different, and weep with Mark Twain, shaking my puny fist along with George Bernard Shaw. I cannot humanly encompass this tragedy myself, except to contemplate the consistent, tragic, biblical formula, extending from Job to Jesus, *a posteriori*: It is because it was. God's will be done, for some higher purpose far beyond our dreams or finite imagination.

By faith the religious have always believed that there is life after life, something far more mysterious than meets our transient eye. Another world, a parallel universe, a transmigration of souls—something else—but life is not the end. All civilizations have believed this throughout recorded history. Over one hundred thousand years before the pharaohs, Neanderthal man provided his buried kindred with clothing and utensils, as if they might prove useful somewhere else. But this is a metaphysical interpretation, a prayer. Death is the horizon of life, but only that horizon which blocks our vision. "The past, present, and future are only illusions," Albert Einstein noted—"even if *stubborn* ones." As he memorably concluded,

"God does not throw dice."

In her terminal despair, Jeanne recalled her voices toward the last: "'Have no care for your martyrdom, for in the end you shall enter the Kingdom of Paradise.' *They have told me this simply, absolutely, and without fail.*" But if we fail to take these words seriously, then we are in jeopardy of never finding Jeanne. We will never really understand Jeanne, but only categorize her out of our existence as a religious embarrassment. In high dudgeon too many scholars have not even allowed Jeanne to be religious on her own terms. They have willfully mauled her own testament to fit their prejudice, no less than her judges at Rouen in 1431. Therein lies her second tragic destruction.

Our hearts follow Jeanne, but our minds resist. In Karen Sullivan's stellar and objective work, *The Interrogation of Joan of Arc,* she honestly conceded her own educational bias. Few others do so, although it is implicit in our collective post-Enlightenment approach:

> Literate, and indeed, academically trained, I necessarily share the clerics' own valorization of logical analysis, rationality, and objectivity. Skeptical of claims to direct contact with a metaphysical realm of reality, I necessarily share their suspicions about Joan's claims to have heard voices from God. Institutionally authorized as a college professor, as they were themselves institutionally authorized as university masters, I necessarily partake in their desire to teach and advise those who might seem to benefit from this instruction. . . . I can attempt to keep in mind the cultural bias this role implies. Even if I cannot transcend the mentality of the educated, I can attempt to remain conscious of what is *excluded* by this mentality. (italics added)[66]

Over a century and a half ago, Jules Michelet lamented the early transition from medieval devotion toward modern despair in *Jeanne d' Arc.* Some believe he remains the most moving interpreter of her essence. Michelet spoke for himself and his new age, with one foot in antique belief, the other stretching toward a fearful future. "We may boast as proudly as we please," Michelet wrote in the 1840s, "we philosophers and rationalists of the present age. But who among us, amid the agitations of the modern world, or in the voluntary servitude of research, in its harsh and lonely quest, who can hear without emotion the sound of these lovely Christian festivals, the voice of the bells touching our hearts, like a mother's gentle reproof? . . . The mind remains firm, but the soul is sad unto death."[67]

God is dead: Friedrich Nietzsche, 1882
Nietzsche is dead: God, 1900

"Our souls are restless, until they find their rest in Thee." So expressed St. Augustine a millennium and a half ago. Eight hundred years later, Thomas Aquinas still acknowledged this same unknowable restlessness, *angustia*, capturing an ever-modern sense of distress and *angst*. The process anticipated existentialism, four hundred years before Descartes let the cat out of the bag with *cogito ergo sum*. "Human beings are directed to God as an end," Aquinas reasoned in *Summa Theologiae*, "that surpasses the grasp of their reason." As Blaise Pascal timelessly expressed, "the heart has its reasons, which reason can never know."

Modern Reason? Science? Objectivity? Truth? All medical explanations have been delved, and all are found wanting, some laughably inadequate by both scientists and pseudo-scientists.

MENE MENE TEKEL UPHARSIN

By Aristotelian logic—spanning three millennia of mankind's maturing logical analysis, rationality, and objectivity—

this leaves us with the single impossible possibility for the source of Jeanne d'Arc's voices. God.

But it is unlikely that the Almighty will submit to intellectual probes and brain scans in His own defense:

For My thoughts are not your thoughts, neither are your ways My ways, says the Lord.

Isaiah 55:8[68]

Notes

Chapter One: Go! Go on! I Will be Your Help—Go on!

1. Beginning of trial, Scott, pp. 63–64, Feb. 21, 1431. Testimony from the Rouen trial is mainly from the translation by W. S. Scott, *The Trial of Joan of Arc*. The second trial transcript utilized is T. Douglas Murray, *Jeanne D'Arc, Maid of Orleans*. The third trial translation consulted is W. P. Barrett, *The Trial of Jeanne d'Arc*. This book includes an additional section on the trial background by Pierre Champion, translated by Coley Taylor and Ruth H. Kerr. Copious information is also available from the Joan of Arc Center website in Albuquerque, New Mexico, directed by Virginia Frohlick, available through both "Google" and "Yahoo" search modes.

The fifteenth-century background of the trial transcripts all derive from various versions in French, translated into Latin several years after Jeanne's death in 1431. They were probably not transcribed before 1435. At least five copies were made, one of which was officially destroyed after Jeanne's trial of Reclamation, around 1456. According to the testimony of Martial d'Auvergne, one copy was sent to Rome, one to Orléans, and one to Paris. Another copy apparently was intended for the king of England, then pre-adolescent. The various trial records show no substantial differences, according to Pierre Champion, considered the greatest twentieth-century collator. In comparing these three complete versions in English, I have found no differences of fact or substance. There are occasional elaborations by one version or the other on the same factual matter. When it seems helpful to add an amplification from one version to another, I have done so, in an attempt to convey as much information as possible. These amplifications are specified in my reference notes whenever I do so.

My depiction of Jeanne's physical appearance is conjectural, as it has been for everyone who has gone before me. No likeness of her exists, despite lingering historical teasers. Every several decades her armor is "rediscovered" as some physical beginning, the most recent case being an *ultra-petite* Parisian claim in 1996, fitting the antique dealer's adolescent daughter. This latest claim is being presently dismissed by Joanastic scholars. Who knows? In her own time Jeanne was described in several voyeuristic male vignettes as having carnal breasts, along with an appealing feminine voice. The only clue to her real appearance might exist literally in a single dark brown hair, stuck in the wax seal of one of her letters, since vanished into the hand of some souvenir hunter. One may envision Jeanne as tall, fair, and beautiful, a trend of the nineteenth century. In the twentieth century the trend has changed toward short, dark, and not remarkably handsome. There appears to be no recorded factual basis for either. She was alluring enough to have survived several molestation attempts by her enemies, as well as to induce lust in the hearts of devout followers, who uniformly were too awestricken to attempt consummation. Certainly Jeanne d'Arc had charisma, the name history remembers her by, although she herself neither heard nor used that designation in her lifetime.

2. Scott: cut off head, 63, Feb. 21; revelation, 66, Feb. 22; not tell all, 71, Feb. 24. Background of Jean Beaupère, Régine Pernoud and Marie-Véronique Clin, *Joan of Arc: Her Story*, 207–08.

3. Scott, first vision, 67, Feb. 22; amplifications from Murray, Feb. 22.

4. "False mysticism," theologian Jean Gerson, Deborah A. Fraioli, *Joan of Arc; The Early Debate*, 21; Gerson on Christ

flying through the air and discussion of theology in the streets, Dyan Elliott, "Seeing Double," 29, 33; execution of diviner Jeanne de Brigue, invoker of the devil with toads, Jan R. Veenstra, *Magic and Divination at the Courts of Burgundy and France,"* 78–80; background on visionaries and sorcerers, Ann LLewellyn Barstow, *Joan of Arc,* 33–40, and on witches, 101–02; sabbats and witches, Marina Warner, *Joan of Arc*, 128–29; *nouer l'aiguillette*, to make men impotent with the "Knot," Bernard Barnett, "Witchcraft, Psychopathology, and Hallucinations," *British Journal of Psychiatry* 3 (1965): 439–45. For an extensive examination of the theology and scholasticism behind the corporal aspects of impotence, witches, and the devil since the time of Thomas Aquinas, see Walter Stephens, "Witches Who Steal Penises," 495–529.

5. Scott, Fairies' tree, 74–76, Feb. 24; additions from Murray, Feb. 24.

6. Scott: voices unclear, 86, Mar. 1; godmother and fairies, 123, Mar. 17. Merlin legend, Fraioli, 62–64.

7. Scott, mandrake, 87–88, Mar. 1; W. P. Barrett, 74, Mar. 1; reviving infant, Scott, 96, Mar. 3; amplification from Murray, Mar. 3.

8. Scott, sword and standard, 81–82, Feb. 27; amplifications on sword from Murray, Feb. 27; Scott, on going boldly, 93, Mar. 3; on butterflies, 95, Mar. 3; did Jeanne hate Burgundians? Barrett, 53, Feb. 24.

9. Scott: first mention of St. Michel, 78–79, Feb. 27; save France, 67, Feb. 22; leave parents, 104–05, Mar. 12; pledge virginity, 103–04, Mar. 12.

10. Scott: St. Michel told Jeanne to be a good girl, 67, Feb.22, also 120, Mar. 15; St. Catherine and St. Margaret, 77–78, Feb. 27, also 85, Mar. 1.

11. Scott: what parts she saw, hair, etc., 85–86, Mar. 1; hanged for telling the truth, 73, Feb. 24, also 121, Mar. 15. Background of saints, Warner, 132–36.

12. Scott: do saints speak English? 86, Mar. 1; hate English?

123, Mar. 17; seven-year prophesy, 84, Mar. 1; prophesy of wound, 83, Feb.27; Had Jeanne ever defeated the English?, testimony of Jean Tiphaine.

13. Scott: not told to take Paris, 110, Mar. 13; capture before St. John's Day, 99, Mar. 10. "Daughter of God, go on," testimony of Count de Dunois, Pernoud, *Joan of Arc*, 131; description of Charles, Pernoud and Clin, 79; evidence of some efforts, versus none at all, by Charles to retrieve Jeanne from captivity provided by Pierre Champion, in supplement to trial transcript by Barrett, 389–90.

The most intractable and influential opponent to Jeanne in Charles's court was Regnault de Chartres, Archbishop of Reims, who presided first over her theological examination at Poitiers, and then at the coronation of Charles VII. He was brilliant and well respected by both competing parties, and acted as the ultimate diplomat who patched France back together after Jeanne's death. Both sides held legitimately different opinions over how to save their country: one by war, the other by negotiation.

14. Letter of Henry VI, Scott, 52, Jan. 3, 1430; accusation of round device over helmet at Jargeau, Barrett, 80, Mar. 3; popular adulation and rings, Scott, 94–95, 132, Mar. 3, 27; I am sent from God, 94, Mar. 3; allegation of children with candles, Elliott, 49–50.

15. Scott: prayer to Christ, 140, Mar. 28; daily contact with voices, 71–72, Feb. 24.

16. Background on the University of Paris and the plight of Rome, Pierre Champion, supplement to Barrett transcript, 484–87, 492–95; also by Barbara W. Tuchman, *A Distant Mirror*, 160, 250–51.

17. Letter from University of Paris to John of Luxembourg, Scott, 49–50, July 14, 1430; letter from Pierre Cauchon to John of Luxembourg, Karen Sullivan, *Interrogation of Joan of Arc*, 109; background of Pierre Cauchon, Vita Sackville-West, *Saint Joan of Arc*, 259–60.

18. Background of judges, Scott, 10–11, Sackville-West, 272–74; list of judges, Sackville-West, 347–53; protest from Jeanne, 279.

19. Scott, God's grace, 73–74, Feb. 24; question, testimony of Jean Lefevre, Pernoud, *The Retrial of Joan of Arc*, 196.

20. Jeanne confused, but answers boldly, Scott, 77, Feb. 27; did not always answer questions, testimony of Nicolas Taquel, rector in diocese of Rouen, Pernoud, *The Retrial of Joan of Arc*, 191.

21. Listens closely to voices, light, Scott, 112, Mar. 14; not recognizing at first, 78, Feb. 27; half-asleep, 72, Feb. 24.

22. Jean Le Maître and "the serenity of his soul," Barrett, 29; general background of Poitiers trial, Fraioli, first assessment at Chinon and Poitiers, *discretio spirituum*, 2; Jeanne "devout, sober, temperate, chaste," 17; Charles might appear ridiculous, 18; Jeanne a possible assassin, 20; evil must make visible eruption, 21; God has power to make revelation, outwit devil by outwaiting him, 22; will be challenged at Poitiers, 45–46; "spiritual moneychangers," Jean Gerson, 47; debated like a second St. Catherine, 49; risk of repelling the Holy Spirit, 207; St. Jerome on Gaul, 14, 91; Amos 7:15, 1 Corinthians 1:27. Sullivan: on *signum*, 62; Moses and John the Baptist, 65; *monstrum, prodigium, portentum, miraculum,* 80. Sackville-West, "I have not come to Poitiers to perform signs," etc., 127–30.

23. Sackville-West, historical background of Charles and Anglo-French politics, 14–20.

24. Embraced from below, Scott, 127, Mar. 17.

25. Scott: St. Michel naked? 88, Mar. 1; loss of virginity? 126, Mar. 17. Physical differences between angels and demons, Warner, 128–30; background on sabbats, the devil, incubi, H. R. Trevor-Roper, *Religion, the Reformation and Social Change,* 92–96; further theological background on physical reality of demons, Stephens, 495–529; *Nullus Deus sine diabolo,* no God without the devil, p. 505; other background from Tuchman, 318–19.

The preacher of apocalypse was named Brother Richard, whom Jeanne met at Troyes. Burgundians claimed that she was actually one of his followers, Vita Sackville-West, *Saint Joan of Arc,* 205–07; also Régine Pernoud, *Joan of Arc,* 145. Jeanne's description of their meeting, Scott, 93, Mar. 3.

26. Scott: do saints have heads? 90, Mar. 3; do saints send letters? 105, Mar. 12. Jean Gerson on proper function of angels, Veenstra, 175.

27. Trial format, Scott, 12; Sullivan, *The Interrogation of Joan of Arc,* 93–96; incapable of error, 5; church in council cannot err, Scott, 122, Mar. 17; "Must I tell you that?" Barrett, 52, Feb.24; Cauchon and personal knowledge of the law, H. Ansgar Kelly, "The Right to Remain Silent: Before and After Joan of Arc," *Speculum*, 68 (Oct. 1993): 1009.

Exhaustive background on the mentality of witchcraft and its persecution was provided by Jules Michelet, *Satanism and Witchcraft: The Classic Study of Medieval Superstition.* This work is a gem for feminist historians, full of insights and examples of repression and the often surprising medieval rationale behind it, exploring dark avenues even of popular incest among the masses. Reading between the lines, much of the primal framework appears mutually erotic. Michelet wrote as if in the post-1960s, instead of the pre-1860s, fast and loose and baroque in his French flamboyance. All in all, *vive Michelet.* A more recent and exquisitely documented work covering most of the same ground is Veenstra's *Magic and Divination at the Courts of Burgundy and France.* If one wishes to trace myth and theology from Aristotle to Aquinas leading to fifteenth-century sorcery, this is the work, brilliantly expressed. If French and Latin are not your first language, like myself, unfortunately long and important segments appear without English translation.

Aspects of the trial format are a compendium of excesses spanning five hundred years, varying by century and country. For example, Satan did not appear as a direct conduit of heresy until the thirteenth century. Although thousands were executed as heretics before the fifteenth century, mass execution of witches by the thousands began a half-century or so after Jeanne's death in 1431, reaching a zenith in the sixteenth and seventeenth centuries. Although the spectrum was the same, degrees of ferocity waxed and waned according to century and locale. Four witches burned in Paris during Jeanne's time appeared a remarkable number, whereas four hundred burned in one French, German, Swiss, or English province would be unremarkable by the following century. Michelet admitted the difficulty in precisely dating the beginning of the process. Yet French historian and novelist Anatole France seemed to telescope everything. He claimed that all of Jeanne's judges had helped burn dozens of witches, amounting to hundreds or even thousands, before showing up at Rouen. His documentation would prove interesting. In fact most of Jeanne's trial appeared a showcase of moderation, even through the over-protracted result of burning her as a heretic and sorceress. The finest tools of medieval highest civilization were amply applied, often fairly, leading to a larger truth that Anatole France maintained: Most of the clerics wished to judge well at Rouen. I share his general assessment, with the exception of repeated occasions on which the judges knowingly played unfairly, for palpable political reasons. George Bernard Shaw utilized this tragic paradox to deadly effect in his play *Saint Joan*. Arthur Miller attained the same effect in *The Crucible,* in which righteousness executes innocence according to the same rules.

28. Beware of judging me, Scott, 70, 72, 113, Feb. 24, Mar. 14: amplification from Barrett, 51, Feb. 24.

29. Refusal to recite the Pater Noster, Scott, 65, Feb. 21; escape in three months? 87, Mar. 1; God's will be done, 90–91, Mar. 3; God helps those who help themselves, 117, Mar. 15.

30. Male attire, Deuteronomy 22:5; short hair, 1 Corinthians, 11:6; Sullivan, medieval aspects of cross-dressing, 45–52;

Scott, male dress needed, 68, Feb. 22; God commanded male dress, Scott, 79–80, Feb. 27; Barrett, 61, Feb. 27; evasive on command to wear male dress, Scott, 91–92, Mar. 3; everything good that I did, 106, Mar. 12.

31. Scott, *passez outre*, 69, Feb. 22; did not see angel, 80, Feb. 27; must not perjure self, 89, Mar. 1; angel with crown and three hundred witnesses, 101–02, Mar. 10; amplifications on perjuring self from Barrett, 48, 51, Feb. 24.

32. Scott, angels invisible among Christian folk, 105, Mar. 12.

33. Scott, extensive story of the sign to Charles, 107–10, Mar. 13.

34. Background on the *Ars Notoria* from Jan R. Veenstra, 70–71, 146–47.

35. "It seems to me," instead of "I am certain," Jean Lohier to Guilluame Manchon, in Pernoud, *Joan of Arc*, 241; testimony from Guillaume Duval about his and Isambard de la Pierre's attempts to guide Jeanne's early testimony, Pernoud, *The Retrial of Joan of Arc*, 198.

36. Scott: destruction of Compiègne, rather die than be prisoner of English, 111–12, Mar. 14; told not to jump, surrender to God's will, 97–98, Mar. 3; wrong to jump, but not a suicide attempt, forgiven, 15, Mar. 14.

37. Scott: sign by deliverance from prison, 102, Mar. 10; it must happen so, 99, Mar. 10; please our Lord to be captured, 103, Mar. 12; will enter heaven, 113, Mar. 14.

38. Scott: salvation a great treasure, 113, Mar. 14; still needs to cleanse soul in confession, 114, Mar. 14.

39. Scott: which is the true pope? 84, Mar. 1; take trial to Rome, 126, Mar. 17, also 149, May 2, and 163, May 24; had transgressed faith of Christ? 118, Mar. 15; obey God over church, 122, Mar. 17; Jeanne did not understand distinction between Church Militant and Triumphant, testimony of Jean Massieu, Pernoud, *The Retrial of Joan of Arc*, 189–90.

40. Background of moving trial to Jeanne's prison on Mar.

10, Murray, Mar. 4; why do you make such a difficulty? Mar. 17.

41. Text of Articles of Indictment, Sackville-West, 289–90; also Murray, Mar. 27–28.

42. Article two (captured in *flagrante delicto* in continued witchcraft); Article four (taught her religion by witches and fairies); Articles five and six (witchcraft around the Fairies' tree); Article seven (the mandrake); Article eight (sleeping with whores and soldiers); Article eleven (boasting of siring children by the Holy Spirit); Murray, Mar. 27; further personal details of charges from Barrett, 144–55, Mar. 27, 28.

43. Scott, submit to church in heaven alone, 131–32, Mar. 27, and 148, May 2; prior answers of Jeanne read to her, to avoid later denial, Mar. 24, Kelly, 1019; on prior objection of Jean Lohier about no council for Jeanne, 1018.

44. Scott: Jeanne on womanly duties, 135, Mar. 27; charge of false prophet, 143, Mar. 28; "by their fruits ye shall know them," Matthew 7: 16–20.

45. Scott: buried in consecrated ground, will die a good Christian, 146–47, Apr. 18; "Let him be unto thee as a heathen," Matthew, 18: 17: exchange about poisoning and whore insult with Master Jean Estivet, testimony of Jean Tiphaine and Guillaume de la Chambre, in Pernoud and Clin, 125.

46. Scott, dangerous curiosity and St. Michel, p. 120, Mar. 15; Gerson on female curiosity, Elliott, 29; demons disguised as angels, 2 Corinthians 11: 13–15; Aquinas on imitative powers of Satan, Michelet, *Satanism and Witchcraft*, 140; legend of Satan at Cluny monastery, Warner, 101; further background on implications of *curiositas*, Sullivan, *Interrogation of Joan of Arc*, 51–53; Scott, not afraid of death, 149, 151, May 2; trial and execution of Jehan de Bar, Veenstra, 67–69, 86–87.

47. Scott, torture would be considered coercion, 151–53, May 9, 12; amplifications, Murray, May 9; the torture episode and vote, Barrett, 303–06, May 9, 12.

48. Scott, censures of the University of Paris, 154–59, May 23; also Barrett, 330–38, May 23.

49. Pernoud, *Joan of Arc,* episode at St. Ouen, 254–55; also Scott, 163, May 24; John 15: 4–6.

50. Pernoud, *Joan of Arc,* further details at St. Ouen, 256–57.

51. Scott, disputed *Cedula* text, 164; Murray, May 24; Pernoud, *Joan of Arc,* disagreements on text by Jean Massieu, Nicolas Taquel, and Guillaume de la Chambre, 258–59.

52. Pernoud, *Joan of Arc,* sent back to prison, 263.

53. Scott, 169–70, May 28; Murray, did not understand abjuration, would reassume women's clothes, May 28.

54. Pernoud and Clin, testimony of Jean Toutmouillé, 133–34; shall be in paradise, Scott, 171, May 29; Cauchon, "it is done," testimony of Isambart de la Pierre and Martin Ladvenu, Pernoud, *Joan of Arc,* 268–69.

55. Pernoud, *Joan of Arc,* testimony of Jean Massieu on public weeping, 277; on excessive haste to burn Jeanne, 279; words of final condemnation, Scott, 173; "if one member suffers, all suffer," 1 Corinthians 12:26; more context on last sermon and excommunication, Barrett, 359–62, May 30.

56. Pernoud, *Joan of Arc:* death of Jeanne according to Maugier Leparmentier and Jean Massieu, 280; story of dove as described to Isambart de la Pierre, 282; survival of entrails and heart from the fire, 283; Jean Riquier's account of confession by Jean Alepée, canon of Rouen, 281; story of name of Jesus written in flames, told to Thomas Marie; account of general weeping, described by Jean de Mailly, Bishop of Noyon; Jeanne's screams to Jesus, description by Jean Riquier, Pierre Daron, Laurence Guesdon, Maugier Leparmentier, Jean Monnet; "We have burned a Saint," English secretary Jean Tressart, confessed to Pierre Cusquel, citizen of Rouen, 282.

57. Versions of Jeanne's final confession about being deceived by voices from Nicolas de Venderès, Martin Ladvenu, Pierre Maurice, Nicolas Loyseleur, Thomas de Courcelles, Jean Toutmouillé, see Murray, June 7, 1431; see also Barrett, 368–72, June 7, 1431.

Chapter Two: Rehabilitation

1. Pernoud, *Joan of Arc,* letter to Noyon, 315–16.

2. Pernoud, descriptions of young Jeannette; godfather Jean Moreau, 65, godmother Béatrice, 67, *Retrial of Joan of Arc;* did not recall herding cattle, Scott, 75, Feb. 24.

3. Pernoud, *Joan of Arc: By Herself and Her Witnesses*: caring for sick, Simon Musnier, full of good ways, too pious, Mengette Joyart, 17; alms to poor, Durand Laxart (Lassois), 18.

4. Pernoud, *Joan of Arc: By Herself and Her Witnesses*: tease her, Colin, 18; no dancing, Isabelette d'Epinal, 18; ringing bells, Perrin Drappier, 19; going to Notre Dame de Bermont, Michel Lebuin, 19.

5. Pernoud, *Retrial of Joan of Arc*: recollections regarding Fairies' tree, Béatrice d'Estelin, Jean Moreau, 65–68; Hauviette, Menguette, Simon Musnier, 72–74.

6. Pernoud, *Retrial of Joan of Arc*: recollections of Jeanne leaving Domremy, Hauviette, 72–73, Mengette, 73–74; prophesy of maid saving France, Michel Lebuin, 75, Durant Laxar, 77.

7. Pernoud, *Retrial of Joan of Arc*: recollections of Jean le Fumeux, 80, Catherine Le Royer, 88, Henri Le Royer, 89.

8. Pernoud, *Joan of Arc*: recollections of Catherine Le Royer, 40; spoke well, Albert d'Ourches, 42; Jean de Metz, 39.

9. Ibid.: born to do this, to Henri de Royer, 41; don't be afraid, to Jean de Metz, 45–46.

10. Ibid.: Jeanne presumptuous, Jean de Metz to Marguerite de Touroulde, 44; no carnal desire, Bertrand de Poulengy, 45; also no desire, Jean de Metz, 46.

11. Ibid.: Alençon on Jeanne's breasts, 74; preferred to sleep with young women, Simon Beaucroix, 74; no carnal desire for Jeanne, Gobert Thibault, 75; *coitus reservatus*, Barnett, 439, 445.

12. Pernoud, *Joan of Arc*: poor little shepherdess, Grandmaster Raoul de Gaucourt, 55; Charles hid himself, Simon Charles, 56, Jean Chartier, 60; told Charles his secret, Jean

Pasquerel, 60–61; nature of secret, anecdote of Pierre Sala, told by Guillaume Gouffier, 61–62; no hope but God, Marguerite de Touroulde, 65, Jean Barbin, 66. Fraioli: Jeanne a possible assassin, 20; told Charles the secret, Pancracio Justininani, 8.

13. Pernoud, *Retrial of Joan of Arc*: anecdote of Pasquerel about man drowning, 161; tearful devotion of Jeanne, according to Pasquerel, 162, according to Louis de Coutes, 57, Pernoud, *Joan of Arc.*

14. Pernoud, *Joan of Arc*: Alençon on Jeanne's horsemanship, 58; also described by Marguerite de Touroulde, 77; denied such prior skills at Trial of Condemnation, Scott, 67, Feb. 22. Fraioli, when not on horse, a "defenseless lamb," 40.

15. Pernoud, *Joan of Arc*: irritation over questions, to Pasquerel, 66; examined for virginity, Pasquerel, Jean d'Aulon, 68; theological examination found a good Catholic, 59.

16. Fraioli, letter to the English, 208; Pernoud, *Joan of Arc;* received armor at Tours, Jean d'Aulon, 69; design of standard, according to Pasquerel, 162, Pernoud, *The Retrial of Joan of Arc.*

17. Battle of the Herrings, Kelly Devries, *Joan of Arc: A Military Leader*, 66–67.

18. Pernoud, *Joan of Arc*: description of army from Blois to Orléans, Pasquerel, 70, Alençon, 94, Jean Chartier, 95; Jeanne on swearing, Louis de Coutes, 73, Duke of Alençon, 74; on looting, Simon Beaucroix, 74.

19. Jean Gerson's secondhand description of Jeanne, *de quadam puella,* 135, Barstow.

20. Pernoud, *Joan of Arc*: Dunois and first meeting with Jeanne, 95–96; letter to English, Mar. 22, 1429, 82.

21. Ibid.: description of entry into Orléans, 97–98, Apr. 29, 1429.

22. Ibid.: Jeanne's anger on delays, to Louis de Coutes, 99.

23. Ibid.: Jeanne confronts Dunois to attack, description by Jean d'Aulon, 101.

24. Ibid.: Jeanne oversleeping, Louis de Coutes, 101–02.

25. Ibid.: Jeanne with no supernatural powers, to Marguerite de Touroulde, 76; weeping over English dead, version of Jean Pasquerel, 102.

26. Ibid.: letter shot on arrow to English, Jean Pasquerel, 102–03; Jeanne attacking with a lance, description of Jean d'Aulon, 104–05.

27. Ibid.: prediction of wound to Pasquerel, 105–06; description of wounding, May 7, 106. Description of Dunois, Marina Warner, 109–110.

28. Pernoud, *Joan of Arc,* Aulon's description of final assault on Orléans, 107–08. Fate of William Glasdale, Jeanne's instruction to let English go, Sackville-West, 184–88.

29. Pernoud, *Retrial of Joan of Arc*: all glory to God, to Jacques l'Ebahy, 132; God's book, to Pasquerel, 167. Warner: disliked adulation, to Simon Beaucroix, 91; letter of Perceval de Boulainvilliers, 119–20. Pernoud, *Joan of Arc*: recollections of a simple and ignorant Jeanne, Thibaut d'Armagnac, 73; Marguerite de Touroulde, 76.

30. Pernoud, *Joan of Arc*, Dunois's description of Jeanne's voice, 131.

31. Pernoud, *Retrial of Joan of Arc,* Jeanne's piety in Orléans, Dunois's sense of chastity around Jeanne, 127–28. Pernoud, *Joan of Arc,* Guy Le Laval's letter to his mother, 132–33.

32. Pernoud, *Joan of Arc*: Jean de Wavrin's letter, June 8, 1429, 133–34; Alençon, fear no multitude, God guided the French, 134–35.

33. Ibid.: Alençon's description of Jeanne at Jargeau, June 10, 1429, 135–36. General description of siege of Jargeau, Devries, 104–06.

34. Devries, Richemont's response to Jeanne, 111.

35. Ibid., Jean de Wavrin on Jeanne's response, 112.

36. Pernoud, *Joan of Arc*: testimony of Dunois on Jeanne's confidence, June 18, 1429, 139–40; Alençon's same opinion, 140. Pernoud, *Retrial of Joan of Arc,* description of Thibault d'Armagnac on Jeanne's tactical prowess, 108.

37. Pernoud, *Joan of Arc*, Jean de Wavrin's description of the Battle of Patay, June 18, 1429, 140–42. Devries, general description of the battle, 116–21.

38. Pernoud, *Retrial of Joan of Arc*, Louis de Coute's description of Jeanne after the battle, 158.

39. Devries, Jeanne's letter to future towns, June 25, 1429, 125. William Shakespeare, *Henry V*, Act 4, Scene 3, *Complete Works of William Shakespeare.*

40. Devries, 126–28.

41. Ibid., 128–30.

42. Sackville-West, Jeanne and Brother Richard, 205–07; also Pernoud, *Joan of Arc*, 145; also Jeanne's description, Scott, 93, Mar. 3; sermon preached against Jeanne and Brother Richard by Jean Graverent in Paris, July 4, 1431, information from Pierre Champion, supplement to trial transcript by Barrett, 408.

43. Pernoud, *Joan of Arc*: Dunois's description of Jeanne at Troyes, 146–47; similar description by Simon Charles, p. 147. Pernoud, *Retrial of Joan of Arc*, Alençon's description of Jeanne and laying out artillery, 142; same evaluation by Dunois, 126.

44. Pernoud and Clin, coronation at Reims, 64–66.

45. Pernoud, *Joan of Arc*: Jeanne wished to be buried in Soissons, according to Dunois, 157; Devries, prelude to Paris, 135–39.

46. Pernoud, *Joan of Arc*, Jeanne's letter to the Duke of Burgundy advising strong peace, 153. Devries, diplomatic double-dealing unknown to Jeanne, 144–45; not advised by voices to attack Paris, Scott, 110, Mar. 13; Pernoud, *Joan of Arc*, Jeanne vows to see Paris closer, put Charles there, version of Perceval de Cagny, 163–64.

47. Pernoud, *Joan of Arc*, description of attack in *Bourgeois de Paris*, 61. Devries, Paris defenses and attack, 148–53.

48. Pernoud, *Joan of Arc*: another description at Paris and wounding of Jeanne, Perceval de Cagny, 164–65. Scott, attacking Paris on feast day, 69–70, Feb. 22, also 111, Mar. 13; Jeanne at

St. Denis, 124, Mar. 17; relics at St. Denis, Sackville-West, 220.

49. Pernoud, *Joan of Arc*: Charles sent Alençon home, 170; Jeanne departs from Charles at Sully-sur-Loire, 177.

50. Ibid., encounter with Catherine de la Rochelle, 171–72; Scott, 96–97, Mar. 3.

51. Ibid., Jeanne confused at St. Pierre-le-Moutier, according to Jean d'Aulon, 172–73; Devries, 157–62.

52. Scott, 97, Mar. 3; letter for aid, Nov. 9, 1429, Devries, 164.

53. Devries, 165–68; Scott, gave up after voice at Melun, 111, Mar. 13; last letter to Reims, Mar. 28, 1431.

54. Scott: used captured sword for "hard clouts," 82, Feb. 27; rationale at Rouen for having Franquet d'Arras executed, 114–15, Mar. 14.

55. Tradition of Jeanne predicting her capture, Michelet, *Joan of Arc*, 54; description of Jeanne's capture by Perceval de Cagny, Pernoud, *Joan of Arc,* 180–81; description of capture by Burgundian Georges Chastellain, 181–82; Jeanne's version at trial of Condemnation, Scott, 99–100, Mar. 10; letter of the Duke of Burgundy, Devries, 182–83.

56. Description of morale after Jeanne's capture by Burgundian Enguerrand de Monstrelet, Pernoud, *Joan of Arc; By Herself and Her Witnesses,* 152; description of Jeanne in prison, by Haimond de Macy, Pernoud, *Joan of Arc,* 186–87; Jeanne and wearing women's clothes offered from Luxembourg's wife, Jeanne de Béthune, 187; payment for capture of Jeanne to the Bastard of Wandomme, Devries, 183.

57. Pernoud, *Joan of Arc,* testimony of Jean Massieu on confusing questions, 204–05.

58. Ibid., testimony of Guillaume Manchon on fatiguing sessions, 205.

59. Ibid., testimony of Guillaume Manchon on spying and inappropriate interrogation, 206–07.

60. Ibid.: testimony of Jean Beaupère on subtlety of women, 231; Jeanne's sound memory, Jean Lefevre and Pierre Daron, 232.

61. Ibid.: testimony of Guillaume Manchon on altered transcripts, 235–36; opposition to proceedings by Jean Lohier, 240–41.

62. Ibid., testimony of physicians Jean Tiphaine and Guillaume de la Chambre on contaminated fish, 242–43.

63. Ibid., account of threatening visit by John of Luxembourg, Stafford, and Warwick, 251.

64. Ibid., clothes had been switched, Jean Massieu; wearing men's clothes to avoid rape, Pierre Cusquel; Martin Ladvenu told of rape attempt by English lord, 265–66; Scott, Jeanne's explanation that men's clothes were more safe around guards, 169, May 28.

65. Pernoud, *Joan of Arc,* perhaps better off in English hands, Martin Ladvenu; bypassing of legal sentencing, Laurent Guesdon; on haste of the English to burn Jeanne, Jean Massieu, 279.

66. Ibid.: description of death in *Journal d'un Bourgeois de Paris,* 290; Cauchon and false recantation, refusal to sign by Guillaume Manchon, 284.

67. Ibid., false Jeannes after her death; Claude des Armoises, 294, 300; Barstow, 66–67; Pernoud and Clin, 234.

Chapter Three: Jeanne in the World Thereafter

1. Warner: on Voltaire, 237–39; on Southey's poem and Covent Garden, 242–43. Comments on Chapelain's work, Charles Wayland Lightbody, *The Judgements of Joan,* 156.

An ancestor of Lafayette had served with Jeanne. The Marquis de Lafayette, descendant of Southey's current salute, had fled France the year before the poem. He wound up a political prisoner in Austria for five years, and a conservative anathema to leaders of the Revolution like Robespierre and Marat. In England Southey's poem was considered subversive, as it was sympathetic to the French Revolution during a time of renewed conflict.

2. Warner, on Amazons, 202–10; William Shakespeare, *Henry VI, Part One*, Act I, Scene II.

3. Daniel Rankin and Claire Quintal, *The First Biography of Joan of Arc*; historical facts in *Henry VI,* Frederick S. Boas, "Joan of Arc in Shakespeare, Schiller, and Shaw," *Shakespeare Quarterly* 2 (Jan. 1951): 36–38.

4. Warner, Jeanne not a durable image as an Amazon, 216.

5. Ibid.: on Christine de Pisan, 220; on Pierre Lemoyne, 225.

6. Ibid., on Friedrich Schiller, 241; excerpts from Schiller's *Die Jungfrau von Orleans*, 1802.

7. Ibid.: on Jules Michelet, 244; on Alexandre Dumas, 268. Additional background on Michelet and French nationalism, Susan Dunn, "Romanticism and the Rise of History," *History and Theory* 35 (1996): 387.

8. Ibid., on Alphonse de Lamartine, 246.

9. Napoleon and background of 1804 statue, Nora M. Heimann, "The Art of Politics in Early Nineteenth-Century France; E.-É.-F. Gois's *Jeanne d'Arc pendant le combat* as Metaphor," *Gazette des Beaux-Arts* 132 (July/August 1998): 31–36.

10. Jeanne on stage post-Napoleon, Sarah Hibberd, "Marianne; Mystic or Madwoman? Representations of Jeanne d'Arc on the Parisian Stage in the 1820s," *Prose Studies* 23 (2000): 90, 93–94; criticism and replacement of Gois's statue in Orléans, Heimann, 37–38.

11. Warner: on Domremy during Franco-Prussian War, 237–38; on Jeanne's house, 258–59. On German geographical claim to Jeanne, Lightbody, 161; German initiative to publish Jeanne's trial records in 1835, Nadia Margolis, "Trial by Passion; Philosophy, Film, and Ideology in the Portrayal of Joan of Arc (1900–1930)," *Journal of Medieval and Early Modern Studies* 27 (Fall 1997): 449; quote from Quicherat to Michelet about truth of Jeanne, 450.

12. Jeanne's equestrian statue by Emmanuel Frémiet, Caro-

line Igra, "Measuring the Temper of Her Time; Joan of Arc in the 1870s and 1880s," *Konsthistorisk Tidskrift*, 68 (1999): 117–25.

13. Brigitte Coste, "Right or Left, Who Owns Joan of Arc?" 105–10; Mary Elizabeth Tallon, *Joan of Arc at the University*; Warner, on Alfred Dreyfus case, 260; conservatives' opinion of Marianne, Martha Hanna, "Iconology and Ideology: Images of Joan of Arc in the Idiom of the *Action Française*, 1908–1931," *French Historical Studies* 14 (Autumn 1985): 216–17.

14. Examples of Vichy propaganda, Eric Jennings, "'Reinventing Jeanne': The Iconology of Joan of Arc in Vichy Schoolbooks, 1940–1944," *Journal of Contemporary History*, 29 (Oct. 1994): 719, 725; words of Marshal Pétain in 1942, Patrick Marsh, "Jeanne d'Arc During the German Occupation," *Theatrical Research Institute* 2 (1977): 140–41.

15. Marxist and fascist literature, Lightbody, 170–71; de Gaulle and his association with Jeanne, Phillip C. Naylor, "Charles de Gaulle and Joan of Arc; A Comparison of Person and Praxis, " in Tallon, 117–28; de Gaulle and silent protest of Vichy government, Joan Tumblety, "Contested Histories: *Jeanne d'Arc* and the *Front National*," *European Legacy* 4 (1999): 17.

16. On divine virtues of the Church, William Searle, *The Saint and the Skeptics: Joan of Arc in the Work of Mark Twain, Anatole France, and Bernard Shaw*, 141.

17. Henry Ansgar Kelly, "Joan of Arc's Last Trial: The Attack of the Devil's Advocate," in *Fresh Verdicts on Joan of Arc*, eds. Bonnie Wheeler and Charles T. Wood, 205–36.

18. William Searle, aspects of canonization trial, *The Saint and the Skeptics*, pp. 140, 142, 171.

19. Searle, 92; Warner, on Jeanne as saint, 264; Karen Sullivan, *Fresh Verdicts on Joan of Arc*, 106.

20. Searle, on Anatole France, 60–66, 74, 79; for contributions of Pierre Champion to Jeanne d'Arc literature, see Margolis, "Trial by Passion," 452–57.

21. Abandonment by Jeanne's voices, Michelet, *Joan of Arc*, 96.

22. Searle, on Anatole France, 71–73, 81, 85, 91–93; Warner, letter to Hussites, 178.

23. Searle, 83–85, 94, 96.

24. Episode of François Thalamas, in Margolis, "The 'Joan Phenomenon' and the French Right," *Fresh Verdicts on Joan of Arc*, 278, also "Trial by Passion . . . ," *Journal of Medieval and Early Modern Studies*, p. 459; Margolis: on reaction to France's work, 461; on betrayal of Brousson, 462; quote on authors own trials and verdict, 484.

25. Searle, on Mark Twain, 15, 44, 47, 153n; Roger B. Salomon, *Twain and the Image of History*, Twain's most sincere work, 168; relationship with daughter Susy, Edith Colgate Salsbury, *Susy and Mark Twain: Family Dialogues*, 311, 318, 360.

26. Searle, 20–21, 34; Mark Twain, *Personal Recollections of Joan of Arc*, 431.

27. Searle, 28–29, 44; Salomon, 174–79; Twain, 313–16; Albert E. Stone, Jr., "Mark Twain's Joan of Arc: The Child as Goddess," *American Literature* 31 (Mar. 1959): 1, 3, 6–8.

28. Salomon, 175–76; Twain, 332–33.

29. Searle, 20–21, 37–38; Salomon, 179–81; Twain, 426; Jeanne and lack of menstruation, Albert E. Stone, Jr., "Mark Twain's Joan of Arc: The Child as Goddess," *American Literature* 31 (Mar. 1959): 6.

30. George Bernard Shaw, *Saint Joan*, 75–77.

31. Searle, 100–101, 119; Anthony S. Abbott, *Shaw and Christianity*, 22–23, 32, 38–39; Shaw, preface, 41.

32. Searle, 100–101; Shaw, 59.

33. Searle, 107, 110–11; Abbott, 32; Shaw, 130.

34. Searle, 105, 122; Shaw, 121–22.

35. Shaw, 95, 99; Lightbody, on Protestant rejection of Jeanne, 155.

36. Brian Tyson, *The Story of Shaw's Saint Joan*, 104; Shaw, preface, 40.

37. Shaw, 147–58.

38. Arnold Silver, *Saint Joan: Playing With Fire,* 71; Shaw, preface, 28, 43.

39. Searle, 53n; Shaw, preface, 25, 27–28, 43.

40. Searle, 116, 126–27; Shaw, 112, 134.

41. Silver, 14–15; Abbott, 169.

42. Tyson, 85, 91, 96.

43. Ibid., 97–99, 100–102, 111; Silver, 9, 17; background of Paris production, Stanley Weintraub, *Saint Joan: Fifty Years After: 1923/24–1973/74*, 15, 21, 202–03, 210.

44. Bernard F. Dukore, *Saint Joan: A Screenplay by Bernard Shaw,* xiii, xxxiv.

45. Ibid., xxxviii, 143–46; Searle, 115; Shaw, 137–38.

46. Dukore, xxxiv, xxxvii, 147; Silver, 112.

47. Kevin J. Harty, "Jeanne Au Cinema," *Fresh Verdicts on Joan of Arc,* 237–64; Dominique Paul Noth, "Burned by Celluloid: Joan of Arc in Film History," *Joan of Arc at the University*, ed. Mary Elizabeth Tallon, preface, 34, and 157–66.

48. Silver, 100–14; Shaw, preface, 34; other essays on Saint Joan and Marxism, "Saint Joan: A Marxist View," Alick West, 106–13, also "Joan as Unhappy Trotzkyist," Arland Ussher, 119–24, Weintraub.

49. Silver, 14; William Scaff, *The Philosophy of T. S. Eliot*, 26, 29–30.

50. John D. McCabe, "Joan of Arc: Saint or Symbol?" *Joan of Arc at the University,* 182–89; Pierre Champion on Jeanne as wildflower of Christian piety, supplement to trial transcript by Barrett, 537; Tyson, 107; Abbott, 164.

51. Warner, on Jeanne and feminism, 263, 275; Barstow, xiii, 131–32; Ronald Edward Zupko, "The Many Faces of Joan," *Joan of Arc at the University,* 20; on feminist historians and women religious figures, Charlotte Allen, "The Holy Feminine," *First Things* 98 (Dec. 1999): 37.

52. Jeanne and virginity, according to feminist Andrea

Dworkin, *Intercourse*, 85, 99; Jean Gerson on ways to avoid sex, *Oeuvres completes*, Monseigneur Glorieux.

53. Victoria Stagg Elliott, 35–38.

54. Marsha Norman, *On Campus,* Agnes Scott College, June 2000.

Chapter Four: Madness: Jeanne Among the Doctors

1. Barstow, 110, concerning Dr. Robert Greenblatt, *Journal of Sexual Medicine*, as reported in *Omni* (April 1982); statement about Jeanne in snakepit by Anatole France, Searle, 81; opinion on insanity of, William W. Ireland, "On the Character and Hallucinations of Joan of Arc," *Journal of Mental Science* (1875): 26.

2. Shaw, on being cracked, 103.

3. Karl Menninger, *The Vital Balance: The Life Process in Mental Health and Illness,* evolution of psychiatric theory from Hippocrates to the time of Jeanne, 421–26.

4. Pernoud, *Retrial of Joan of Arc*; not uncanny, according to Marguerite la Touroulde, 110; testimony of priests that Jeanne was of sound mind, Murray, June 7, 1431; Gerson on women with repeated visions, Dyan Elliott, 29.

5. Madness of Charles VI, Desmond Seward, *The Hundred Years War*, 143–44; also Tuchman, 513–15; more background in Veenstra, 64–70, 115; depravity of Gilles de Rais, most background by Mark Gribben, *The Crime Library*, Courtroom Television Network, available on the internet.

It has been speculated that Charles VI may have suffered from porphyria, a rare chemical disorder retrospectively offered up to explain everything from medieval werewolves to mad King George III of England. A decent case beckons for the hereditary abnormality of porphyria, since George III was a descendant of Charles VI. Both of them suffered from periodic madness punctuated with long interludes of normalcy.

6. Scott: Jeanne's denials of sorcery, lost glove, 95, Mar. 3;

lost cup, 110, Mar. 13; godmother not a wise woman, 123, Mar. 17. For a sophisticated and lucid description of the confusing aspects of theology versus magic, see Veenstra: 7–20; Cardinal Pierre d'Ailly (1350–1420) and his religious horoscope, 11–12, 110; small superstitions since at least the time of Saint Augustine, 105–06.

7. Scott: *passez outre* concerning angel, 69, Feb. 22; did not see an angel, 80, Feb. 27; Jeanne might perjure herself about sign of angel, 89, Mar. 1.

8. Sullivan, *Interrogation of Joan of Arc,* contradiction about the sign to Charles, 73–74, concerning contradiction about angel, May 30, 1430; also Murray, June 7, 1431, also Barrett, 368–72, June 7, 1431; Jeanne's confession of being deceived by voices, Pernoud and Clin, 140; for one example, among many others not cited, of denial of suspect last confession, see George H. Tavard, *The Spiritual Way of St. Jeanne d'Arc,* 184.

9. Karen Sullivan, "'I Do Not Name to You the Voice of St. Michel': The Identification of Joan of Arc's Voices," 85–111, in *Fresh Verdicts on Joan of Arc;* made up names of saints, 88, 102; Fraioli, Jeanne under pressure changed her tune, 198; Michelet, on Jeanne's fallible inconsistencies, *Joan of Arc,* 75, 89.

10. W. S. Scott, on angel coming from God, p. 72, Feb. 24; Sullivan, *Fresh Verdicts on Joan of Arc,* p. 97.

11. Scott, my voices are Saint Margaret and Saint Catherine, 77, Feb. 27; also Murray, Feb.27; also Barrett, 58, Feb. 27; Sullivan, *Fresh Verdicts on Joan of Arc;* God, my Lord, and *messire*, 91; "the Lord who redeemed us from hell," Barrett, 52, Feb. 24; St. Francis and Christ through Passion as God transformed, Emmanuel Le Roy Ladurie, *Montaillou: Cathars and Catholics in a French Village, 1294–1324*, 299, 303; to examine an incredible range of medieval Christian belief and practice spanning Catholic orthodoxy, Catharist heresy, and atheistic scatological blasphemy among common villagers in southern

France, read "Fate, Magic, and Salvation" and "Religion in Practice," 287–326.

12. Bertrand de Poulengy, describing Jeanne's stimulating voices on way to Chinon, Pernoud, *Joan of Arc*, 45.

13. Saint Catherine and Saint Margaret, "believe me if you will," Barrett, 61, Feb. 27; letter of Alain Chartier, Cynthia J. Brown, "Allegorical Design and Image-making in Fifteenth-Century France; Alain Chartier's Joan of Arc," *French Studies* 53 (Oct. 1999): 385; Fraioli, concerning *De Mirabili Victoria*, 209–12 (text), 126–49 (discussion).

14. Scott, Jeanne vowed her virginity, called Daughter of God, 103–05, Mar. 12.

15. On spiritual aspect of virginity, *Jean Gerson, Oeuvres complétes*, (Monseigneur Glorieux, Paris, 1968–1973).

16. Andrew Lang, *The Maid of France: Being the Story of the Life and Death of Jeanne d'Arc,* on theory of Anatole France, 11, 316.

17. Scott, Jeanne desired to believe voice, 120, Mar. 15; concerning background of Francis Galton, Henri F. Ellenberger, *The Discovery of the Unconscious: The History and Evolution of Dynamic Psychiatry,* 168–69, 524, 691.

18. Shaw, all Christendom mad, preface; Jeanne with possible eidetic imagery, F. E. Kenyon, "The Life and Health of Joan of Arc," *Practitioner* 207 (Dec. 1971): 835–842.

19. Sackville-West, Jeanne's voices not from within herself, 256.

20. Scott, 72, Feb. 24.

21. Warner, Jeanne's views different from her voices, 131; Scott, voices do not come from Jeanne's head, 145, Mar. 31; testimony of Guillaume Manchon on underhanded spying of Nicolas Loieleur, Pernoud, *Joan of Arc*, 206–07.

22. Text of abjuration, Pernoud and Clin, 140.

23. August Piper, Jr., "Multiple Personality Disorder," *British Journal of Psychiatry* 164 (1994): 600–612; additional background of CIA controversies, false memory, etc., 166 (1995): 281–83; and 167 (1995): 263–70.

24. Colin A. Ross, *Multiple Personality Disorder: Diagnosis, Clinical Features, and Treatment.*

25. Quotation on problems with defining time from physicist Max Tegmark of the University of Pennsylvania, "A Hole at the Heart of Physics," George Musser, *Scientific American* 287 (Sept. 2002): 48; other background on conflict between philosophy and physics in exploring consciousness, "Consciousness Studies Swell From Stream to a Flood," James Gorman, *New York Times* (Apr. 29, 1997): B7,9; Augustine on consciousness, Garry Wills, *Saint Augustine*, 53–54.

26. Peter A. Bick and Marcel Kinsbourne, "Auditory Hallucinations and Subvocal Speech in Schizophrenic Patients," *American Journal of Psychiatry* 144 (1987): 222–25.

27. Freud and persistent voice of the intellect, Fred H. Johnson, *The Anatomy of Hallucinations,* 77–78; thoughts of Plato and Aristotle on dreams, Veenstra, 176–78; Jung and subconscious slips, Anthony Storr, *The Essential Jung,* 39.

28. Scott, Jeanne recounted father's dreams, threat to drown her, 105–06, Mar. 12.

29. Ross, account of eighteenth-century exorcism, 20–21.

30. Mark 9: 25–29; J. M. Bramwell, *Hypnosis: Its History, Practice and Theory,* Freud on psychosis, 17.

31. Pernoud, *Joan of Arc,* Jeanne delusional about fifty thousand troops, 172–73.

32. Dietrich Blumer and Earl Walker, "Sexual Behavior in Temporal Lobe Epilepsy," *Archives of Neurology* 16 (1967): 37–43; G. W. Roberts et al., "A Mock-up of Schizophrenia: Temporal Lobe Epilepsy and Schizophrenia-like Psychosis," *Biological Psychiatry* 28 (1990): 127–43; David C. Taylor, "Factors Influencing the Occurrence of Schizophrenia-like Psychosis in Patients With Temporal Lobe Epilepsy," *Psychological Medicine* 5 (1975): 249–54; S. K. Currie et al., "Clinical Course and Prognosis of Temporal Lobe Epilepsy: A Survey of 666 Patients," *Brain* 94 (1971): 173–90.

33. Jeanne and theories on tuberculosis, John Butterfield

and Isobel Butterfield, "Joan of Arc: A Medical View," *History Today* 8 (1958): 628–33; J. M. Nores and Y. Yakovleff, "A Historical Case of Disseminated Tuberculosis, " *Neuropsychobiology* 32 (1995): 79–80; R. H. Ratnasuriyia, "Joan of Arc, Creative Psychopath: Is There Another Explanation," *Journal of the Royal Society of Medicine* 79 (1986): 234–35; H. M. Dastur and A. D. Desai, "A Comparative Study of Brain Tuberculomas and Gliomas Based Upon 107 Case Records of Each," *Brain* 88 (1965): 375–96.

34. Elizabeth Foote-Smith and Lydia Bayne, on musicogenic epilepsy, "Joan of Arc," *Epilepsia* 32 (1991): 810–15; David C. Poskanzer et al., "Musicogenic Epilepsy Caused Only by a Discrete Frequency Band of Church Bells," *Brain* 85 (1962): 77–92; Shaw, use of bells, 102–03; Jeanne's testimony on occasional association with voice and bells, Scott, 69–70, Feb. 24; Pierre Maurice in attempt to get Jeanne's confession about bells, Barrett, 370, June 7, 1431; also Murray, June 7, 1431.

35. D. Landsborough, "St Paul and Temporal Lobe Epilepsy," *Journal of Neurology, Neurosurgery, and Psychiatry* 50 (1987): 659–64; biblical description of Paul's conversion on the road to Damascus, Acts 9: 1–19; 22: 6–13; 26: 9–16; heavenly visions, 2 Corinthians 12: 2–5, 7–9.

36. Saint Paul, Mohammed, Van Gogh, et al. and temporal lobe epilepsy, Jeffrey Saver and John Rabin, "The Neural Substrates of Religious Experience," *Journal of Neuropsychiatry and Clinical Neurosciences* 9 (Summer 1997): 501–02; Anthony J. De Luca, *Freud and Future Religious Experience*, Freudian theory and Dostoyevski, 112–14; on religion and Oedipal complex, 180–82; Paul's explanation of Christ as "second Adam," Romans 4: 12–21.

37. Religious experiences of patients, "Sudden Religious Conversions and Temporal Lobe Epilepsy," Kenneth Dewhurst and A. W. Beard, *British Journal of Psychiatry* 117 (1970): 497–507.

38. Opinions of Georges Dumas, Searle, 68–69; Andrew

Lang, 328; Michelet on Jeanne's common sense and creation of her own reality, *Joan of Arc*, 3, 9.

39. Subject of "gynecological massage," Rachel Maines, "Hysteria, the Vibrator and Women's Sexual Satisfaction," reviewed in *Journal of the American Medical Association* (Jan. 12, 2000): 262; other details from Greek thought on hysteria, Menninger, 421–23; opinion of Sybil Thorndike on female hallucinations and menstruation, Holly Hill, *Playing Joan: Actresses on the Challenge of Playing Shaw's Saint Joan*, 107.

40. Ross, voices in M.P.D. versus schizophrenia, 161–64; David Hellerstein et al., "The Clinical Significance of Command Hallucinations," *American Journal of Psychiatry* 144 (Feb. 1987): 219–21.

41. Schizophrenics not prone to interrupt voices, Bick and Kinsbourne, 222–25; M. A. J. Romme et al., "Coping With Hearing Voices: An Emancipatory Approach," *British Journal of Psychiatry* 161 (1992): 99–103.

42. Opinions of Wilson Van Dusen, in James Fadiman and Donald Kewman, *Exploring Madness: Experience, Theory and Research*, 122 ff.; study on good and evil voices, Paul Chadwick and Max Birchwood, "The Omnipotence of Voices: A Cognitive Approach to Auditory Hallucinations," *British Journal of Psychiatry* 164 (1994): 190–201.

43. Jung on treating schizophrenics, Storr, 44.

44. Johnson: schizophrenics think less, not more, 61–62; discourse of one patient, 133. New theory on nicotine and schizophrenia, "Brain-Tied Gene Defect May Explain Why Schizophrenics Hear Voices," Denise Grady, *New York Times* (Jan. 21, 1997): B14.

Concerning cigarettes, most schizophrenics are well-documented heavy smokers. Recently it has been postulated that nicotine might give fleeting relief to distractions that interfere with a schizophrenic's ability to concentrate. Past studies suggest that a certain receptor in the brain may be responsible for blocking out irrelevant sounds. This receptor responds to the chemical messenger acetylcholine—and to nicotine. Much research is needed to confirm this, but if it proves valid it might lend intriguing support to the possibility that schizophrenics suffer from an overinclusion of stimulation, which is normally blocked out.

45. Julian Jaynes, *The Origin of Consciousness in the Breakdown of the Bicameral Mind.*

46. C. Helmstaedter et al., "Right Hemisphere Restitution of Language and Memory Functions in Right Hemisphere Language-dominant Patients With Left Temporal Lobe Epilepsy," *Brain* 117 (1994): 729–37.

47. Jaynes, 405.

48. Zechariah 13: 3–4; Albert Schweitzer, *Psychiatric Study of Jesus*, various psychiatric opinions, 34–44.

49. Fadiman and Kewman, Jung on insanity, 109.

50. Interview with schizophrenic Marilyn Mitchell, on "Ockham's Razor," National Public Radio, May 26, 2002, with Robyn Williams.

51. Evidence that right hemisphere may be superior in perception, S. D. Smith et al., "The Right Hemisphere as an Anomaly Detector: Evidence From Visual Perception," *Brain and Cognition* 48 (Mar.–Apr. 2002): 574–79.

52. Difference in personalities of temporal lobe epileptics, David M. Bear and Paul Fedio, "Quantitative Analysis of Interictal Behavior in Temporal Lobe Epilepsy," *Archives of Neurology* 34 (Aug. 1977): 454–47; opinions of Roger Sperry on split-brain consciousness: R. W. Sperry, "Hemisphere Deconnection and Unity in Conscious Awareness," *American Psychologist* 23 (1968): 723–33, 1968; and "Changing Concepts of Consciousness and Free Will," *Perspectives in Biology and Medicine* (Autumn 1976) : 9–19.

53. Jaynes, 346 ff., 321 ff., 341, 405–06; Socrates and Aristotle, Johnson, 2–3; ancient to mediaeval transition of epilepsy, Saver and Rabin, 499–500.

54. Wilder Penfield and Phanor Perot, "The Brain's Record

of Auditory and Visual Experience," *Brain* 86 (Dec. 1963): 595–695

55. Pierre Gloor et al. "The Role of the Limbic System in Experiential Phenomena of Temporal Lobe Epilepsy," *Annals of Neurology* 12 (Aug. 1982): 129–44.

56. Eric Halgren et al. "Mental Phenomena Evoked by Electrical Stimulation of the Human Hippocampal Formation and Amygdala," *Brain* 101 (1978): 83–117.

57. Toshimi Ishibashi et al. "Hallucinations Produced by Electrical Stimulation of the Temporal Lobes in Schizophrenic Patients," *Journal of Experimental Medicine* 82 (1964): 124–39.

58. Jaynes, 111–12.

59. D. A. Silbersweig et al., "A Functional Neuroanatomy of Hallucinations in Schizophrenia," *Nature* 378 (Nov. 9, 1995): 176–79; Sharon Begley, "Lights of Madness," *Newsweek* (Nov. 20, 1995): 76–77; K. J. Friston et al., "The Left Medial Temporal Region and Schizophrenia," *Brain* 115 (1992): 367–82; thoughts of Jay Ingram, "When Hearing Is Believing, *Equinox* (Jan.–Feb. 1996): 16–18.

60. Clifford Allen, "The Schizophrenia of Joan of Arc," *Historical Medicine* (Autumn–Winter 1975): 4–9.

61. Donald W. Goodwin et al., "Clinical Significance of Hallucinations in Psychiatric Disorders: A Study of 116 Hallucinatory Patients," *Archives of General Psychiatry* 24 (Jan. 1971): 76–80.

62. Fred Henker, "Joan of Arc and DSM III," *Southern Medical Journal* 77 (Dec. 1984): 1488–90.

63. Roger Money-Kyrle, "A Psycho-analytic Study of the Voices of Joan of Arc," *British Journal of Medical Psychology* 13 (1933): 63–81.

64. Quotations from Francis Crick and Angela Hegarty appeared in *Los Angeles Times* (Apr. 26, 1998), article by Robert Lee Hotz. Background information is diverse and inchoate for various neurocientific searches for religion. For studies of the brain during meditation, plus thoughts at large, see

Andrew Newberg et al., *Why God Won't Go Away: Brain Science and the Biology of Belief.* For an overview in the popular press, see "Religion and the Brain," *Newsweek* (May 14, 2001); also David C. Noelle, "Searching for God in the Machine," *Free Inquiry* (Summer 1998). The studies of M. A. Persinger with his magnetic helmet may be found in an article by C. M. Cook and M. A. Persinger, in *Perceptual and Motor Skills* 92 (2001): 447–48. For a brief description of a personal trip under the helmet, see Susan Blackmore, "Alien Abduction," *New Scientist* (Nov. 19, 1994): 29–31.

65. Shaw, preface, 14.

66. St. Paul, Romans, 1: 22–23; Sullivan, *Interrogation of Joan of Arc,* xxiv-xxv.

67. Michelet, *Joan of Arc,* 94–95.

68. "Be resigned," Murray, Mar. 14, 1431; Scott, p. 113, Mar. 14; *MENE MENE TEKEL UPHARSIN,* "you have been weighed in the balance and found wanting," Daniel 5: 27; "For my thoughts are not your thoughts," Isaiah 55:8.

Bibliography

Abbott, Anthony S. *Shaw and Christianity*. New York: Seabury Press, 1965.

Allen, Charlotte. "The Holy Feminine." *First Things* 98 (Dec. 1999): 37–44.

Allen, Clifford. "The Schizophrenia of Joan of Arc." *Historical Medicine* (Autumn–Winter 1975): 4–9.

Arthur, A. Z. "Theories and Explanations of Delusions: A Review." *American Journal of Psychiatry* 121 (Aug. 1964): 105–15.

Artz, Frederick B. *The Mind of the Middle Ages, A.D. 200–1500: An Historical Survey.* Chicago: University of Chicago Press, 1980.

Aston, Margaret. *The Fifteenth Century: The Prospect of Europe.* New York: W. W. Norton, 1979.

Baetzhold, Howard G., and Joseph B. McCullough. *The Bible According to Mark Twain.* New York: Simon and Schuster, 1996.

Barnett, Bernard. "Witchcraft, Psychopathology, and Hallucinations." *British Journal of Psychiatry* 3 (1965): 439–45.

Barrett, W. P. *The Trial of Jeanne d'Arc Translated Into English From the Original Latin and French Documents.* New York: Gotham House, 1932.

Barstow, Anne Llewellyn. *Joan of Arc: Heretic, Mystic, Shaman.* Lewiston, N.Y., and Queenston, Ontario: Edwin Mellen Press, 1986.

Bear, David M., and Paul Fedio. "Quantitative Analysis of

Interictal Behavior in Temporal Lobe Epilepsy." *Archives of Neurology* 34 (Aug. 1977): 454–67.
Begley, Sharon. "Lights of Madness." *Newsweek* (Nov. 20, 1995): 76–77.
Bentall, R. P. "The Illusion of Reality: A Review and Integration of Psychological Research on Hallucinations." *Psychological Bulletin* 107 (1990): 82–95.
Bick, Peter A., and Marcel Kinsbourne. "Auditory Hallucinations and Subvocal Speech in Schizophrenic Patients." *American Journal of Psychiatry* 144 (1987): 222–25.
Blackmore, Susan. "Alien Abduction." *New Scientist* (Nov. 19, 1994) 29–31.
Blumer, Dietrich, and Earl Walker. "Sexual Behavior in Temporal Lobe Epilepsy." *Archives of Neurology* 16 (1967): 37–43.
Boas, Frederick S. "Joan of Arc in Shakespeare, Schiller, and Shaw." *Shakespeare Quarterly* 2 (Jan. 1951): 35–45.
Bramwell, J. M. *Hypnosis:Its History, Practice and Theory.* Reprint. New York: Julian Press, 1956.
Brown, Cynthia J. "Allegorical Design and Image-making in Fifteenth-Century France: Alain Chartier's Joan of Arc." *French Studies* 53 (Oct. 1999): 385–404.
Butterfield, John, and Isobel-Ann Butterfield. "Joan of Arc: A Medical View." *History Today* (Sept. 1958): 628–33.
Chadwick, Paul, and Max Birchwood. "The Omnipotence of Voices: A Cognitive Approach to Auditory Hallucinations." *British Journal of Psychiatry* 164 (1994): 190–201.
Cleghorn, John M., Sheryl Franco, Barbara Szechtman, Ronald D. Kaplan, Henry Szechtman, George M. Brown, Claude Nahmias, and Stephen E. Garnett. "Toward a Brain Map of Auditory Hallucinations." *American Journal of Psychiatry* 149 (1992): 1062–69.
Cook, C. M., and M. A. Persinger. *Perceptual and Motor Skills* 92 (2001): 447–48.
Currie, S., K. W. G. Heathfield, R. A. Henson, and D. F.

Scott. "Clinical Course and Prognosis of Temporal Lobe Epilepsy: A Survey of 666 Patients." *Brain* 94 (1971): 173–90.

Dastur, H. M., and A. D. Desai, "A Comparative Study of Brain Tuberculomas and Gliomas Based Upon 107 Case Records of Each." *Brain* 88 (1965): 375–96.

De Luca, Anthony J. *Freud and Future Religious Experience.* New York: Philosophical Library, 1976.

Devries, Kelly. *Joan of Arc: A Military Leader.* Gloucestershire, England: Sutton Publishing, 1999.

Dewhurst, Kenneth, and A. W. Beard. "Sudden Religious Conversions in Temporal Lobe Epilepsy." *British Journal of Psychiatry* 117 (1970): 497–507.

Duby, Georges. *France in the Middle Ages, 987–1460: From Hugh Capet to Joan of Arc.* Oxford and Cambridge: Blackwell, 1997.

Dukore, Bernard F. *Saint Joan: A Screenplay by Bernard Shaw.* Seattle: University of Washington Press, 1968.

Dunn, Susan. "Romanticism and the Rise of History." *History and Theory* 35 (1996): 384–90.

Dworkin, Andrea. *Intercourse.* 1987. Reprint. New York: Free Press, 1997.

Egdell, H. G., and I. Kolvin. "Childhood Hallucinations." *Journal of Child Psychology and Psychiatry* 13 (1972): 279–87.

Ellenberger, Henri F. *The Discovery of the Unconscious: The History and Evolution of Dynamic Psychiatry.* New York: Basic Books, 1970.

Elliott, Dyan. "Seeing Double: John Gerson, the Discernment of Spirits, and Joan of Arc." *American Historical Review* 107 (Feb. 2002): 26–54.

Elliott, Victoria Stagg. "Our Lesbian Saints." *Lesbian News* 24 (Dec. 1998): 35–38.

Evans, Joan. *Life in Medieval France.* London: Phaidon Press, 1957.

Fadiman, James, and Donald Kewman. *Exploring Madness: Experience, Theory and Research*. Monterey, Calif.: Stanford, Brooks/Cole Publishing, 1973.

Falconer, Murray A. "Reversibility by Temporal Lobe Resection of the Behavioral Abnormalities of Temporal Lobe Epilepsy." *New England Journal of Medicine* 289 (Aug. 30, 1973): 451–55.

Fish, D. R., P. Gloor, F. L. Quesney, and A. Oliver. "Clinical Responses to Electrical Brain Stimulation of the Temporal and Frontal Lobes in Patients with Epilepsy." *Brain* 116 (1993): 397–414.

Foote-Smith, Elizabeth, and Lydia Bayne. "Joan of Arc." *Epilepsia* 32 (1991): 810–15.

Fraioli, Deborah A. *Joan of Arc: The Early Debate*. Rochester, N.Y.: Boydell Press, 2000.

France, Anatole, *Vie de Jeanne d'Arc*. Paris: Calmann-Lévy, 1908.

Friston, K. J., P. F. Liddle, C. D. Frith, S. R. Hirsch, and R. S. J. Frackowiak. "The Left Medial Temporal Region and Schizophrenia." *Brain* 115 (1992): 367–82.

Geschwind, Norman. "Behavioural Changes in Temporal Lobe Epilepsy." *Psychological Medicine* 9 (1979): 217–19.

Gladwell, Malcomb. "The Naked Face." *New Yorker* (Aug. 5, 2002): 38–49.

Gloor, Pierre, André Olivier, Luis F. Quesney, Frederick Andermann, and Sandra Horowitz. "The Role of the Limbic System in Experiential Phenomena of Temporal Lobe Epilepsy." *Annals of Neurology* 12 (Aug. 1982): 129–44.

Goodwin, Donald W., Philip Alderson, and Randall Rosenthal. "Clinical Significance of Hallucinations in Psychiatric Disorders: A Study of 116 Hallucinatory Patients." *Archives of General Psychiatry* 24 (Jan. 1971): 76–80.

Gorman, James. "Consciousness Studies Swell From Stream to a Flood." *New York Times* (Apr. 29, 1997): B7,9.

Halgren, Eric, Richard D. Walter, Diana G. Cherlow, and

Paul H. Crandall. "Mental Phenomena Evoked by Electrical Stimulation of the Human Hippocampal Formation and Amygdala." *Brain* 101 (1978): 83–117.

Hanna, Martha. "Iconology and Ideology: Images of Joan of Arc in the Idiom of the *Action Française*, 1908–1931. *French Historical Studies* 14 (Autumn 1985): 215–39.

Heimann, Nora M. "The Art of Politics in Early Nineteenth-Century France: E.-É.-F. Gois's *Jeanne d'Arc pendant le combat* as Metaphor." *Gazette des Beaux-Arts* 132 (July–Aug. 1998): 29–46.

Hellerstein, David, William Frosch, and Harold W. Koenigsberg. "The Clinical Significance of Command Hallucinations." *American Journal of Psychiatry* 144 (1987): 219–25.

Helmstaedter, C., M. Kurthen, D. B. Linke, and C. E. Elger. "Right Hemisphere Restitution of Language and Memory Functions in Right Hemisphere Language-dominant Patients With Left Temporal Lobe Epilepsy." *Brain* 117 (1994): 729–37.

Henker, Fred. "Joan of Arc and DSM III." *Southern Medical Journal* 77 (Dec. 1984): 1488–90.

Hibberd, Sarah. "Marianne: Mystic or Madwoman? Representations of Jeanne d'Arc on the Parisian Stage in the 1820s." *Prose Studies* 23 (2000): 87–98.

Hill, Holly. *Playing Joan: Actresses on the Challenge of Playing Shaw's Saint Joan*. 26 interviews. (n.p.: Theater Communications Group, 1987).

Huizinga, Johan. *The Waning of the Middle Ages*. Chicago: University of Chicago Press, 1996.

Igra, Caroline. "Measuring the Temper of Her Time: Joan of Arc in the 1870s and 1880s." *Konsthistorisk Tidskrift* 68 (1999): 117–25.

Ingram, Jay. *The Barmaid's Brain; and Other Strange Tales from Science*. New York: Henry Holt, 1998.

———. "When Hearing Is Believing." *Equinox* (Jan.–Feb. 1996): 16–18.

Ireland, William W. "On the Character and Hallucinations of Joan of Arc." *Journal of Mental Science* (1875).

Ishibashi, Toshimi, Hiroshi Hori, Koh Endo, and Tokijiro Sato. "Hallucinations Produced by Electrical Stimulation of the Temporal Lobes in Schizophrenic Patients." *Journal of Experimental Medicine* 82 (1964): 124–39.

Jaynes, Julian. *The Origin of Consciousness in the Breakdown of the Bicameral Mind.* Boston: Houghton-Mifflin, 1976.

Jennings, Eric. "'Reinventing Jeanne': The Iconology of Joan of Arc in Vichy Schoolbooks, 1940–44." *Journal of Contemporary History* 29 (Oct. 1994): 711–34.

Johnson, Fred H. *The Anatomy of Hallucinations.* Chicago: Nelson-Hall, 1978.

Kelly, H. Ansgar. "The Right to Remain Silent: Before and After Joan of Arc." *Speculum* 68 (Oct. 1993): 992–1026.

Kenyon, F. E. "The Life and Health of Joan of Arc: An Exercise in Pathography." *Practitioner* 207 (Dec. 1971): 835–42.

Kretzmann, Norman, and Eleonore Stump. *The Cambridge Companion to Aquinas*. Cambridge: Cambridge University Press, 1993.

Ladurie, Emmanuel Le Roy. *Montaillou: Cathars and Catholics in a French Village, 1294–1324.* Translated by Barbara Bray. Middlesex, England: Penguin Books, 1980.

Landsborough, D. "St Paul and Temporal Lobe Epilepsy." *Journal of Neurology, Neurosurgery, and Psychiatry* 50 (1987): 659–64.

Lang, Andrew. *The Maid of France: Being the Story of the Life and Death of Jeanne d'Arc*. London: Longmans, Green and Co., 1908.

Lang, Jonathan. "The Other Side of Hallucinations." Parts 1, 2. *American Journal of Psychiatry* 94 (1938): 1089–97; 96 (1939): 423–30.

Lightbody, Charles Wayland. *The Judgements of Joan: Joan of Arc, a Study in Cultural History*. Cambridge: Harvard University Press, 1961.

McGuire, P. K., G. M. S. Shah, and R. M. Murray. "Increased Blood Flow in Broca's Area During Auditory Hallucinations in Schizophrenia." *Lancet* 342 (Sept. 18, 1993): 703–6.

Mahl, George F., Albert Rothenberg, Jose M. R. Delgado, and Hannibal Hamlin. "Psychological Responses in the Human to Intracerebral Electrical Stimulation." *Psychosomatic Medicine* 27 (1964): 337–67.

Margolis, Nadia. *Joan of Arc in History, Literature, and Film: A Select, Annotated Bibliography*. New York and London: Garland Publishing, 1990.

———. "Trial by Passion: Philosophy, Film, and Ideology in the Portrayal of Joan of Arc (1900–1930)." *Journal of Medieval and Early Modern Studies* 27, no. 3 (Fall 1997): 445–93.

Marsh, Patrick. "Jeanne d'Arc During the German Occupation." *Theatrical Research Institute* 2 (1977): 139–45.

Menninger, Karl. *The Vital Balance: The Life Process in Mental Health and Illness*. New York: Viking Press, 1963.

Michelet, Jules. *Joan of Arc*. 1853. Translated and edited by Albert Guérard. Ann Arbor: University of Michigan Press, 2000.

———. *Satanism and Witchcraft: The Classic Study of Medieval Superstition*. Translated by A. R. Allinson. New York: Citadel Press Book, 1992.

Money-Kyrle, Roger. "A Psycho-analytic Study of the Voices of Joan of Arc." *British Journal of Medical Psychology* 13 (1933): 63–81.

Murray, T. Douglas. *Jeanne D'Arc, Maid of Orléans, Deliverer of France: Being the Story of Her Life, Her Achievements, and Her Death, as Attested on Oath and Set Forth in Original Documents*. London: William Heinemann, 1903.

Musser, George, "A Hole at the Heart of Physics." *Scientific American* 287, no. 3 (Sept. 2002): 48–49.

Newberg, Andrew, Eugene D'Aquili, and Vince Rause. *Why God Won't Go Away: Brain Science and the Biology of Belief*. New York: Ballantine Books, 2001.

Nores, J. M., and Y. Yakovleff. "A Historical Case of Disseminated Tuberculosis." *Neuropsychobiology* 32 (1995): 79–80.

Norman, Marsha. Commencement speech on Joan of Arc. *On Campus*. Atlanta: Agnes Scott College, June 2000.

Paulesu, E., C. D. Frith, and R. S. J. Frackowiak. "The Neural Correlates of the Verbal Component of Working Memory." *Nature* 362 (Mar. 25, 1993): 342–44.

Penfield, Wilder, and Phanor Perot. "The Brain's Record of Auditory and Visual Experience." *Brain* 86 (Dec. 1963): 595–695.

Pernoud, Régine. *Joan of Arc*. Harmondsworth, England: Penguin Books, 1964.

———. *Joan of Arc: By Herself and Her Witnesses*. Lanham, Md.: Scarborough House, 1994.

———. *The Retrial of Joan of Arc*. New York: Harcourt, Brace and Co., 1955.

Pernoud, Régine, and Marie-Véronique Clin. *Joan of Arc: Her Story*. New York: St. Martin's Press, 1998.

Piper, August, Jr. "Multiple Personality Disorder." *British Journal of Psychiatry* 164 (1994): 600–12.

Poskanzer, David C., Arthur E. Brown, and Henry Miller. "Musicogenic Epilepsy Caused Only by a Discrete Frequency Band of Church Bells." *Brain* 85 (1962): 77–92.

Rankin, Daniel, and Claire Quintal, trans. and eds. *The First Biography of Joan of Arc*. Pittsburgh, Penn.: University of Pittsburgh Press, 1964.

Ratnasuriyia, R. H. "Joan of Arc, Creative Psychopath: Is There Another Explanation?" *Journal of the Royal Society of Medicine* 79 (1986): 234–35.

Restak, Richard M. *The Brain: The Last Frontier*. New York: Warner Books, 1979.

Roberts, G. W., D. J. Done, C. Bruton, and T. J. Crow. "A Mock-up of Schizophrenia: Temporal Lobe Epilepsy and Schizophrenia-like Psychosis." *Biological Psychiatry* 28 (1990): 127–43.

Romme, M. A. J., A. Honig, E. O. Noorthoorn, and A. D. M. A. C. Escher. "Coping With Hearing Voices: An Emancipatory Approach." *British Journal of Psychiatry* 161 (1992): 99–103.

Ross, Colin A. *Multiple Personality Disorder: Diagnosis, Clinical Features, and Treatment.* New York: John Wiley and Sons, 1989.

Sackville-West, Vita. *Saint Joan of Arc.* 1936. Reprint. New York: Image Books/Doubleday, 1991.

Salomon, Roger B. *Twain and the Image of History.* New Haven, Conn.: Yale University Press, 1961.

Salsbury, Edith Colgate, ed. *Susy and Mark Twain: Family Dialogues.* New York: Harper and Row, 1965.

Saver, Jeffrey L., and John Rabin. "The Neural Substrates of Religious Experience." *Journal of Neuropsychiatry and Clinical Neurosciences* 9 (Summer 1997): 498–510.

Scaff, William. *The Philosophy of T. S. Eliot: From Skepticism to a Surrealist Poetic, 1909–1927.* Philadelphia: University of Pennsylvania, 1986.

Schweitzer, Albert. *The Psychiatric Study of Jesus: Exposition and Criticism.* Translated by Charles R. Joy. Boston: Beacon Press, 1948.

Scott, Walter Sidney, ed. *The Trial of Joan of Arc: Being the Verbatim Report of the Proceedings From the Orléans Manuscript.* London: Folio Society; Westport, Conn.: Associated Booksellers, 1956.

Searle, William. *The Saint and the Skeptics: Joan of Arc in the Work of Mark Twain, Anatole France, and Bernard Shaw.* Detroit: Wayne State University Press, 1976.

Seward, Desmond. *The Hundred Years War: The English in France, 1337–1453.* New York: Atheneum, 1982.

Sexsmith, Dennis. "The Radicalization of Joan of Arc Before and After the French Revolution." *RACAR* 17 (1990): 125–30.

Shakespeare, William. *Henry V,* Act. 4, Scene 3. *The Complete*

Works of William Shakespeare. New York: Avenel Books, 1975.

Shaw, George Bernard. *Saint Joan.* London: Penguin Books, 1924, 1956.

Silbersweig, D. A., E. Stern, C. Frith, C. Cahill, A. Holmes, Sylke Grootoonk, J. Seaward, P. McKenna, S. E. Chua, L. Schnorr, T. Jones, and R. S. J. Frackowiak. "A Functional Neuroanatomy of Hallucinations in Schizophrenia." *Nature* 378 (Nov. 9, 1995): 176–79.

Silver, Arnold. *Saint Joan: Playing With Fire.* New York: Twayne Publishers.

Skaff, William. *The Philosophy of T. S. Eliot.* Philadelphia: University of Pennsylvania Press, 1986.

Smith, S. D., W. J. Tays, M. J. Dixon, and M. B. Bulman-Fleming. "The Right Hemisphere as an Anomaly Detector: Evidence From Visual Perception. *Brain and Cognition* 48 (Mar.–Apr. 2002): 574–79.

Sperry, R. W. "Hemisphere Deconnection and Unity in Conscious Awareness." *American Psychologist* 23 (Oct. 1968): 723–33.

———. "Changing Concepts of Consciousness and Free Will." *Perspectives in Biology and Medicine* (Autumn 1976): 9–19.

Stephens, Walter. "Witches Who Steal Penises: Impotence and Illusion in *Malleus maleficarum.*" *Journal of Medieval and Early Modern Studies* 28 (Fall 1998): 495–529.

Stolpe, Sven. *The Maid of Orleans.* New York: Pantheon Press, 1956.

Stone, Albert E., Jr. "Mark Twain's Joan of Arc: The Child as Goddess." *American Literature* 31 (Mar. 1959): 1–20.

Storr, Anthony. *The Essential Jung.* Princeton: Princeton University Press, 1983.

Sullivan, Karen. *The Interrogation of Joan of Arc.* Minneapolis: University of Minnesota Press, 1999.

Tallon, Mary Elizabeth, ed. *Joan of Arc at the University.* Milwaukee: Marquette University Press, 1997.

Tavard, George H. *The Spiritual Way of St. Jeanne d'Arc*. Collegeville, Minn.: Liturgical Press, 1998.

Taylor, David C. "Factors Influencing the Occurrence of Schizophrenia-like Psychosis in Patients With Temporal Lobe Epilepsy." *Psychological Medicine* 5 (1975): 249–54.

Tien, A. Y. "Distributions of Hallucinations in the Population." *Social Psychiatry and Psychiatric Epidemiology* 26 (1991): 287–92.

Trask, Willard. *Joan of Arc: In Her Own Words.* New York: Books & Co., 1996.

Trevor-Roper, H. R. *Religion, the Reformation and Cultural Change*. New York: Macmillan, 1972.

Tuchman, Barbara W. *A Distant Mirror: The Calamitous 14th Century*. New York: Ballantine Books, 1978.

Tumblety, Joan. "Contested Histories: *Jeanne d'Arc* and the *Front National*." *European Legacy* 4 (1999): 8–25.

Twain, Mark. *Personal Recollections of Joan of Arc.* 1896. Reprint. New York: Gramercy Books, 1995.

Tyson, Brian. *The Story of Shaw's Saint Joan*. Kingston-Montreal: McGill-Queen's University Press, 1982.

Veenstra, Jan R. *Magic and Divination at the Courts of Burgundy and France: Text and Context of Laurens Pignon's Contre les devineurs (1411).* Leiden, New York, and Köln: Brill Publisher, 1998.

Walter, Richard D., Charles H. Markham, Robert W. Rand, and Paul H. Crandall. "Memory Changes Induced by Stimulation of Hippocampus or Amygdala in Epilepsy Patients With Implanted Electrodes." *Transactions of the American Neurological Association* 92 (1997): 50–56.

Warner, Marina. *Joan of Arc: The Image of Female Heroism.* 1981. Reprint. London: Vintage Books, 1991.

Weintraub, Stanley, ed. *Saint Joan: Fifty Years After: 1923/24–1973/74.* Baton Rouge: Louisiana State University Press, 1973.

Wheeler, Bonnie, and Charles T. Wood. *Fresh Verdicts on Joan of Arc*. New York and London: Garland Publishing, 1996.
Wills, Garry. *Saint Augustine*. London: Phoenix Publishing, 1999.

Index